Erich Leinsdorf.

Photograph: Anthony Crickmay.
From the collections of the Theatre Museum, V&A.

Erich Leinsdorf on Music

by Erich Leinsdorf

AMADEUS PRESS
Reinhard G. Pauly, General Editor
Portland, Oregon

The essay entitled "To Cut Or Not To Cut?" first appeared
in *The Opera Quarterly*, Volume 10, No. 1 (Autumn 1993): 5–12.
It is reprinted here with kind permission.

The article entitled "Opera: What Constitutes Longevity" is reprinted
by permission of *Daedalus*, Journal of the American Academy
of Arts and Sciences, from the issue entitled
"The Future of Opera," Fall 1986, Volume 115, No. 4.

Published in 1997 by Amadeus Press (an imprint of Timber Press, Inc.)
The Haseltine Building
133 S.W. Second Avenue, Suite 450
Portland, Oregon 97204, U.S.A.

ISBN 1-57467-028-X

Printed in Singapore

Library of Congress Cataloging-in-Publication Data

Leinsdorf. Erich. 1912–
    Erich Leinsdorf on music / by Erich Leinsdorf.
        p.   cm.
    Includes index.
    ISBN 1-57467-028-X
    1. Music–History and criticism.   I. Title.
    ML60.L348   1997
    780–dc21   96-52635
                                                                                    CIP
                                                                                    MN

All in all, I feel that *we* musicians are privileged,
having contact, at a time and place of our choosing,
with the greatest creative minds in drama,
poetry, and musical composition.

—Erich Leinsdorf

Contents

7

Photographs follow page 192.

Preface

Usually when one opens a book the first pages are written by the author introducing it and thanking those associated with it for their help and cooperation. While I try to put myself in those larger-than-life shoes, I am in my apartment surrounded by all the objects that Erich loved and needed in his daily writing: his desk, his comfortable chair, his telephone, his fax machine, and of course his beloved books. I am in the peculiar situation of trying to capture the interest of all those who will be entertained by the pages that follow, and who will delight in Erich Leinsdorf's knowledge, intellect, wit, and humanity.

Although intimately familiar with Erich's thoughts about his profession and all that encompasses this large radius related to the performing arts, I must confess that I was surprised at times in reading his words how ahead of his time his ideas were. His preoccupation with the future of music, symphony orchestras, and musicians in general was ever increasing. He had an extraordinary array of fresh ideas and a sharp mind and tongue to formulate them.

In more than twenty-five years of our life together hardly a day went by, in spite of all his other commitments, that Erich did not jot down, wherever he was, on every scrap of paper available, his own interpretation of history, political happenings, tongue-in-cheek poetry, some unprintable opinions, and puns of all sorts. However, his profession remained his passion and prime interest and music the center of his life. These subsequent pages are but a segment of his written legacy.

Soon after Dr. Reinhard Pauly, general editor of Amadeus Press, approached my husband with the idea of publishing this book, Erich became ill and the project was put on hold. When Dr. Pauly subsequently contacted me again to propose that we continue with the project, I was grateful to make the acquaintance of Ms. Lucia Staniels, who had the opportunity to talk to my husband on the telephone. Her patience, flexibility, and professional integrity made the meeting of all concerned in this most important project for me a reality, notwithstanding that the primary voice, Erich Leinsdorf, was silent.

Along came Mr. Andrew Long, whom I know Erich would have liked meeting. He had the incalculable and difficult task as literary editor to link earlier writings with new ones, while keeping the idiom of Erich's "second native language" fluid.

I have been privileged to share Erich's life for more than a quarter of a century and am sad beyond solace to no longer be able to do so. In making this book come to fruition, my immediate purpose is not only to keep Erich Leinsdorf's name alive, but also, and perhaps more importantly, to bring to the fore an artist completely dedicated to his calling and one with a most original and free-floating imagination.

—Vera Leinsdorf

Introduction

When, in 1993, I approached Erich Leinsdorf about writing another book based on his long career as a conductor of opera and symphony, his response was positive and enthusiastic. We agreed that this volume should be "a collection of essays on a variety of loosely connected topics," and that it should address the general reader. In this it would differ from his two previous books, one of which was largely autobiographical (*Cadenza: A Musical Career*, Houghton Mifflin Company, 1976), the other one intended for students of conducting (*The Composer's Advocate: A Radical Orthodoxy for Musicians*, Yale University Press, 1981).

Sadly, the maestro's death prevented further consultation, leaving us with the task of assembling this volume from the material he had left behind. Some of it consisted of fragments; all of it had to be organized and arranged in the most logical sequence.

These are the thoughts of a distinguished musician. Many of them were jotted down during the last weeks and months of his life. They reveal his strong feelings and convictions, his likes and dislikes, and they reflect his deep love for the masterworks of music from Bach to Stravinsky.

Understandably they also are conditioned by his Central European heritage. (Leinsdorf was born in Vienna in 1912 and made his American debut in 1938.) His thoughts also are based on his many years of conducting and teaching at some of America's most prestigious musical institutions. Some essays more strongly than others tell of his frustrations with some aspects of today's world of music, especially its commercial side.

Leinsdorf loved America (including baseball and other sports), in spite of his at times scathing and sarcastic pronouncements. We have not tried to eliminate or tone down these remarks; had he been with us while this volume was taking shape, he no doubt would have wanted to amplify and perhaps qualify some of his statements, whether positive or negative.

As a sequel to Leinsdorf's two earlier books, this volume rounds out our acquaintance with a man whose artistry provided profound musical experiences and much pleasure to music lovers at home and abroad.

—Reinhard G. Pauly

Chronology of
Erich Leinsdorf's Life

1912	4 February. Erich Leinsdorf is born at Kochgasse 21, Vienna, to Julius Ludwig Landauer and Charlotte, née Löbl.
1915	Leinsdorf's father dies. Leinsdorf and his mother move to nearby Haspingergasse 4, where they live with his aunt, Tante Jetti.
1918	Enters the local music school.
1920	Begins piano studies with the wife of Paul A. Pisk.
1923–28	Studies with Paul Emerich.
1929–30	Studies with Paul A. Pisk.
1930	Graduates from high school.
1931–33	Studies at Vienna's State Academy of Music, making his conducting debut upon his graduation.
1933	Becomes rehearsal pianist for Anton Webern's Singverein der Sozialdemokratischen Kunststelle.
1934	Appointed assistant to Bruno Walter and Arturo Toscanini at the Salzburg Summer Festival. Returns to Salzburg in 1935 and 1936.
1937	Appointed assistant conductor at Metropolitan Opera. Moves to New York.

1938	21 January. Makes his professional conducting debut with Wagner's *Die Walküre*.
1939	Becomes head of the Metropolitan Opera's German repertoire (succeeding Artur Bodanzky). Marries Anne Frohnknecht. They have five children: David (b. 1942), Gregor (b. 1944), Joshua (b. 1945), Deborah (b. 1948), Jennifer (b. 1952).
1942	Becomes an American citizen.
1943	Succeeds Artur Rodzinski as conductor of the Cleveland Symphony Orchestra.
1943	December. Is inducted into the United States Army. Is discharged in 1944.
1944–45	Returns to the Metropolitan Opera as guest conductor.
1947–55	Serves as conductor of the Rochester Philharmonic Orchestra.
1956	Appointed music director of the newly created New York City Opera.
1957	Returns to the Metropolitan Opera as conductor and music consultant.
1962	Appointed music director of the Boston Symphony Orchestra (succeeding Charles Munch).
1968	Marries violinist Vera Graf.
1969	Leaves Boston to embark upon a freelance career, during which he conducts orchestral and operatic works in many major music centers of America, Europe, Asia, and Australia.
1993	11 September. Erich Leinsdorf dies in Zurich, aged eighty-one.

The Life of a Musician

By Way of Introduction

Rather like the trapeze artist who devotes his entire life to the perfection of his only act, I have written throughout my life essentially on one topic only: the urgent need for musical literacy. If we are ever again to enjoy a healthy musical world, it is essential that we learn to read music. It is a sad fact that, while concerned citizens everywhere lament the low functional literacy of the American population, few people extend similar worries to the dismal lack of literacy in music. This includes, alas, many professional musicians.

One major reason for the decline in musical literacy has been the rapid decline in home music-making by amateurs (four-hand piano, voice and piano, chamber music for two, three, or four people). This active musical participation has been largely replaced by the passive activity of listening to recorded professional performances. I have no wish to exaggerate the glories of a bygone age, but I do think it significant that today's concert audiences are strikingly different in character from those of the years before the First World War. Audiences in Central

Europe were at that time still composed not only of lay connoisseurs (such as those whom we still today count among our patrons), but also of numerous amateur musicians, who might well have prepared themselves for the concert with four-hand practice of the symphony to be played, and might even be found checking what tempos the quartet was taking in the Second "Rasumovsky," or whatever piece was being played. Those audiences were, in a sense, rather like today's sports spectators, many of whom have played, in their schools or in their backyards, the games that they watch either in the stadium or in the comfort of their living rooms. Music, stuck in a deep crisis for most of the twentieth century, is today characterized by a mistrust between composer and public, with the performer squeezed rather uncomfortably in between the two. This situation is obviously unacceptable, but it will not change until we make literacy in music part of the basic public education syllabus. In my previously published writings I have attempted to guide professionals (mainly conductors) toward their own reading, and to steer them away from reliance on recordings by prominent performers. In this, my third book, I have chosen to address the lay reader and to discuss several topics related to our musical world. Before I mount the pulpit, however, I feel I should give you at least some idea of my qualifications for the task.

Vienna

When I was six years old, I was marched off to my neighborhood music school. Nobody at that point had the slightest intention of making a professional musician of me; music was simply considered an essential part of one's education in those days. At home, however, there was a large heap of sheet music that my father, like all amateurs of his generation, had purchased to play at home. There were popular tunes from operas and operettas, overtures, the lighter variety of piano music (such as "Für Elise"), and other standard fare for amateurs, in pleasing arrangements for untrained fingers. As I mastered the techniques of recognizing notes and of making such recognition manifest by hitting the right keys (eventually even in the right time), I began to find that heap of light piano transcriptions increasingly beguiling. It was by going over those pieces time and time again (though not really practicing) that I learned the single most helpful tool of a musician's musical existence: the instant recognition of sight reading.

After three years, the Pfriemer music school, as it was called, apparently found me too adventurous (or just unruly, or just too plain ornery) to be tolerated any longer. My mother was therefore advised that I be subjected to the stricter discipline of a second, more professionally inclined teacher. How my mother found Mrs. Frank-Pisk I do not recall, but one day we duly found ourselves seated on the No. 13 trolley, en route to that lady's apartment. By the standards of transportation in the 1920s, it was a long journey.

During the few years (I do not remember exactly how many) of these lessons, my teacher began to suggest to my mother that serious music study might be appropriate for me. Now this was a rather surprising development for my mother, since her insistence upon her son's taking piano lessons had been a mere part of a much larger design: she had been grooming me for a career as a musical journalist! Since she did not have sufficient money either to set up a business or to finance lengthy graduate studies in disciplines such as medicine or law, she had naturally been planning to elicit the help of the cousin who had made *the* prominent career among his brothers and other relations.

Uncle Emil was the editor-in-chief of the *Neues Wiener Tagblatt* (the "other" of the two conservative daily newspapers). My mother evidently believed that with my musical background it would be a cinch and a shoo-in to get a job as a music critic. Looking back on the mercifully few visits I did make to Uncle Emil, I believe I already had my doubts then whether my mother's optimism would ever be fulfilled. He is certainly not remembered as an endearing character.

By 1927 I was with yet another piano teacher, called Paul Emerich. He had been recommended by Mrs. Frank-Pisk, who evidently felt that I was a handful designed for a hand larger than hers. I remained with Emerich for some five years before deciding that the piano was not going to be my chosen instrument. Emerich was one of those music teachers who, having only a limited technique, are more interested in overall musicality.

After one year of instruction, he concluded that I should also be studying theory, harmony, counterpoint, and the whole syllabus necessary for an all-round music professional. Having granted a favor to Mrs. Pisk, he now in turn asked her husband, Paul A. Pisk, to take me on as a composition student. I would be his pupil between the ages of fifteen and nineteen. Not one of these three tutors charged money, by the way, and even as I try to reconstruct the past in my mind, I am quite dumb-founded how my mother achieved this. I did, of course, pay a certain amount of "tuition" as a gofer for my tutors, but that was entirely appropriate.

Both Emerich and Pisk provided a wealth of information and stimuli. Emerich (like many serious musicians) was a part-time composer and had set to music a few poems by the eccentric Karl Kraus. Pisk had been a disciple of Arnold Schoenberg, and their relationship was somewhat reminiscent of that between Alfred Adler and Sigmund Freud.

Pisk's compositions were atonal, without having followed into dodecaphonic ways. He also worked as a critic for the *Arbeiter Zeitung*, the organ of Vienna's powerful Social Democratic party, and was a respected official in that party's cultural services. Our studies together embraced the customary four-year course of harmony, counterpoint, and form.

In Vienna there was also a thriving arts council, which sought to involve the working classes in the very middle-class club that is the classical music world. The council was called the Sozialdemokratischen Kunststelle (Social Democratic Arts Council), and I took many small jobs as a performer at council-sponsored events. Those jobs lasted until 12 February 1934—a key date in my life as well as in the political history of Austria. On that day a short civil war brought an abrupt end to democracy, parliament, the Social Democratic party, and indeed my work for the arts council (the source of most of my income). I heard the cannon at dusk on the outskirts of the city as I walked to my apartment from a music lesson.

Among the many jobs I did at that time, one in particular was of the utmost value to my musical and critical development. In 1933 I became the rehearsal pianist for the composer Anton Webern's Singverein der Sozialdemokratischen Kunststelle (Choral Society of the Social

Democratic Arts Council). The council had organized a chorus of amateurs among the blue-collar citizens of Vienna, and I accompanied the chorus, in rehearsals, at the piano. Webern was the conductor.

By a curious coincidence one of the rare pieces Webern rehearsed was Zoltán Kodály's *Psalmus Hungaricus*, which would later serve me as an introduction to the conductor Arturo Toscanini. Any musician will understand what working with Webern would mean to a twenty-year-old student. Webern, like many composers, conducted as a means to earn the money that his compositions did not earn. He also had his ideas about the interpretation of standard classical and romantic repertoire. Vienna, being exceedingly fixated on "the way we have always done it," did not always agree with Webern's ways (although our group did, as required by loyalty to the faction).

Among the more serious disagreements was one that occurred after Webern had conducted, in a workers' symphony concert, Brahms's *A German Requiem* (*Ein Deutsches Requiem*). I happened to discover many years later that certain directions of Brahms, which had been deleted after the first printing of the score, showed that it was Webern, not the traditionalists, who had been following the composer's wishes.

To have been exposed, in such an arch-conservative city, to a group of elders who habitually reexamined everything and took nothing for granted, was a blessing. It enabled me to become my own person, so to speak, and a person who never accepted received opinion without subjecting it to severe scrutiny. I am indebted to Paul Emerich for having fed me the works of Johann Sebastian Bach, not in mere spoonfuls, but in liberal portions. By my fourth year of tuition, I had studied and played all Bach's clavier music, the organ works in transcription for piano, and all the harpsichord works. I freely confess that some of this music is playable only by a sort of digital witchcraft (crossing hands) that I never mastered, but I do still try occasionally to negotiate the *Goldberg Variations*.

The influence of Paul A. Pisk was of a different nature. Being a former disciple of Master Arnold, Pisk was necessarily a composer of an embattled style. He was atonal and polyphonic, without many (or indeed any) audible links to the past, and yet he still taught music the old-fashioned way (and the only effective way), using centuries-old rules to show me how to put notes on paper. My lessons with Pisk were shared by two other young musicians, and this provided stimuli that are impossible to find in a solo class. We brought our compositions to class and were subjected to rigorous discussion. I felt close to the heart of modern music.

Through Pisk's good offices and through his position on the cultural council of the Social Democratic party, I once received a commission to compose a cantata. The commission was for the inauguration of a new auditorium in a low-income apartment house. The writer chosen for the project was another protégé of the council. His text was uninspiring hack work; he was simply a good bourgeois who, like myself, earned a few shillings doing things without thorough conviction. I detested then, and I detest now, the abuse of any art for the purposes of propaganda. I am happy to report that after I had completed my commissioned cantata and played the piano for the two singers engaged to perform it, I was left with the kind of aftertaste one should have after having undertaken an exercise that lacks honesty and conviction. In those early days I even used to try my hand at composition. Once I was inspired by a beloved novel that was, among all literary works, probably the least likely candidate for musical treatment. My chosen text, Jaroslav Hasek's *The Good Soldier Schweik*, was as unlikely a candidate as the political hack poetry of my cantata author. My creation never did see the light of day (certainly no great loss to the world of music), and yet the exercise did show me that a great text does not necessarily make great music.

It is an unfortunate fact of life that one's journey of self discovery often leads inevitably to a break with one's teachers. This was true of my relationship with both Emerich and Pisk, who doubtless had nothing but terrible things to say about my character ever since. Ungrateful, ungrateful, ungrateful!—and yet those breaks were inevitable, because both men, after having taught me to take nothing for granted, were less than delighted when I began to disagree with their findings and follow my own path. This is one aspect of my career that troubles me, and yet it seems that such breaks must occur whenever teachers or other mentors consider the pupil's bid for independence as an act of betrayal or disloyalty.

Aided by my connections with these various composers and teachers I found a job collating modern scores with orchestral material. The scores were in composers' manuscripts, the parts by professional copyists. It was my task to uncover as many copyists' mistakes as possible. Correcting errors can be very expensive with a whole orchestra sitting around; it is better to have it done before rehearsals by one poorly paid musician. Important as the small stipend was, what I learned was more significant: how to read modern full scores without the aid of an instrument. No conservatory could provide such a course and it is a fact, perhaps hard to believe, that there are numerous active professional conductors who do not read modern scores without the aid of a recording.

The publishing house Universal Edition, for whom I did my collating jobs, was then effectively the center of modern music, as it had exclusive contracts with Schoenberg, Berg, Webern, Zemlinsky, and a host of lesser-known composers, including Pisk. Its house organ, *Der Anbruch* (The Dawn), was, by virtue of a few outstanding contributors, incomparably better than most house organs, which peddle their wares without much imagination. All told, our group of "progressives" appears, in retrospect, as a splendid ghetto in an ultra-conservative musical city. Most of the material I prepared for Universal Edition went to German opera houses, which, then as now, accepted new music more readily than establishments elsewhere.

At that time there was a growing awareness of how difficult it was for working people to trudge back and forth between their homes and the inner city to listen to music or go to the theater. Newly built small auditoriums were therefore constructed, and it was in one of these that I made my debut as a performer. At fifteen years of age, I began work as an accompanist, playing mostly for dance recitals, conventional singing, violin, and so forth. I was also employed as a pianist for political cabaret, a marvelous form of entertainment that is little-known in the English-speaking world because there are no real political antagonists (an indispensable premise for the fun and games to be played on the powers that be). In America the nearest equivalents to this form of entertainment are the stand-up comedians and the political satirists of the newspapers. In my view, however, they are not nearly as funny or as effective as the artists of political cabaret.

My love of theater, comedy, acting, mimicry, and so forth is an old Leinsdorf family trait, even if it was manifested mostly in passive theater-going and a general fascination with show business. One of my mother's cousins was with the police department and always had house seats to the big shows, so my mother and aunt were able to see everything that was playing in the subsidized houses. Perhaps my greatest moment as an accompanist came when I was called upon to stand in for a leading actor who had become ill. Having played the piano for the show in so many of these neighborhood auditoriums, I knew every line of the piece in question. But what would happen to the piano accompaniment if I was to perform in beard and morning coat? One of our group found the solution: the piano would be placed in a spot where a curtain covered both it and me. There I sat, playing in costume and makeup; then, in two leaps, there I was suddenly on stage, acting; and then there I was back again at the keyboard. It was wonderful. (Actually, it was probably terrible, but for me, at least, it was wonderful!)

Pisk was a member of the Second Viennese School, and even if he was less dogmatic than most, he still evaluated composition and performance according to doctrine passed down from on high. When one is eighteen years old, one is not generally inclined to toe the party line, but my resistance to his methods represented more than just the rebellion of the teenager. I had continued to work for Universal Edition, and in reading a large amount of music I had developed the capacity to distinguish between solid composition and the less honest kind of musical writing that had flourished ever since strict rules of voice leading and harmony were first broken.

My break with Pisk occurred just as I graduated from high school. My mother felt that my chances of achieving a successful journalistic career—a career that she gamely continued to map out for me—would be much improved by my earning a doctorate (the Viennese have quite a penchant for titles). The musicology department at the University of Vienna then enjoyed a first-class reputation, thanks to its former principal, Guido Adler, and I was therefore more than happy to oblige my mother. In the fall of 1930 I began to attend university seminars, mainly in music but also in philosophy and German literature.

I quickly discovered that my indiscriminate browsing through my father's assorted sheet music had made me an effective sight reader, and yet this discovery proved to be a decisive factor in my electing to cut short my university career. I soon found, to my surprise, that I was the only student willing to accept the professor's invitation to step forward and illustrate the meaning of the music by playing it on the piano. This continued for many weeks, and while I was gratified to receive compliments for my ability to sight read, I could not remain indifferent to the spectacle of a dozen or so young musicologists unable or unwilling to sit before their fellow students and give their impressions of a piece of music.

I therefore decided that I would be wasting my time by remaining there. Since I was already being engaged as a voice coach for local singers and accompanying dance recitals, it seemed to me that I could function quite well as a musical performer and that a degree in musicology would be little more than an ornament to me. As time went on, I received more calls for my services as coach and accompanist, and formal schooling later continued with my enrollment at Vienna's State Academy of Music, where I found a large orchestra and many opportunities to conduct it. I studied there between 1930 and 1933.

When the Austrian fascist party ousted the Social Democrats in February 1934, all my arts council engagements ended, and I became entirely dependent on private coaching. It so happened that an opera singer client of mine, Luise Helletsgruber, was engaged to sing at the Salzburg Summer Festival, and asked me to coach her in Italian for the role of Donna Elvira in Mozart's *Don Giovanni*. I had been taking Italian lessons for three years and had been studying original Italian opera scores. In Vienna all opera was sung in German, and since the Salzburg Festival was run by the staff of the Vienna Opera, I had hoped there might be a niche for a musician who knew Italian. My lucky break indeed came when the Italian singers found the prompter from the Vienna Opera unable to prompt them properly. One of those singers, the great Ezio Pinza, asked me to take on the job, and for the next three summers I prompted all the operas conducted there by Toscanini.

Five Minutes to Midnight

In 1937 I left for New York to take up an appointment as assistant conductor at the Metropolitan Opera. My move from Vienna occurred at five minutes to midnight, so to speak. Within four months of my arrival in the United States, Germany annexed Austria. I had been aware of what the future might hold for a Jewish musician in Vienna, but I now knew that I had been lucky beyond belief. Had I remained I would doubtless have become either a refugee or another of Hitler's victims. I have always felt infinitely grateful for that lucky break.

It is often instructive to see how the image-building industry can blur a person's true identity (sometimes even to himself). I was touted as the chosen assistant to Toscanini and Bruno Walter, but my engagement was due entirely to the failure of a conductor who had been specifically recommended by Walter. Somebody at the Met then apparently decided to take a gamble on me, since they could not possibly have seen me conduct. My entire observable musical work up to that point had been as coach, rehearsal pianist, and prompter. It is true that in 1933 I had conducted the State Academy's orchestra for a public graduation concert, but as I do not recall having directed any other instrumental or vocal group up to that point, I fail to see how any Met talent scout might have seen me perform.

Various people have claimed the credit for my appointment, and I confess I was never entirely certain who was responsible for what. I do know, however, that the two great conductors most frequently mentioned in the Leinsdorf publicity literature over the years played no active part in it whatsoever. Toscanini's name was freely used, I am sure, by Lotte Lehmann, who was without doubt the most important celebrity beating a drum for me. Lotte had a young lady named Constance Hope doing her publicity in America, and I suspect Constance was the real mover and shaker in this affair. How she persuaded Edward Johnson and Artur Bodanzky of the Met to appoint an untried person to such an important post still puzzles me today!

By 1936 I had already had enough of Vienna and quite enough of the growing and unmistakable threat from the Third Reich. I had spent the winter of 1936–37 in Italy, where I was engaged to assist in the preparation of German works (*Die Meistersinger* and *Die Walküre* in Bologna, *Arabella* in Trieste, *Figaro* in Florence). In Bologna, where the *stagione* (season) was subsidized, it was compulsory for the impresario to produce one contemporary work. During my engagement, it was the turn of a score by the director of the Bologna conservatory. I have been unable to locate either author or opera in the latest edition of the *New Grove*

Dictionary of Music and Musicians (which suggests that either my memory or the *New Grove Dictionary* is full of holes). The title of this *capolavoro* was *Imelda*. After two days of rehearsal, however, every musician on the staff was referring to the work as *Imerda*.

My next significant encounter with twentieth-century music came somewhat later, when I was working as music director of the Philharmonic in Rochester, New York. This was a very fine situation in which a remarkably inventive manager had devised a way of running a very fine symphony orchestra that relied for its big events on a group of first-rate graduate students at the Eastman School of Music. The negative side of this ingenious system was the director of the school, Howard Hanson, who felt himself to be not only the "American Sibelius" (as his admirers fondly referred to him) but also the ordained music director of the orchestra. For some reason that I still do not understand, Koussevitzky performed Hanson's music as if it were the best of Sibelius (whom Koussevitzky performed gloriously).

During those years, with seasons in Rochester agreeably short, I was able to accept several fine guest engagements. In Chicago I conducted Louis Gruenberg's *The Emperor Jones*, in San Francisco the American premieres of Walton's *Troilus and Cressida* and Poulenc's *Dialogues des Carmelites*. Thinking of these three works, with their undistinguished scores, I am reminded that one reason for their acceptance by an opera manager was that each had a corker of a libretto. Eugene O'Neill, William Shakespeare, and Georges Bernanos provide so much potential for great notes and highly emotional dramaturgy that it is fair to state that the deeper qualities of the scores were, at most, of secondary importance.

Mozart refused even to start composing *Die Entführung aus dem Serail* until Count Orsini-Rosenberg had approved the libretto. In a letter to his father he wrote that he did not "wish to waste his time, if upon his return the count should disapprove of the libretto." Concert music for instruments has, unfortunately, no such provision for ensuring the quality of a score, and it is no surprise that three truly great works of the period immediately following the First World War were based upon literary masterpieces. In chronological order, these were Igor Stravinsky's *L'Histoire du soldat* (1919), Alban Berg's *Wozzeck* (1925), and Kurt Weill's

The Threepenny Opera (*Die Dreigroschenoper*, 1928). I consider myself fortunate to have conducted inventive stagings of *L'Histoire du soldat* with Paul Draper and of *Wozzeck* with a wonderful cast at the Teatro Colòn in Buenos Aires (and a splendid orchestra of Tanglewood "fellows"). Of *The Threepenny Opera* I could only indulge in a concert version called *Kleine Dreigroschen Musik*, a marvelous arrangement for fourteen musicians, which has everywhere produced the same enthusiasm provoked many years ago by the complete stage version.

Curiously enough, the only orchestra with which I had considerable difficulties in getting the style of Weill's music right was the famous, wonderful, peerless Berlin Philharmonic. The European career of Kurt Weill was associated entirely with Berlin, and it was a strange and somewhat eerie sensation that while American orchestras had no problems with the work, the Berliners of the 1980s just could not manage that utterly simple and obvious work. To me it was as if the twelve years of the Third Reich had succeeded in ruthlessly isolating whatever the Nazis considered cultural bolshevism. It is a sad fact that political history has irrevocably altered the perception of a great deal of music (particularly nineteenth-century music).

My relationship with modern music has influenced my career whenever I have had to make hard choices, and this was particularly the case whenever a job as a music director loomed large. During my years as music director of the Boston Symphony Orchestra (BSO), I discovered that many decisions about musical policies, among them the huge issue of "modern music," were no longer to be decided freely by the music director. Like most musicians I enjoyed performing the great modern masterpieces, such as Berg's Violin Concerto, Schoenberg's *Variations*, or Webern's various Pieces for Orchestra. Although it was also personally enjoyable to discover creative talent, to do so was no longer enough to keep one out of trouble.

It had become something akin to an oath of loyalty for a conductor to be demonstrably a champion of fashionable musical styles. It was not fashionable to play the music of the great composers, such as Béla Bartók and Igor Stravinsky. Some colleagues who held onto their posts did their best to produce satisfactory statistical figures on their cultivation of the latest styles. Unwilling to learn that music themselves, however, they more or less compelled guests on the podium to take the load off the music director's shoulders. When I saw, during my Boston incumbency, that I could never reach an understanding with the politicos of the various composers' alliances, I gave up and became a freelancer. From that point onward I appeared only as an occasional guest, and then only with organizations where a subjective policy of choosing and performing music was considered an asset.

Many years later I received confirmation of my suspicion that my record of tackling complex modern music refused by others had won me no other label than that of a European Anti-Modern. I had chosen and scheduled for the New York Philharmonic Benjamin Britten's song cycle, *Nocturno*. At rehearsals, the tenor (who has appeared with me in many concerts and in a great variety of repertoire) told me of a conversation he had had with someone who had read that he was to sing the cycle. "And who is the conductor?" was the question. "Leinsdorf," answered the tenor. "I didn't know Leinsdorf conducted modern music," came the reply. It was genuinely amusing to me to have my suspicions confirmed. To be labeled European and capable of doing justice to the great classical masterpieces implies, without any need of evidence, an anti-modern stance. Like any other party-political label, however, this type of generalization not only disregards the facts, it is also pure prejudice.

Until 1943 I was exclusively a conductor of opera. When I began to venture into the symphonic field, I became aware that there were lobbies that counted how many minutes of new American music a conductor programmed for his orchestra. During the war years the Indianapolis orchestra played a new American piece at the beginning of every concert. As a young man at the beginning of his concert career, I was certainly not immune to the pressures from lobbies, but I never had any time for the notion that you were either for or against modern music, nor, for that matter, am I either for or against classic or baroque music.

As a performer who chooses and selects, I must also show a critical capacity to establish a standard by which my values can be measured. The ability to be critical is indispensable for composers and performers, not just for critics. Perhaps it would be better to replace the word *critical* with the word *selective*. I feel that Richard Strauss, for example, often devised themes and tunes that he wrote down without much critical examination. An honest musician does not know what it means to be wholly for or against any genre or style. That idea stems from the world of politics and has no place in aesthetic or artistic matters. Yet, the lobbyists evidently feel it is necessary to conquer the conservative "establishment" audiences with such political steamrollers. Should such a policy ever be crowned with success (and let us not forget that such success is difficult to define anyway), its moment of triumph will be short-lived. There is ample historical precedent to show that such effects may win a short burst of wider public approval but will surely fade within a few years.

It is unfortunate that the notion of the champion has not remained where it belongs: with the National Baseball League, Wimbledon, and Muhammad Ali. In those heady realms, a victory in the finals brings a trophy for the mantelpiece, a pocketful of cash, and the right to call oneself a champion until some other team or individual takes the title away. In music, the term *champion* is often employed in its other sense and has been adopted as one of the milder forms of brainwashing employed by publicity agents hoping to peddle their client as the "champion of Spontini" or the "champion of Lebanese music." In such a way they hope to establish an unassailable authority whose career will be greatly enhanced and whose number of engagements will be greatly multiplied.

The trouble is that the notion of the champion can really be a factor only in sports competitions. There are, regrettably, ever more competitions in piano, violin, voice, and other musical disciplines, and yet these competitions have never represented anything of real value. When I was given the opportunity to become a "champion," simply by virtue of having conducted certain scores at an earlier age than others, I wanted none of it. The misnomer was too blatant. When my agent began to spread the good word that I was a champion of modern music, for example, I objected that I was nothing of the sort. Although I have been close to modern music, I have been close only to compositions with which I could identify. I can also state without regret that, as music director, I sometimes had occasion to select certain modern pieces without conviction. It was part of the job. Those conductors who palm modern scores off to guest conductors rather than conduct them themselves are not honest. In any programming configuration today, guest conductors are asked to include something from the repertoire that will promote recognition of a true American school of music. European orchestral associations play the same game, but I have generally been lucky whenever I received a score under such circumstances.

I shall deal more fully with the problems of modern music in later chapters; the present chapter is designed merely to perform the same function as those framed licenses one often sees in doctors' offices. Just as those licenses are designed to reassure the nervous patient that the doctor is entitled to extract a tooth or administer a shot, this chapter is an attempt to show the reader why I feel qualified to talk about modern music, the staging of operas, and other topics related to the world of classical music.

Endorsements in the performing arts are displayed in many forms— foremost among which is the framed photograph on the wall. Given the quantity of modern, offbeat music I have performed, it might be argued that my wall should be adorned with unsolicited snapshots of composers, complete with their dedications. If I am derelict in this respect, I plead laziness. Had I indeed decked my walls appropriately, perhaps the tenor's friend (he who did not know that Leinsdorf conducted modern music) might have known better. If I needed any kind of defense, I might say merely that I take an attitude identical to that which I take toward many composers of the past. Even with contemporary composers whom I admire greatly, I have usually avoided works that do not appeal to me. I do not, for example, find it a sign of disloyalty that I have bypassed Berg's *Three Pieces for Orchestra* while seeking every opportunity to perform many other works for large orchestras.

My entire conducting career has been devoted to a large complex of music, and there has been no distinction made between classic, modern, or any other large stylistic form. My approach has been the same whether the menu offered Beethoven's Violin Concerto or Berg's Violin Concerto. Just as I do not seek the *Three Pieces* by Berg, I have never sought to conduct Beethoven's *Triple Concerto*, Op. 56. Even Beethoven's most partisan admirers are honor-bound to declare that by the yardsticks of Op. 55 and Op. 57 (the works preceding and following the *Triple Concerto*), Op. 56 is not on quite the same exalted level.

It is incumbent upon a conductor to select the program with a clarity of mind that excludes the notion of partisan championship. In 1964 I

arranged at Tanglewood for a retrospective of Richard Strauss to com-
memorate the centenary of his birth. In my endeavors to do more than
repeat for the umpteenth time the symphonic poems, I picked some
lesser-known works such as his *Parergon to the Sinfonia Domestica* for left-
hand piano and orchestra. This dismal piece was produced by Strauss
after he accepted a commission from pianist Paul Wittgenstein (brother
of the famous philosopher) who had lost his right arm in the First World
War. Wittgenstein also commissioned the better-known concerto by
Ravel and scores from other composers rather less skillful than Ravel.

I knew that *Parergon* had never made much impact, but when one
prepares a retrospective, one is compelled to hope that critical ears might
change with the passing of time. I still perform offbeat music if it is by
twentieth-century composers, but not if it is by eminent figures of the
past. Unlike some of my colleagues, who continue to believe that the
libraries must hold neglected treasures by Mozart, Schubert, and others,
I have more respect for the critical faculties of the listeners of the generations in which those composers lived (and indeed the listeners of the
generations immediately succeeding them).

There have always been people whose talents were misunderstood in
their lifetimes, but one cannot conclude from this that all genius was
misunderstood or that all critique in this regard has been mistaken. Every
art is in urgent need of mature critical opinion expressed through various
media (newspapers, magazines, and books). One must balance extremes
of partisan or prejudiced opinion. Critique that is of value must also have
the courage to state clearly, albeit with the respect that an accomplished
composer deserves, when age has taken its toll. One composer who illustrates this point well is Richard Strauss, who without doubt composed
several works of pure genius, in both a modern, forward-looking style
and in a purposefully archaic manner. I admire both styles, yet I also recognized as a fairly young person (long before the *Parergon* of my retrospective) that for some mysterious reason Strauss produced little after his
fiftieth birthday that could be deemed original or forward-looking.

Just as *Ariadne* was totally different from *Elektra*, and this within the
space of a few years, by a similar yardstick many of my colleagues have
little to laud in Bartók's *Concerto for Orchestra*, which they consider a
step backward. While that is an argument I understand, I have nonethe-

less enjoyed that work more than *The Miraculous Mandarin*, which is the choice of those colleagues who downgrade the concerto. Maybe the onset of age or illness turns a creative personality back toward the past; certainly nobody acquainted with Bartók would believe that he would go into reverse just because he needed a particular commission.

In my continuing debates with the avant-garde, and the rear-guard (and with divers other *gardes*), I have tried to take or leave any score without casting aspersions or shadows on other scores. There are certain long scores, for example, in which one finds shocking discrepancies between movements or sections. One such score is that of Mahler's Seventh Symphony, whose three middle sections are worthy to be included among the finest music ever composed by Mahler. Those wonderful passages are preceded by a first section that is merely a conventional, somewhat meandering attempt at a sonata. If, however, the first section is at least bearable (if one knows what is to follow), one certainly cannot say the same of the finale!

A Brave New World Deferred

I feel very fortunate with the fruits of my life in music, but I have also witnessed first hand the crises developing within America's musical life.

I see how the American establishment—the organizations that used to be irresistible magnets for all and sundry—is now frequently second choice whenever other, more attractive venues beckon. In the late 1980s three of the five most famous and prominent orchestras appointed new chief conductors (whom they obediently call music directors), although not one of the three had a sufficient grasp of the singular problems facing American orchestras. Those new music directors were selected as if it were fifty or sixty years earlier in our history, when orchestras might well have welcomed a new music coach raised on the classic and romantic musical repertoire. If (heaven forbid!) I had been chairman of those boards, I should surely have engaged all three of those maestros for extensive conducting assignments, but never as music directors. Musical talent is incompatible with the peculiarly American problems of the music director, but this fact has been lost on boards and on many managers.

On the last day of November 1990, I received an early Christmas card from a retired music publisher. Of German background and long American experience, he had been the chief representative of a prominent music publishing name of fine vintage. He wrote: "I am sorry indeed, that I had to miss your attractive programs. To drive from the upper end of Westchester County into town on a dark evening—it is possible only in a car—is always an enterprise, particularly in winter."

When, in the mid-1960s, the collective contract of the BSO eliminated Sunday afternoon concerts from the regular schedule, I received not one, but many such letters from people too old or impaired to drive at any time but on a holiday during daylight. After having digested the meaning of the new collective contract, I ventured the opinion that we would soon be banned from playing concerts in prime time, when we should all be at home watching television with our children.

This did not contribute to my popularity, but the episode demonstrated clearly to me that if one could not serve the interests of the local public in all its diversity, one could not be called a music director in the full and true sense of those words. The aforementioned letter also had this to say: "For me, the greatest problem of our musical life is the overuse of the standard symphonic literature."

The new appointees did indeed begin by offering all-Brahms programs, promises of more Dvořák, and more of the same predictable cuisine, simply prepared and served by a new chef. Why, some of you may ask, is that the wrong road? Because it disregards a fact expressed most bluntly in Leonard Bernstein's famous assertion that symphony is dead. The broader meaning of that sweeping statement is that the whole format of symphonic programs is tired, and if it continues to be overused it will appeal to ever fewer patrons.

Before I discuss contemporary composers I should explain where the musical Zeitgeist currently lies regarding the programs of American symphony orchestras. Prior to the publication of Beethoven's "Eroica" Symphony in 1805, instrumental concert music did not need the stand-up conductor—opera yes, but concert music no. It was done with the first violin leading and earlier still with the continuo player leading. This is all very well documented. As music became more complex, with the addition of more instruments and other complexities of rhythm and meter, it gradually became essential to have a person standing front-center, facing the players, and turning his back to the public. Unfortunately, those people began to consider themselves divinely inspired. Romantic composition steadily augmented the size of the orchestra to the point where a hundred and more players were required by Richard Strauss's tone poems. The ever more complex rhythms of Stravinsky and the abandonment of straight-laced, metric continuity in composers such as Debussy also ensured that conductors became indispensable.

After Stravinsky's *The Rite of Spring* (*Le Sacre du printemps*), the very large orchestra became a hallmark of many inferior compositions, while the great works of the twentieth century owed much to the smaller, leaner, less fattening sounds familiar to listeners in the eighteenth century. Some of my most beloved modern compositions are for fewer instruments (for example, Stravinsky's works for twenty or so wind instruments). The revival of Vivaldi's works and of a host of lesser baroque compositions, nowadays to be heard day-in, day-out on the radio, is a telling indication of modern tastes. Yet, in the face of this clear and unmistakable trend, our symphony orchestras stay with a regular contracted complement of up to 106 members, when it would be more productive to have these 106 contracts awarded to two groups (perhaps one group of sixty-six and the other of forty).

This is but one small solution to what has become a major problem: namely, the absence of young people in our audiences. It is also a solution that no self-possessed maestro would readily understand, since it would bring an unwelcome reduction of his (the stand-up conductor's) importance. Yet a music director who is not bitten by the bug of being *the* indispensable mediator between Genius and Listener, a music director who does not conduct, a music director who comes from producing recordings or from writing critiques, will quite easily come to this and other necessary conclusions. I had wanted to mix large orchestrations with smaller ones as early as my first orchestral appointment in 1943. A manager kindly informed me, however, that his board members had always wondered why, whenever there was a reduced orchestration on the platform, "we paid so many people."

One is forced to conclude that, while the conductor as star performer may be the high point of a festival, he is not essential to the continuity of a musical organization or for the commissioning of instrumental compositions. He is welcome, necessary, and an enhancement for complex compositions, such as *The Rite of Spring*, the works of Bartók, and others, but that is not to be confused with a music directorship. Trend and fashion in music are, then, moving away from the large ensemble. Colleagues who schedule, for their openings and closings, blockbusters such as Mahler's Eighth, Schoenberg's *Gurre-Lieder*, Bruckner's Eighth, and so on, are simply demonstrating that they are afflicted with what might be called the Rip van Winkle syndrome. It is certainly not easy to contemplate one's lifelong professional activity in terms of its diminishing significance.

In 1900 the Vienna opera house did not even list an opera's conductor on posters or in playbills. Former denizens of the opera's standing room have even described to me how they would crane their necks forward when the house lights dimmed to see whether it was indeed Mahler who had walked into the pit. It is also a historical document that the famous orchestra of the Grand Duke of Meiningen, under Hans von Bülow's celebrated guidance, consisted of forty-nine musicians who played Liszt and Brahms among other earlier scores. If you suggested to a modern conductor that he play a Brahms symphony with forty-nine musicians, he would be offended. Status and prestige, you see, require at least sixty.

The late Artur Rodzinski fought his board of directors in Cleveland for the entire decade of his incumbency to get more strings (seen as the acme of achievement for a music director of a major American symphony orchestra). By 1980, a century after von Bülow went to Meiningen, the movement to play early music on old instruments (or reconstructions of them) produced the United Kingdom's much-publicized Roger Norrington, who has also returned to historic numbers. I seek neither to praise nor criticize Norrington and his ilk; I say simply that in my view the mammoth orchestration that produced the mammoth conductors and the mammoth public relations machines has over those one hundred years outlived its usefulness (notwithstanding pieces such as that Super Bowl of works, *The Rite of Spring*).

Returning now to those living composers, except for two masterpieces by Stravinsky, the symphony as a form of composition died with

Gustav Mahler in 1911. As for the question, Why is the symphony dead? there are two answers, one for the musicologist, the other for the humanist. First, the symphony as a form—four movements: sonata, lied, danse, and rondeau—is inextricably tied to tonality. Now, tonality is gone, but even with the extended chromaticism of Wagner's *Tristan und Isolde* no symphony could have been accomplished. Any competent analysis of harmonic structure in compositions before and after 1900 would make this clear. Second, the death knell for music in the civilized world was sounded when the European monarchies of the Habsburgs, Romanovs, Hohenzollerns, Wittelsbachs, and the lesser duchies were obliged to quit at the end of the First World War. The remaining monarchies of Northern Europe, Belgium, Spain, and principalities such as Liechtenstein, are what one might call cottage nobility. Having never been influential in the arts, they probably took as their culture model the great constitutional British monarchy, with its devotion to horses and gardening.

Symphonic form, as the term is generally understood, reigned for more than 150 years (say between the Haydn of 1760 and the Mahler of 1910). To this form belong most of the concertos for solo instruments with orchestra, the great overtures in sonata form, and the entire canon of chamber music, ranging from the eighty-three string quartets by Haydn to the singular works of Verdi, Debussy, and Bartók. In other words, symphonies could be called sonatas for orchestra just as trios, duo-sonatas, and so on could be called symphonies for small groups or even for one instrument (Beethoven's "Hammerklavier" Sonata, Op. 106 is a prime example). Incidentally, the interdependence of symphony and tonality was best expressed by Alban Berg in his introduction to his opera *Wozzeck*. Whatever our contemporary composers choose as their formal structure for any composition, it should not be for ensemble with large string sections—not with forty-eight, nor with twenty-four. Massed strings play well together only in tonal music. The violin and viol families are not built for chromatic music, which is based on a set of compromises that are quite easily managed by solo players, but rarely by choric groups. This is an old story, yet too many composers, lured by the glamour and publicity of the big band, ignore the most compelling principles of music's autonomous development to win extra attention.

The autonomous development of musical composition represents, in the broadest terms, the end of romanticism and its attached nineteenth-century European cultural values. It has led to a return to music *qua* music and the principles of the eighteenth century, but within a harmonic and rhythmic language that is post-chromatic and post–*The Rite of Spring*.

I should, by the way, stress that in my view *The Rite of Spring* marks not a beginning, but an end. The beginning of the "modern" was, in my view, marked by those three seminal works to which I referred earlier: Stravinsky's *L'Histoire du soldat*, Alban Berg's *Wozzeck*, and Kurt Weill's *The Threepenny Opera*. The authors of their texts are, respectively, C. F. Ramuz, Georg Büchner, and Bertolt Brecht. Again, political factors were paramount, and these works are wondrous examples of what might have been had the Weimar Republic lasted and the Nazis not taken over Europe for twelve years (a period from which music has yet to recover).

The world of music—at least the well-funded world of music—operates essentially from within a booth equipped with a pair of superb earphones emitting the loveliest noises from the finest prerecorded tapes and CDs. It is thus obvious to me that the leaders of today's musical world are poorly qualified to lead music into the future. The prevailing musical expertise is counterproductive, and appointments made today by the major organizations of the musical establishment seem to typify the prevailing retrospective policy. Basic policy has been determined by musicians and committee members who strive to do an ever more "perfect" job of rendering the music of several different styles. The perfection they seek is embodied (alas!) in a telling phrase that I seem to hear every time an enthusiast comes backstage after a good performance: "This should have been recorded."

There is the rub: recording now sets our standards. Recordings, though, are documents of perfection. They are not to be confused with performances, which change from Thursday to Friday because a performance is a form of entertainment that is based on mutuality between audience and performer. (If you wish to challenge my use of the word *entertain* you may look it up in the dictionary, where it is defined first as "to hold mutually" [French *entre tenir*, German *unter halten*]—always there is this central concept of holding something together.)

If music as performance is again to become a healthy and health-giving activity, the dominant striving for more perfection must be replaced by a new priority, that of honesty. The "star" system and the obvious overuse of the great classic masterpieces have opened the box-office doors to many kinds of dishonest dealing.

The absentee musical leader is a dishonest dealer. The scheduling of programs merely because a record company wants to tape them is dishonest dealing. The overbooking of artists is dishonest, since such artists arrive at their engagements in a state of fatigue. The cancellation, by famous tenors, of concert or opera appearances merely because a recording session is offered unexpectedly is dishonest. And organizations that reengage dishonest artists are ipso facto choosing to condone dishonesty.

The great beauty of this argument is that those laypeople who "know nothing about music" (as they are wont to say) are nevertheless extremely sensitive to symptoms of dishonesty. This I know from many conversations with acquaintances who do not know the difference between C major and C minor. Such people do know when the soloist is tired and goes routinely through the program, they see through the conductor who poses as educator by frowning on his audience, and they can sense whether the musicians are fully involved with the music. In fact, they notice everything that escapes those quixotic experts who listen so attentively for perfection.

So there are two overrated concepts: those of perfection and competition. As for the former, I would suggest that we replace the pursuit of perfection with the pursuit of "good enough." We should be asking ourselves questions such as: Is this commissioned composition good enough for the occasion? Is this concert good enough for my family and me? Is this soloist good enough to play Beethoven's Violin Concerto? That is all. As for competitions and prizes, Grammies, Tonys, Oscars, and the like may be good for publicity, but they should be reserved for the world of sports, in which solid documentation exists as myriad statistics: batting averages, earned runs, games finished pitching, fielding chances missed, runs scored, and so forth. While prizes and competitions are doubtless here to stay, they are what they are: pleasant for the recipient but meaningful only if the public agrees with the award ten years or so later. Mozart was recognized as a genius by his contemporaries and two hundred years later I think we can safely say that most people still agree with that judgment.

In September 1986 a music critic of *The New York Times* wrote an introductory essay about a forthcoming festival to be held at the city's Museum of Modern Art. This festival, said the critic, would feature the creative high points of *fin de siècle* Vienna, and he went on to stress that the music of Berg, Webern, and particularly of Schoenberg "was still anathema to mainstream audiences." This statement is not only sweeping, it is also erroneous on two counts: Schoenberg was certainly not anathema in Europe, and New York's symphony subscribers are not the mainstream audience of the twentieth century. At the time of his fiftieth birthday in 1924, Arnold Schoenberg was recognized as a major master of musical composition. His work had met with receptions varying from ecstatic responses by sold-out houses to loud scandals and protests. I believe that his endeavors to merge the classical (symphonic) forms of composition with atonality and twelve-tone composition have led us nowhere. In fact, the eminence associated with his name derives mainly from his early and late periods of composition.

Whereas it is unreasonable to expect a brief article in a daily paper to give a balanced report of an adventurous musical explorer, there is less excuse for misrepresenting the public of New York, vintage 1986. This is a fragmented culture with a fragmented public that is very hard to pin down with definitions. The status of contemporary composition is without doubt problematical, and the fate of the Weimar Republic has been a very influential factor.

Perhaps, though, we might approach the puzzles of our time by looking at two key questions that are rarely the subject of serious critical debate, namely, Who is the public? and What exactly constitutes success? Most musicologists do not touch such questions, while most sociologists do not consider music sufficiently important to raise pertinent questions about it. The leaders of our music establishment therefore have to rely, for the most part, on public opinion polls to aid them in their marketing decisions. While such polls may be valid for the pretzel industry, I would argue that they are not quite so valid for the world of serious music.

One

Conducting: The View from the Podium

What Is a Conductor?

The word is indeed *what*, and not *who*. To the question, Who is a conductor? the proper reply might be, "Anybody who stands or sits, in front of or with, a group of singers or musicians; who motions to them, with or without the aid of a baton, in more or less familiar gestures; who appears to preside over the passage of the music from the first to the last note."

Few, however, know what a conductor is, and the ranks of the unknowing include many who have written about music and even some who conduct music and are paid for it. I can assure the reader, by the way, that this last, apparently outrageous, view is the fruit of countless seminars, symposia, and what are euphemistically known as master classes.

As in the case of other puzzling items of nomenclature, a good look at the language may help both to clarify things and entertain the curious. In the English-speaking world the word *conductor* is used variously for a person who drives a streetcar, for one who examines and punches your ticket on a train, and for the musician who, as described above, motions the necessary directions to singers and/or instrumentalists.

The German word *Dirigent* is applied only to the music director of a chorus, symphony orchestra, or opera ensemble. No streetcar navigator or train controller has any linguistic relationship with the *Dirigent*. In French the word is *chef*, a word also used to identify the fellow who prepares the spaghetti, the fattening sauce, the soufflé Grand Marnier, and so forth. In French job advertisements, confusion is avoided by referring to the musician as the *chef d'orchestre* and to the other guy as the *chef de cuisine*. I might add that whereas I never heard of a soufflé tasting like a fugato, there have been occasions when a French orchestra's rendition was like the thickest sauce of chef Lucullus.

The fate of the German term *Kapellmeister* is a classic example of the vagaries of language. The term obviously derives from the original Italian expression *Maestro di cappella*, which was used to describe a distinguished and demanding church position. Since the end of the eighteenth century, however, the word has become more or less synonymous with a routine time-beater more reminiscent of the traffic cop than the charismatic dreamboat so handsomely modeled by Leopold Stokowski. To understand just what a Kapellmeister was and what he had to deliver, one need look only at the contract established between the Council of St. Thomas's church in Leipzig and Johann Sebastian Bach. The Kapellmeister was composer, organist, continuo player, conductor, teacher of boys in music and in Latin, escort of those boys [to the funerals at which they sang], and general tutor. A Kapellmeister was responsible, in short, for anything musical that took place at that particular church. There were also Kapellmeisters, such as Joseph Haydn, whose function was to serve princes on their estates. How, when, or why the term came to denote a humdrum musician I do not know, but opera houses on the German provincial circuit gradually established the following ranking of titles: Generalmusikdirektor, First Kapellmeister, and (according to the size of the establishment) Second and Third Kapellmeister. I suspect that the "general music director" increasingly took on all the new productions and gave the less important shows to the First or Second Kapellmeister. The almost inevitable consequence was that the Kapellmeisters were obliged to direct performances either with very few, if any, rehearsals. They therefore tended to slide into the kind of routine approach that repertoire opera makes almost mandatory by its somewhat chaotic premises. It seems a pity that a term formally describing a very noble position should have been relegated to the status of dismissive epithet. The first requirement for a conductor of the great musical masterpieces of three centuries is a thorough knowledge of composition. This knowledge is best learned as part of a broader curriculum embracing harmony, counterpoint, and forms of composition. Without such a background it is unlikely that one will be able to read a score, and without score reading there can be no individual interpretation. Asked once to participate in an ambitious training project for young conductors, I insisted that all those who wished to study with me should have a comprehensive knowledge of composition. Although my condition was not rejected outright, be assured that I shall not be participating in the project.

Now, let us attempt to answer the question posed by our title. First, a conductor is primarily a musician, whose only instrument is his body (with or without baton). With early music it is now again the correct custom to conduct from an instrument, be it keyboard continuo or first violin. For music after 1800 the stand-up conductor uses no instrument (with the notable exception of the violinist-conductor of the Johann Strauss *Stehgeiger* tradition). Second, there are four kinds of specialist conductors: choral, popular (or "pop"), operatic, and symphonic. There are also conductors who are competent in all four specialist areas, but very few choose to do this and even fewer are entirely at home with it.

Few of the world's choral conductors are equally good with orchestral music; some just cannot lead oratorios prepared with chorus in a performance that also includes orchestra and soloists. Conductors of pop music are often frustrated exiles from the so-called classic repertoire, and generally find that they cannot go back once they have crossed the artificial divide that separates those two musical disciplines. Many opera conductors are lost when they stand on a concert podium to perform symphonic music. The same is true of symphony conductors, who often become totally confused if they try to conduct an opera. A "complete" conductor must be at home in all four specialties, however, because those specialties are each part of the overall whole that is music.

The choral conductor must have infinite patience because a vocal ensemble is harder to achieve than an ensemble of instruments. In opera, furthermore, the chorus members are expected to memorize their parts. This is a time-consuming procedure and, for the conductor, a tedious one. Since few if any opera conductors have ever done more than visit chorus rehearsals for a quick check before an orchestra's general rehearsals, choral preparation has been delegated to musicians who either have no desire to perform or who have been compelled by circumstances to be content with such an unsatisfactory assignment.

Over a period of decades this procedure bred generations of musicians who had a good ear for vocal training but no knack for conducting. During many rehearsals these choral trainers develop a set of motions that are stimulating to the singers but entirely unorthodox when applied to instrumental ensembles. Put more bluntly, orchestras cannot follow the Svengali-type contortions so prized by conductors of choral performances that are either a cappella (entirely without instrumental accompaniment) or accompanied by piano only. Like all nonscientific specialties, that of the choral conductor has a deteriorating effect. As the old saying goes: The specialist knows more and more about less and less. The choral specialist learns more and more about producing the best and most appropriate sounds, but less and less about diction and tempo.

The two best-known American classical pop-concert specialists were frustrated symphony concert conductors who discovered that when they had scored hits and acquired popularity, the so-called classical podium was suddenly no longer their domain. This I judge from acquaintance with both conductors. I have no idea what their original musical tastes and orientation were, but it is against my best instincts to assume that some musicians are talented only for marches or the glitz of Tin-Pan-Alley arrangements. At moments such as this I generally like to assail the German stuffed shirts of the Victorian era who succeeded in constructing a wall between music that "elevates" and music that merely "amuses." The road is long indeed from the B minor Mass to the sounds of lederhosen-clad bandsmen in a Bavarian beer garden, but when the Bavarian bandsmen blow in tune and work up a decent bounce, it is still music. Like Dom Perignon and Coca Cola or soufflé and potato latkes, the two are clearly related in some way. The general perception of the pop music conductor is mistaken, and was created largely by prejudice. Whereas lowly "entertainment" music requires a depraved character, the great spiritual feast of "Olympian" music requires the opposite—so prejudice would have us believe. This notion was common in the nineteenth century, and the popular images it has inspired have generally been as misleading as the most whimsical creations of Madison Avenue's finest.

My experience has shown that the pop music conductor stands or falls by the caliber of his music library (meaning the caliber of his arrangements of the latest hits and the caliber of the editing in the orchestral parts). Pop programs must be prepared in one-fourth of the rehearsal time allotted to classic pieces of comparable length. There may be an occasional short passage that runs by itself, so to speak, but the preparation of a pop program with a symphony orchestra is generally more complex than that for music played for the regular subscribers. It is always trickier to organize a sequence of eight or ten pieces than to organize the more familiar standard program of short opener, concerto, intermission, and major symphonic work. Another crucial point is that the instrumentation for short pieces within the same program is often very diverse. Those players who have nothing to do in a particular piece should be aware of that fact, or you may otherwise find your percussionist opening the piece with a loud crash of the cymbals although it has a soft, tender opening and no cymbal part in sight.

Given the number of technicalities involved, a two-and-a-half-hour rehearsal leaves scarcely any time to discuss finer musical points, special effects, or indeed anything much beyond the dreaded routine of the recording process. Moreover the "pop" conductor does not always enjoy the services of the senior principal players, and rare indeed is the orchestra that can field a reserve squad of the same caliber as the first team. Having said that, I do know one American symphony orchestra that after two decades and hundreds of concerts finally achieved the unique distinction of a woodwind section without the slightest weakness. There is, by the way, an octet by Stravinsky that betrays in the first ten minutes of the first rehearsal where a wind section's weaknesses lie.

To return to my central point, however, I would suggest that those music snobs who love to dismiss "popular" classical music do not have the faintest notion how difficult it is. As in all serious performing arts, the comic and light-hearted are often based on premises that are more delicate than those of the tragic. Opera and symphony need not, and should not, be regarded as mutually exclusive specialties. Whenever it seems that they are, it is because of the conductor's weakness. The opera specialist who feels lost in front of a symphony orchestra is the type who functions best with the voices acting as lead music to an orchestral accompaniment. The operatic music director can, however, thrive for many years, in what is an extremely taxing profession, without ever being found out.

A prime example of this was a certain conductor who was an undisputed master in opera and who knew a large repertoire (really *knew* it right down into the bowels of the score). I recall one occasion when he proudly told another, very well known, conductor that he had found a mistake in the fourth horn part of a work that the other conductor had conducted many times from the same orchestra material. This was, of course, a matter of no consequence, since in heavy and chromatic musical settings certain misprints sometimes endure because they constitute the kind of "error" that is noticed by the eye but not the ear. The incident merely showed that the conductor who discovered the printing error was a more thorough reader, but not necessarily also a better interpreter. This particular opera conductor felt intense frustration at the limitations of his range and did everything in his power to win symphonic engagements. On one occasion, when we happened to find ourselves in the same town, he asked me to attend one such engagement. I did so, and confess that I cannot, in retrospect, explain quite what was wrong. Everything was in its place, all the right notes were there at the right time, but somehow those notes were devoid of content. More I am unable to explain.

I might add that, whereas this particular conductor is no longer among the living, one could cite similarly baffling cases of living giants of the opera pit who are curiously unwilling to achieve the same convincing and extraordinary projection in symphonic works. I say "unwilling" because I simply cannot believe that a conductor capable of giving a masterful rendition of an opera score should not be able to do the same for symphonic works. Perhaps such conductors refuse concert engagements partly because they feel it is too late in their career to learn the repertory. Perhaps they never tried to treat the solos in symphonic music as they treat the sung solos of opera, or perhaps the absence of a text inhibits the imagination of those who have been exclusively active in music that has an explicit poetic or dramatic text.

The opposite phenomenon, that of the concert maestro who cannot get through an opera, is easily explained. There is no psychology involved, and it is rarely a case of being unable to read the score or any similar musical limitation. The problem is a lack of technique, and yet since there is no teachable technique of conducting, it is not easy to explain, in nontechnical language, exactly what "lack of technique" means. Readers should note that my opinions about technique are far from being entirely accepted by others. In my view the teaching of the unteachable is going on all around us and I fear only the musicians themselves know the full horror of what they go through.

Technique, in conducting, equals flexibility. Flexibility is possible only when the conductor listens *before* the next gesture of the timer, which is that part of the body that takes care of the metric flow. The timer can be either left or right arm, left or right hand, a nodding head, or a stamping foot. The latter is not quite the "done thing," by the way, for polite indoor events. I once had to tell a chorus master who rehearsed with much loud foot time-beating that he might as well find some other way since there was little point in doing something in rehearsal that could not be repeated in public concert.

The concert conductor needs this flexibility for the greatest musical masterpieces, but it is not indispensable for very good renditions of great scores. In an opera house it is a rather different story: one cannot negotiate act 1 of *La Bohème* without the crucial ability to listen to a singer or singers before conducting. I would caution that if this principle is taken too far, that same flexibility degenerates into obedient trailing behind the lead of whomever or whatever carries the tune. We then have the opera conductor who has, for all intents and purposes, abdicated the classic task of conducting.

As I mentioned earlier, there is no reason why a traditionally trained musician should not be able to master the entire spectrum (can one use the word *spectrum* for something so completely auditory?) of choral, pop, operatic, and symphonic music. One point should, however, be made in this context: would-be conductors of that daunting spectrum should certainly learn other languages besides their own, because those languages can bridge the culture gaps that keep conductors trapped within those specialties. The old Metropolitan Opera management used to employ a German conductor for German operas only, an Italian conductor for Italian, and (*faute de mieux*) a French-Canadian for French opera.

Some of the artistic troubles of modern American musical institutions result from their having no casting or programming director. Any conductor, regardless of how talented and devoted he or she may be, needs a casting director. Not having a casting director was not a problem as long as every great or second-echelon orchestra had a real music director (by "real" I mean one who stays with the orchestra for most, if not all, its working season). Since this is now very rarely the case, however, one rarely sees these days any evidence of proper casting. Conductors assert their limited repertoires by insisting on their party pieces, and the result is an overall program for the season that makes no sense. In trying to please too many, such programs end up by pleasing very few. Most of these problems are due to a deterioration in the morale—and indeed the morality—of conductors. The same deterioration is also partly responsible for the dreadful misdeeds of operatic stage directors. Returning to our title, however, let us ask two further questions: What is a conductor's overall task? Under what circumstances and according to what premises does the conductor work?

The role of the conductor began in the opera house, where it quickly became indispensable. It then moved over into the concert hall, but did not become indispensable there until the nineteenth century, when the ensemble that had sufficed for Haydn, Mozart, and the early Beethoven began to include more instruments and larger string bodies, and the music became metrically and rhythmically more elaborate.

Whereas every simple metric division can certainly be rendered perfectly without a stand-up conductor, no composite meter can be so rendered unless there is a stand-up conductor. Even now, any permanent ensemble trying to play classical symphonies with the first violin "leading" would be shipwrecked when it tried the first movement of Beethoven's "Eroica" symphony. Why? Because the meter alternates between three-in-a-measure and one-in-a-measure, and the rhythm contains so many hemiolas (at times a combination of three-in-a-measure against a hemiola) that no ensemble could possibly negotiate these passages unaided. The "Eroica" symphony might, in this sense, be credited for bringing the concert conductor into the world. (One of the best spots, by the way, is the passage just after measure 620.) I would also add that many younger conductors are uncomfortable with composite meters and consequently subdivide the phrase in a rather clumsy fashion. This awkwardness is instantly transferred to the ensemble. A rhythmically unstable musician who will "beat" the $\frac{12}{8}$ section of the Adagio in Beethoven's Ninth in twelve, instead of letting it float in four large metric units, does nothing less than butcher one of the most sublime passages in the history of music.

The problem of composite meters exists in opera scores too, and yet, whereas certain butchers of the opera podium are just as merciless in their savagery as some of their concert hall counterparts, the nature of opera is such that fewer people notice it. There can also be one or two handy alibis in the opera world. A singer who drags the tempo, one might argue, practically forces the chopping up of the rhythmic line. Without rehearsal time and after a lapse of twenty days since the previous performance, one might further argue, nobody can be expected to conduct the grand line, sweeping with the most elegant bravura through the score.

There are elements of the conductor's task that can be negotiated. A glance at the documentation in musical biographies often reveals, for example, that a great deal of effort has been put into negotiating the basic conditions for good musical performances. Self-confidence in rhythmic and metric breadth, however, is not a negotiable item and cannot be taught. It is quite amusing to read, in music reviews, eloquent descriptions of a conductor's "insight," "charismatic perceptions," or "unidiomatic yet convincing liberties," when the truth is that the peerless leader in question cannot conduct the Adagio of the Ninth in four. Of course, if the critic really did recognize the "insight" for what it was, the critic would have to be a fully equipped conductor. In that case, I would venture to suggest that he might well prefer to conduct rather than write reviews.

It may not have helped my popularity when I wrote in a book for conductors that, whereas most listeners recognize the difference between a good and a bad pianist or singer, few (including licensed experts) know the difference between a good and a bad conductor. The critics go straight into the grander and more glamorous issues of interpretation without stopping first to tell the reader whether the fellow in question knows how to conduct.

We know, for example, that Stravinsky made many changes in his early scores when he found it necessary to conduct them (this I heard from Ernest Ansermet). Like many modern composers, and notwithstanding his gigantic stature as (probably) the greatest of the great twentieth-century figures, Stravinsky wrote many things in his scores that are not necessary for that particular "spelling." When he began to conduct he simplified those passages, even though more experienced conductors had already learned to deal with the complexities in question.

There is more to rhythmic and metric security than an unteachable inner pulse. The issue concerns the entire relationship between the conductor and those who play with him. I avoid, by the way, the usual term *under*, because if musicians find themselves playing *under* a conductor, it generally means something is amiss. An accomplished conductor has people playing *with* him, while a good faker will have an experienced orchestra play *in spite of* him. The faker's priority is to impress the least sophisticated among the crowd. To him, the appearance of being a commanding figure is easily accomplished by memorizing the score just enough not to wreck the ship. Memorizing a few cymbal crashes and similar prominent attacks does not do any harm either, of course. The appropriate majestic-looking gesture, followed by the crash itself, will convince many onlookers that there has never been a better sound or a more dramatic reading. In such cases the poor players, seated at supper, might be heard recalling how "tonight Tchaikovsky got the kiss of death," or some such account of the proceedings.

Beyond the orchestra members, though, it often seems that little or nothing is known about *what* conducting is or about *what* a conductor is, does, and does not do. A youngish Met opera conductor once came to me with a specific problem he had encountered at a tricky climax in an Italian opera's most dramatic scene. Since I had conducted the same opera at the same opera house, he wished me to tell him what to do. We looked at the score and I told him: "Do nothing, just stop conducting." The day after his next performance he called me and said simply, "It worked," although he was still laughing at the fact that "doing nothing" could solve a tricky conducting problem. This advice could not have worked in another opera house; it was based on my acquaintance with that company's orchestra and with the acoustic conditions of the place. In different circumstances my advice might have caused a total disaster. Confidence in the ears and musicianship of the players is one of the criteria for a mutual understanding between conductor and ensemble.

The common pulsation must, however, be there. No faking is possible in that area, and no signal of hand or arm will be of any use if it is mechanically learned and does not come from a sense of inner security. The hand or baton (or meat cleaver) does only what the brain commands. I have often encountered cases in which musicians find it impossible to play "together" although the conductor has the clearest and most meticulous "beat."

Thus it becomes more complicated to explain adequately *what* a conductor is. Perhaps one might try to explain it by describing what happens when the conductor is not in charge. Once I was asked to run through the final movement of Mozart's "Jupiter" Symphony as an acoustic experiment. New foam-rubber cushioning was being tried out and the management wanted to record a well-known piece, of simple sonic fabric, and later compare it with the pre-foam-rubber acoustic. The occasion was a rehearsal with a top-quality orchestra that was not terribly familiar with me (and vice versa). We went through the movement, and it went so well that the resulting tape might easily have been sold as a first-class commercial recording. It was a very familiar piece, and the orchestra had regularly played and recorded the piece with conductors who had no problem doing Mozart in style. Nonetheless, the sound was also due to the nature of the exercise. My task for that run-through was merely to let them be, let them play as they had been used to, and this meant, in effect, that I did virtually nothing.

That German orchestra, incidentally, once sent a committee of players to my room, during the intermission of a second rehearsal, to declare that they felt unable to learn Debussy's *Ibéria* within the scheduled rehearsal time. This was despite the fact that the scheduled time was as long as that usually planned for any American orchestra. In America Debussy is a repertoire composer, in Germany he is not, but it still took them a lot longer than it would take an American ensemble to learn what they did not know. The Germans do not consider Debussy an important composer (perhaps the pianists do, but not the conductors). No conductor could have made that orchestra learn the piece without doubling the rehearsal schedule and that was simply not possible.

The point of this tale is that the conductor cannot correct such a situation on a short visit. I had been asked specifically to do *Ibéria*, but had failed to inquire when the work had been played most recently. My excuse, had I needed one, might have been that I had such confidence in the orchestra from previous encounters that it did not occur to me that Debussy might be an unknown composer to them.

At this point readers may have noted that the word *interpretation* has not cropped up very much in this essay. That is because the essay seeks rather to explain misconceptions about conducting and replace them with intelligible definitions and descriptions of the skill and (sometimes) art of the conductor. The preparation of singers and players requires physical coaching. In opera the conductor is the coach of singers, some of who may need a patient pianist who will play the score while the singer learns and memorizes the role.

A conductor who is more than an obedient accompanist of the vocalists will not only coach them, he will insist on doing so. Coaching in the music world is in many ways very similar to coaching in the world of sports. In music, as in sports, the coach aims to bring together, as a team, a number of individuals who will, in public performance, demonstrate unanimity of purpose. Those individuals must learn the same phrasing, the same pronunciation of the language sung, and the same emphasis on similar themes and tunes. They must produce a balanced sound that requires a flexible reading of dynamic markings and a few hundred other items concerning nuance, special effects, and whatever else the score and work may require.

It is among the more regrettable aspects of the present international music circuit that the entire process of coaching opera has gone to seed. What a melancholy tale might be told of the reasons for the lopsided and musically insufficient preparation of certain operatic shows! In symphonic music there has as yet been no attempt to delegate coaching (rehearsing) to substitute or assistant conductors. Only legitimate illness will ever bring an assistant before the orchestra for a "reading" rehearsal, and the results are rarely satisfactory. The central requirement is the same for opera and symphony alike: that of having a conductor who acts as coach and performer, without any separation of the two tasks.

There are many well-documented examples of why this is so. There was the case of the opera production for which there were staging rehearsals, under a "producer," for several weeks. When the great conductor subsequently appeared, one day before the first general rehearsal of the orchestra, he found the entire cast set in their ways (not only in matters histrionic but also in matters musical). This was because they had been rehearsing for weeks with a pianist whose job it was to do what the stage director wished. During that process numerous habits develop and many tempos and positions become so well established that the great conductor finds there is very little space (or time) to make the necessary corrections (let alone bring his reading to the fore).

Talk about interpretation is therefore very often nothing more than fanciful. The critic or lay observer who indulges in debates over this or that may simply take a combination of haphazard contributions from several individuals as a consciously planned and arrived interpretation when it is nothing of the sort. In this context, the preliminary interview revealing "what the new production of *Don Giovanni* has in store for us" turns out to be mere brainwashing. If in opera the conductor was, once upon a time, responsible for the work's interpretation, this is no longer the case. In the wonderful language of the Italians he is nonetheless still listed as Maestro Concertatore e direttore d'orchestra. A symphony concert is simpler, but here the Concertatore, or permanent coach, has turned into an occasional coach whose tasks are carelessly covered by the title of music director.

A conductor of a symphony orchestra used to be a true coach, forming a true permanent ensemble that knew how to react to a downbeat (in the present world of peripatetic conductors this is not, I regret to say, to be taken for granted). Today's symphony orchestras are rapidly losing whatever unanimous style they had back in the days when they still functioned with a bona fide conductor. So here the answer to the title query is: A conductor *was* a musician who coached an orchestra to achieve unanimity when performing orchestral compositions. Now, however, most conductors (and all conductors of major international orchestras) are part-time operators. They still coach when they rehearse, but their coaching cannot endure beyond the day when the next guest conductor takes the podium—whether this is a matter of two or six weeks later makes little difference. The reasons for this most significant change are, like most developments in our classic music cultivation, largely a matter of sociology.

The two essential functions of the music conductor are first to coach and second to be a leading performer when the coached group appears before the public. To continue the (for me, irresistible) parallels between the musical ensemble and the sports team: a good conductor is like certain player managers in baseball who are in charge of the team both on and off the field. Similarly, just as athletes are fond of saying, "you can't win 'em all," so the musician must acknowledge that "you can't always have perfection."

The parallels quickly run out, though. Whereas the baseball manager who hits a losing streak will be swiftly fired, musical leaders who "lose" too many performances (demoralizing too many musicians along the way) may carry on with impunity for many years. Whereas a professional baseball club has owners who make a profit on their investment only if they have a winning club with a winning slugger, a professional orchestra generally has no owners and is organized as a nonprofit organization. Whereas every small child after the age of four knows the difference between a game won and a game lost, few think of musical concerts in the same terms. It is not that those terms do not apply; it is simply that those who have always seen classical music as a kind of holy rite would find such a notion altogether too shocking.

Unfortunately for my argument I have no inside knowledge of religious corporations such as churches or synagogues. I therefore have no idea whether any member of the clergy has ever been fired for losing too many parishioners. Church leaders do, however, seem to fire preachers, rabbis, and so forth only rarely, and only if they cause public scandal (even then most reluctantly). In music we do not seem to have scandals of quite the same nature. The relationships of musical personalities, for example, appear to elicit virtually no interest beyond a narrow circle of gossipmongers. Yet, musical organizations seem to be as helpless as their

ecclesiastical counterparts in dealing with a losing streak. I suspect that
few lay members of directors' boards could ever tell the difference
between two conductors of their orchestras. Critics who are otherwise very well schooled in music and whose musical judgments are
often otherwise quite unexceptionable are quite lost when it comes to
conductors.

The term *interpretation* touches upon many different aspects of a
performance or performer (particularly a conductor). One often hears
questions such as, How does she play Mozart? How does he conduct
Tchaikovsky? or How do they sound in Debussy? It is generally the job of
the critic to reply to such questions, but I suspect that few self-respecting
editors would allow the following "critique," for example, to reach the
printer unedited:

> Maestro uses a six-eight pattern of time signal, which creates in
> every other measure an involuntary ritard because he eschews
> the Italian manner which divides the six-eight meter from a
> basic "two." The Germans signal the third eighth in the same
> manner as the second eighth note in $\frac{4}{4}$, namely, to the left.

This sentence does mean something very real if it is demonstrated to
a class of students who think that one can learn how to "beat" the metri-
cal flow of a piece of music, but in writing for the public, such descriptions invariably meet a well-deserved end on the editor's spike.

So what else is there then to report and review? Why, interpretation,
of course, and yet interpretation is, to put it bluntly, a matter of fashion.
I recall one review written by a well-known New York critic about a well-
known conductor performing with his well-known orchestra the well-
known sixth symphony of Beethoven. I know the critic, the conductor,
and the orchestra. The critic is a very bright, honorable person who has
an encyclopedic knowledge of all things pianistic and who absorbed most
other music during many years as a meticulous, attentive, and open-
minded critic. After the usual general comments he came to the symphony, calling what he had heard "an old-fashioned performance." I
understood what he meant, although I doubt many lay readers did. I was
intrigued because I do agree that interpretations change with impercep-

tibly changing fashions. Perhaps those changes are even more perceptible to critics, who have to go to more concerts than I.

While we are on the subject of fashion, I hope I may be allowed a (very brief) digression into the world of men's clothing fashions (which I confess has never been my primary concern, but which does have a certain impact on musical life). While I do not generally notice when lapels get narrower, I have noticed the fashion of wearing one's black bow tie outside the collar. I have also noticed that it has become very difficult to find a bow tie that has not been sewn by the manufacturer. Now I, for one, had always thought that a pre-sewn butterfly was considered bad form!

So what exactly is an old-fashioned performance of the "Pastoral" Symphony? I suspect that the maestro in question conducted the work as he had learned it forty years before. Judging from my acquaintance with that maestro, I would say that he does not like to reexamine old, thrice-familiar scores, but prefers to steer a safer, more familiar course. I am certain that this was true in this instance, since the same conductor once stated quite openly to his musicians that he, as a teacher of so many years' standing, had no wish to learn new things; and yet, if one does not learn new things, then one does not relearn old things. If one does not constantly relearn the great works of the repertoire, then one cannot keep pace with how *they* change. Beyond the notion of fashion, interpretation essentially amounts to every person's individual idea of a piece (provided that there is a preconceived idea). Perhaps the critic is even more of an interpreter than the performer, in the sense that it is his or her function (at least nowadays) to "interpret the interpretation."

Right now in musical history the height of fashion is to play ever older music in a so-called authentic style. This is (please forgive the expression) bull. The term *authenticity* sometimes seems to be little more than a catchword masking a convenient method of making a fortune out of re-recording the great repertory of Mozart and Beethoven. Of course, the members of the authentic-music movement have as much right as any other musician to perform Bach and Mozart in the way they see fit. In November 1984, in Vienna, I heard Nikolaus Harnoncourt's rendition of the Bach C minor mass. I found it very enjoyable and I compliment him, but let no one try to convince me that this was the authentic, or only, way of doing it.

Similarly, there is more than one Toscanini, or Walter, or Klemperer. Interpretation by conductors is a very personal, fluid affair. The conductor Wilhelm Furtwängler, for example, was one of the cult figures on the Viennese podium in the late 1920s, when I began to attend concerts regularly. I watched him change as an interpreter over the years just as almost every conductor changes. In this respect, conductors as interpreters are much like actors. Whereas some actors are instantly recognizable, regardless of their makeup and costume, others are so completely transformed that their identity is hidden. Still, I believe quite strongly that even if some interpretation may be very faithful to the more explicit symbols of the composer, the variables involved are too numerous for interpretation to be the object of critique. The criticism that one does see is mostly superficial and does not even tell us how good the interpreting conductor is.

I earlier referred to Igor Stravinsky and the changes he made in his early scores after he began to conduct regularly. This, I maintain, is perhaps the definitive illustration of how even a composer of works of genius may not find the best way of interpreting his scores if he is not a good conductor. I have boundless admiration for Stravinsky, whose works I perform whenever and wherever possible, and yet I believe Ernst Ansermet was quite right to be angry at Stravinsky when that great composer rejected the tempos of Pierre Monteux and of Ansermet himself.

Those two conductors were among the earliest prominent interpreters of Stravinsky's ballet scores and had a clear recollection and understanding of those early tempos. The two master conductors obviously knew the tempos from the days of the earliest public showings (the word *knew* here means something quite fixed). Their disagreement arose because the great composer, who later conducted *concert* performances of his ballets, was (unlike Monteux and Ansermet) unconcerned with the split-second timing of the *fouetté*.

A composer may quite rightly make many other changes to his score, besides those he makes to his original directions. Changes are made due to numerous factors that affect a musical score just as the aging process affects the human body. Richard Strauss, unlike Stravinsky, came to orchestra conducting early in his adult life and was as great a conductor as any of the maestros then or since. At the Vienna Opera he conducted sublime performances of *Tristan*, *Così fan tutte*, *Fidelio*, and of his works. With his compositions it was a different story. Other conductors were more loving, more attentive to detail, and better interpreters than Strauss, who perhaps was a little tired of his music. If these eye-witness accounts of Strauss and Stravinsky are to be trusted, one can imagine how much more remote is the composer's original intention when one deals with works a hundred years older than those of the twentieth-century master.

Now to answer our original question: musical literacy, a lively imagination, and that crucial ability to act as kind of "refracting lens" (to borrow Hermann Hesse's description of the artist)—these are the essential components of the conductor as artist. Although the notion of interpretation is central to any discussion of what a conductor does, it remains a very nebulous concept. It is a mysterious phenomenon involving a musician's immersion in the mind of a composer. The interpretations of performing musicians—including instrumentalists, conductors, and even singers—are just not sufficiently manifest to be readily described or subjected to critical review or analysis.

Interpretation of music is but one branch of hermeneutics. Hermes, messenger of the gods, has many colorful incarnations on the podiums of opera pits and concert stages. Whereas all seem quite convinced that they bring musical messages from the gods, those messages are too often conveyed by scholars whose ears cannot hear what they read, antiquarians who believe that old or reconstructed hautbois and corni will do more than play out-of-tune, or worshipers at the altars of the recording companies. One thing most modern conductors seem to remember about Hermes is that he is the god, and protector, of travelers. This is presumably the reason they all fly so swiftly from one spot to the next before their repertory has been fully exposed for its limitations!

To Young Conductors

The Zurich weekly newspaper *Weltwoche* published a lengthy report and commentary, written by its music editor, on three young conductors of exceptional promise. The three are employed as Generalmusikdirektoren (the title is Germany's equivalent of the American music director) in smaller towns often scoured by scouts acting for larger venues.

In the first half of this century the ladder from Aachen or Ulm to Berlin took about eight years to climb. Today's giddy ascent from the musical world's second echelon to an engagement at a London recording studio may take as little as eight weeks. According to *Weltwoche*, something does not seem to be working for these young men despite their "exceptional" talents (one of the trio had apparently suffered a breakdown as he began a rehearsal in London with the BBC).

It was suggested by one of the three that an early taste of international glamour, acquired through guest engagements, constituted a forced speeding up of normal development. Another commented that he and his colleagues were reluctant to refuse tempting offers lest they be forced to remain stuck in their provincial cities, doing solid and "worthy" work, with no chance of hitting the big time. The 1991 winter season of the New York Philharmonic contributed a footnote to this story. Several young conductors bit the dust in quick succession, canceling their appearances after a couple of innings. One must assume that all those in question had a legitimate indisposition, and that none was playing the kind of games so beloved of certain vocal artists, conductors, and pianists. It is, sadly, often the case that the more lucrative the career, the more frequent the artist's failures to appear. The *Weltwoche* article is important because it addresses the issue of the current shortage of conductors. This shortage is often reported to us by the orchestra managers and music administrators who are in charge of filling the guest conductor spots. Since musicians today, at least in America and on the European continent, have tenure, they tend to speak openly and critically of such matters as the shortage of young conductors who show more than just "talent."

The terribly destructive promise of instant fame is as prevalent in music as it is in sports (even if it is much more visible in the media-crazy world of sports). Whereas the world of sport has been progressively modernized over the decades, in music nothing has changed to accommodate the modern preference for a quick fix. I well recall that in the 1960s a certain foundation issued a report showing that, unlike more efficient branches of civilization, music had not moved on from the point it reached two hundred years ago. It gave one exquisite illustration of this point, noting that two centuries ago it took five people thirty-five minutes to perform a Mozart quintet for strings, and yet it still took five people thirty-five minutes to perform the identical task in 1966.

In other words, the great advances made in the era of jet travel have not changed the human brain, the human psyche, human stamina, or anything else that goes into the making of a public performer. This principle is especially true of an artist who is responsible for several dozen other human beings, up to one-hundred instruments, or two-hundred with voices. To preside (and I believe this is the proper word) over such a body of people one needs more than talent. Conducting an ensemble of musical performers (from a large chamber music combine to a giant ensemble such as those required for Schoenberg's *Gurre-Lieder* or Mahler's Eighth) is a task understood by very few people. Let me state unequivocally again: While many aspects of music are teachable, conducting is not.

Some years ago, an opera manager sent me a young conductor who was slated to lead a new *Salome* production by his company, asking whether I would help him. The conductor arrived with a score, and we went over the structure, the relative movements, and the relation of musical themes to the characters and to the action. I also advised him to have a good long look at other scores by Richard Strauss to learn a general awareness of how Strauss wrote down his intentions. I told him that every composer has his peculiarities (one might call them personal "spelling" or syntactic special effects), and that he should find representative samples of the composer's style and familiarize himself with the period of the work in question.

No matter how clever the young man was, and how good a job he did, his study constituted, at best, a cramming of something which one of his counterparts in Europe would have taken several years to prepare. The European would never have been allowed near the podium for *Salome* unless he had been a member of an opera house's musical staff, a coach, a chorus master, a ballet conductor, or a combination of all of them. As a coach, the European would have played the piano scores of *Salome*, *Elektra*, *Der Rosenkavalier*, perhaps also of *Arabella*, *Daphne*, or *Capriccio*, so that the style would be familiar right down to the last detail.

That is not to say that there is any significant difference between the notes and fabric of a *Don Juan* and a *Salome*. It would not take an expert graphologist-musician to determine that both have the same master's signature.

All three conductors cited in the *Weltwoche* report were General-musikdirektoren in opera companies. Among their main problems was the fatigue of having to travel (in a hurry, on a short leave-of-absence) to foreign capitals. Another was that they were conducting a concert repertoire for which, because of their nearly exclusive occupation with opera, they were simply not prepared. There is also an immense difference between standing in the pit of one's familiar opera house and standing in front of eighty-five players in a London concert hall. To the continental European, the latter may seem an utterly different world, alien, perhaps slightly hostile, and devoid of those familiar vocal protagonists who, no matter how vain they may be, at least endow the young maestro with an identity that he does not have without a stage. When I say "perhaps slightly hostile," I refer to the several musicians in each orchestra who are conductors of local ensembles or have unfulfilled ambitions to conduct. Such people become curiously alert whenever a new boy appears before them, and their swift and merciless negativism is familiar to any experienced professional.

That negativism does not stop with beginners and youngsters. Once, while rehearsing a certain European orchestra (I have no intention of identifying the orchestra or gossiping about it), I followed an internationally successful conductor of early middle age. I confess I never thought of this man as anything more than a solid practitioner who could perform the very difficult task of handling musicians but who did not have much interpretive imagination. Nevertheless, the concertmaster's opinion about this conductor would certainly be deemed slander if expressed in print by a professional music critic.

To be comfortable on the international circuit, a conductor must have experience. I know that may sound like an old cliché, and I know that as a youth I regarded such remarks as little more than the psychological defense mechanism of older conductors who felt the hot breath of youthful heirs and successors down their necks. I might still feel a little squeamish about stressing experience as the ultimate credential were it not for the cold, hard evidence. Young musicians of undoubted talent can crumble if they are exposed too early to the klieg lights (which really do burn brighter in New York and Munich than they do in Wichita and Augsburg).

Experience is gained by having an open mind. This means one must be capable of asking oneself, for example, "Why was I constantly a fraction behind the soloist in that variation of Rachmaninov's *Rhapsody on a Theme of Paganini?*" I once observed this very phenomenon and was able to tell the conductor that he did the variation as two-beats-to-the-bar, which is clumsy and makes it almost impossible to be in sync with a solo that phrases the same piece at one-in-a-measure. Such questions often crop up in briefing sessions with young conductors. The answer I gave to the conductor, telling him how to avoid being "behind," may not help him at all if he does not know (really *know*) the solo part. It is only by knowing the solo well that one can anticipate and feel what the phrasing is like.

Rental scores of concertos often contain so many pencil markings in blue, red, and yellow, and so many markers to accentuate the lead voice, one might often mistake them for road maps. Why so many markings? Because conductors are often simply informed that the pianist (or violinist) will play such and such a concerto, which they do not generally know. The conductor's main preoccupation is with "his" pieces (the symphony, the overture, and so forth) and he considers the solo piece of only minor importance. He consequently prefers to look it up in a rental score on the night before the orchestra rehearsal. The unfortunate result is that the soloist interrupts the rehearsal to ask the orchestra (either directly or through the conductor) for this nuance, that tempo, or indeed anything that was not suggested by the conductor. If this should ever happen, the conductor's credit with the orchestra players immediately suffers.

Other manifestations of inexperience are more decisive and often very subtle. A conductor must know, either beforehand or by instant perception, whether an orchestra is at home in a piece being prepared for performance. Some young conductors, who evidently believe that they are God's gift to music, start rehearsing a familiar work as if the town had never heard it before and everything ever done by others was a waste of time. Even if this should be true (and it is unlikely to be the case) it makes a very bad impression and causes instant resentment and resistance from the orchestra. Whether an orchestra is at home with a given work can be recognized within two minutes. If it is not, then an open mind and some experience will enable the conductor to run through a first reading to give them a brief synopsis of the piece. Such a reading might give information on the length of the piece, its difficulties, and its dominant themes.

How to apportion available time is often a major stumbling block for all conductors—even those with considerable experience. It can be very difficult to estimate the available time and distribute it in such a way that every piece will be sufficiently prepared. The process involves judging which pieces will be easy, difficult, or very difficult for a particular orchestra and taking account of the available rehearsal time. It often happens that either the conductor is inexperienced (and so underestimates the difficulties) or the composer writes his or her compositions in such a complex manner that no available rehearsal time will do. The evaluation of what is possible within the various parameters is better dealt with by an experienced conductor. Part of the conductor's experience comes from a thorough acquaintance with the players and with conducting an ensemble in a specific style. Also, young conductors should do their best to avoid the two extremes of the repertoire: the very familiar and the unknown. These can be very stormy seas indeed, and are better navigated by an old sea dog.

Orchestras have an uncanny knack of knowing when rehearsal time is being wasted to cover the conductor's uncertainty and insecurity. Experience shows that final rehearsals on the day of the first concert in a series of several repeats should be wisely planned. The program for the eve of the final rehearsal may, for example, include a work that demands the type of intensity string players generally do not like very much. Some of Bruckner's works are typical examples of this. If that should be the case, I recommend doing the final run-through on the previous day and spending the morning of the concert with other, less demanding matters of detail. There should be frequent, brief rest periods that make it clear to everyone that the show is not until the evening.

It is imperative not to attempt to nail down too much before the performance. One cannot, and should not, nail down everything, lest the indispensable spontaneity of the concert be weakened. The better an orchestra, the better it is to leave a few things to the spur of the moment. That does not mean being vague about tempos or transitions, but merely allowing flexibility. Each audience produces an individual ambiance that is sensed by stage performers and collective orchestra alike—flexibility is therefore necessary.

Conducting, unlike playing an instrument, can be done quite successfully by faking. Whereas it is impossible to fake at the keyboard or with the bow, the music world has seen quite a few fakers on the podium. Many of these performers are still very much with us, to judge from the brochures of certain secondary or part-time orchestras around the world. The layperson may well ask how it is possible to fake conducting. It is quite easy if you are clever, have a good ear, and select music that your orchestra knows. There is also the crucial element of the metric raw material. Music has either a steady pulse or a changing pulse, and the latter can be difficult for some conductors to achieve. It is exemplified by the freedom of romantic vocal composition (with Giacomo Puccini the foremost exponent), but may also refer simply to frequent changes of meter. No faker will get through the coda of Stravinsky's Violin Concerto without overt mishap, just as no faker will get through act 1 of La Bohème; however, a clever faker (meaning any faker who manages to secure more than one public performance) will easily get through the entire "Great" C major Symphony of Schubert or almost any Beethoven symphony.

By "getting through" one should understand getting from the first to the last measure without any mishaps that are noticeable by the casual listener. Even musicians of distinction who have been recognized as interpreters of some consequence are known to flounder when the meters change too rapidly. It is on such occasions that one often observes the phenomenon of the musical "flat tire." The conductor suffering from this is strangely unable to perform for a bewildering variety of reasons—the material mysteriously fails to arrive, the material is incomplete, the Marimba falls victim to a short circuit, and so forth. If, however, such a conductor is also a fine interpreter of music in classic metric patterns, it is because his range is limited only by his limited experience. I do not believe that a genuinely distinguished interpreter of Schumann or

Bruckner should be defeated by *The Rite of Spring*, but this is sometimes the case. Having risen to fame by conducting great music in $\frac{4}{4}$ and $\frac{3}{4}$, a prominent conductor may not relish having to go back to school to prepare the more complex works he had not been able to learn in his younger days.

So a lack of true experience can result when a conductor climbs the ladder of success too quickly, but it can also result from an incorrect approach to learning. Experience has to be *active* experience. Passive presence, such as witnessing rehearsals, is no substitute for activity. If this were not so, every concertmaster would be a first-rate conductor, as would every orchestra musician with the ambition to lead. A thorough knowledge of the music does not necessarily make a conductor. This point is generally well understood, but bears repeating.

Conductors should, then, gain experience in opera before venturing into the more demanding field of concert music. If we are to judge from the three conductors referred to in the *Weltwoche* article—all music directors of opera companies—there must be a little more to it than that. Nonetheless, there is no doubt that those European conductors who have conducted opera regularly for a few seasons know how to conduct opera. In the German houses this invariably includes the highly demanding scores of Wagner and Strauss, and a constant flow of new and complex works.

The Vienna Opera invites (either through conviction or necessity) a stream of guest conductors for their repertory. One young person after another arrives, rehearses on a rehearsal stage with the singers, and assists with a couple of quick staging sessions (briefings for guest artists). They hardly ever rehearse with the orchestra, and their number includes certain daring youngsters who accept such shows without ever having stood in that particular pit before. Nevertheless, it seems that shows directed in this manner do proceed from the first to the last with very few mishaps of the kind that often occur in well-rehearsed performances.

I recall how one evening, a few years ago, I walked through the stage door of the Vienna opera house for a piano rehearsal to be told that the conductor for that evening's performance (a ballet with a contemporary score) had not shown up. The show was to proceed with a recording in place of the orchestra. It appeared that the young guest conductor had simply mistaken the week of the performance, and he was welcomed back for the next show just the same. In everyday opera the conductor is of minor significance; in everyday instrumental music the conductor is of first importance. The conductor's principal importance in opera has historically been the preparation of the cast and the orchestra.

Arturo Toscanini would often tell the following story from his early days as principal cellist. During a long opera season in Buenos Aires the conductor for Gounod's *Faust* was a maestro who used a piano-vocal score in rehearsal (implying that he could not know the full score). The young cellist therefore decided to double the violin solo from the tenor aria in the lower octave. The conductor, not having a score, did not know that this was a gratuitous addition. When in performance the cellist played his true part, the conductor became upset—something that he had been used to was now missing.

I heard this story several times—Toscanini never tired of manifesting his utter contempt for almost all conductors who were not Toscanini. This and other stories illustrate that in those days the preparation of opera was interminable, with orchestra readings of eight or ten sessions for operas that these days are given two rehearsals at most. Whereas the better orchestras for modern opera companies do not need six or more rehearsals for *Faust*, new works are given a more-than-adequate allotment of preparation time. A Generalmusikdirektor in a German opera house usually has the largest percentage of new productions and is given (within reason) much rehearsal time. He also has to coach singers and is present at some staging rehearsals. He is therefore given enough time to learn and penetrate into the smallest nuances of score and libretto—far more time than is given to a conductor rehearsing a concert program.

I have experienced both extremes of rehearsal conditions. At the Met in 1938 I conducted several operas similar to the Vienna model, without orchestra rehearsal. The shows ran in a well-prepared sequence, with myself slated simply to take over, at a certain point, what another guide had already coached and rehearsed. On the other hand, when I prepared a premiere production of an Ernst Krenek opera in Vienna, I had at least fifteen orchestra rehearsals and was present for the staging throughout several weeks. For a new production of Richard Strauss's *Arabella* at the Met in 1983 I spent three weeks in the rehearsal room.

Preparation for a new opera production is rather like the progress of a convoy of ships, which can proceed only at the speed of its slowest member. In opera this usually means that the performance can proceed only after the stage director has learned the work and the less alert singers or conductors have finally understood what it is all about.

Imagine the plight of a young Generalmusikdirektor in opera, venturing on a program of concert music with a Berlioz overture, a Brahms concerto, and a Dvořák symphony. The poor fellow finds himself having to tackle three works known to the orchestra but less familiar to him. If he could count on the equivalent of the rehearsal days commonly accorded a new production of an operatic score, he would have time to learn every smallest nuance and tradition of the piece, as well as the soloist's part. In fact, he is lucky if he gets five sessions of two or two-and-a-quarter hours (including deductions for intermissions determined by collective agreement). Five rehearsal sessions might even be seen as generous by the prevailing standards of major orchestras. It can be counted on occasionally in one of the big radio orchestras in Europe, but concert orchestras rarely have more than four rehearsal sessions.

London holds some sort of record with three sessions, of which two will be three-hour sessions held on the same day in a church that serves as rehearsal hall for all the London groups. On the concert day there will be a three-hour dress rehearsal, held where the concert will take place later that evening. So even if a young conductor is esteemed as a music director in a respectable operatic environment, he may find himself suddenly promoted to an entirely different league. He may have just eight hours of actual rehearsal time, two-thirds of which will be under acoustic conditions different from those of the concert. He may find himself in front of a madly overworked group of musicians who cannot be expected to enjoy being drilled in a symphony by Dvořák or Tchaikovsky.

Two

Notes on the Staff:
Interpreting a Musical Score

The Edition Can Be Critical

It is often assumed that a brilliant composer must necessarily be a brilliant orchestrator. This assumption shows admirable faith in the composer's genius, but it usually implies a lack of objective criticism. The old complete editions of the great composers' works were genuinely critical, and for one perfectly good reason: their editors wanted them to be ready for performance. Of course, those editors' ideas were different from ours, but that does not mean that they were necessarily wrong (or at least not as wrong as modern, uncritical observers wish us to believe).

A critical decision is needed, for example, in the first movement of Mozart's "Haffner" Symphony. Most editions of this work show no repeat sign after the exposition. The facsimile of the manuscript can be read either way, but I find it most peculiar that in one of the shortest of symphonies the obligatory sign to repeat the exposition should have been canceled. There is agreement between both major publishers, but it still makes no sense. This is a case in which the decision should be made by common sense, not by interpreters of the manuscript.

The editors of the *Neue Mozart Ausgabe* (NMA) succeeded in getting their "complete Mozart" accepted as an indispensable authority. Yet, while it shows the usual differences of scholarship and judgment (ranging from excellent to just plain bad), the NMA should by rights be called "An Uncritical Edition of the Complete Mozart."

The NMA is the ultimate achievement of what might politely be called the "positivist" school of musicology (and I did not invent that term, I borrowed it from the musicologist Joseph Kerman). If I understand the word *positivist* correctly, it refers to a compendium of texts, which are faithfully copied (with modern clefs replacing old C-clefs; tenor voice parts printed *à la Ricordi*: treble clefs with an 8 underneath; and, in some volumes, printed appoggiaturas and suspensions from below).

Whenever I plan to perform a work by Mozart I consult the relevant volume of the NMA (of which I am an original subscriber), but I cannot use any NMA symphony parts without considerable editing. They are no more performable than the Haydn editions of Robbins-Landon. Some volumes must have been edited by people who knew nothing about violin bowing or the habits of composers who indicate a specific phrasing only on its first appearance, leaving it to the performer to apply the pattern whenever the same or a similar phrasing returns. The academic nonperformers among musicologists, who know nothing of these conventions, appear to believe that painstaking observation of the printed text is all there is to playing, singing, performing, and interpreting. This is not the case at all. The old Breitkopf edition of Mozart's works was edited throughout, and every score in that edition was therefore performable. Realizing that the Breitkopf text was edited, every competent performer was at liberty to re-edit according to his (or her) lights. This is as true of the entire vast library of pre-1800 music as it is of most post-1800 music. Every conductor knows that violin soloists treat printed violin parts very freely, and in my opinion this is certainly better than pedantically following an uncritical edition.

To Cut or Not to Cut?[1]

The word *cut,* which we use in musical circles, has not the same meaning as the same word uttered at a delicatessen counter. It is rather a convenient, colloquial, substitute for the more ponderous but more accurate *abridgement.* A cut is shown on a musical score by taking the Latin word *vide* and putting the first syllable *VI* at the beginning of the intended cut and the second syllable *DE* where the cut ends and the music continues.

That this usage still survives is, I suppose, simply evidence that modern languages have found no useful or satisfactory substitutes. Opening my old vocal score of *Der Rosenkavalier,* I see the syllable *VI* at measure 223 and the syllable *DE* at measure 233. I don't think that it would look right if *VI-DE* were replaced by *LO-OK.*

My most recent encounter with the issue of cuts came with an article in the *New York Times* by its then senior music critic, Donal Henahan, discussing some horrible cuts made in Wagner's music dramas at the old Met. As one who was a member of the conducting staff during the Edward Johnson regime, I felt that my then chief, Artur Bodanzky, was being made the target of strictures, half a century after the fact, when neither he nor most of the others involved could explain or defend what happened at the time.

I wrote a letter whose essential points were graciously printed by Mr. Henahan. Most pertinently, I said that the cuts made at the Met were the same as those made in many European houses, which not only insisted on substantial cuts but also performed Wagner's works with a reduced orchestration, having neither the space to seat quadruple woodwinds and eight horns in their small orchestra pits, nor, in all likelihood, a sufficient pool of able instrumentalists in their towns.

The old Met had the instrumentalists, but it also catered to a very large public among whom were not only Wagnerites who wanted the complete scores, but also many others who attended operas to savor the highlights sung by the finest vocalists of the time.

---

[1] This essay first appeared in *The Opera Quarterly,* Volume 10, No. 1 (Autumn 1993): 5–12. It is reprinted here with kind permission.

Great vocalists are not necessarily purists offended by any omission. Wagner had to contend with the tenor Joseph Tichatschek (1807–86), the first *Tannhäuser*, who refused to sing all three strophes of the "Hymn to Venus" in act 1. They are among the most renowned tenor killers in the repertory, going, with short intervals, from D-flat to D-natural to E-flat, only to land in the singers' contest of act 2 in E. Wagner preferred to cut the second strophe and keep Tichatschek. This and similar stories of pragmatic decisions by musicians of integrity and authority do not, however, entitle us to consider omissions *per se* as a must, just to pamper singers wishing to avoid fatigue. That would be as if a starting pitcher might sign a contract only if baseball games were reduced to six innings instead of nine. Pitching is tiring, and so are leading roles.

The Met, during the periods when I was a regular conductor there (1937/38–1942/43), had cuts in all evening performances of Wagner, but not in matinees of the *Ring* cycle. The reasons for the difference were financial, as was to be expected at a time of economic depression. Overtime for all hands in the pit and backstage cost a fortune—and still does.

There have been traditional cuts in non-Wagner and non-German operas as well. They are numerous, and if I cite one particular set of cuts in Massenet's *Manon*, it is because of a true story attached to it. The New York City Opera, on tour in Chicago, gave Massenet's masterpiece under the direction of Jean Morel. He had reopened the "Cours-la-Reine" scene, usually, or often, omitted, as it lengthens the work, too much in the opinion of some. The then general director of the company, Josef Rosenstock, attended the performance and, visiting Morel afterwards, said to him: "Jean, this *Manon* now is as long as *Götterdämmerung* without cuts." "Yes," said Morel, "but not nearly as funny."

When I recorded *Le nozze di Figaro* in 1958 we made no cuts. When I conduct the same opera in the opera house, be it New York or Vienna, I omit the arias of Marcellina and Basilio in act 4. This has been traditional, and for reasons more historical and dramaturgic than purely musical.

From the evidence offered by *Le nozze di Figaro* and *Don Giovanni* we may conclude confidently that Mozart was in the habit of writing at least one aria for every member of the cast. Most operagoers do not know that in the first production of *Le nozze di Figaro* in 1786 there was only one tenor for both Basilio and Curzio and only one bass for both Bartolo and Antonio. A look at the libretto will show that this could be done. That it is not done today has no bearing on the topic at hand. (The Commendatore in *Don Giovanni* was also the Masetto, in which guise he got his aria.)

The real reason why the Basilio and Marcellina arias should be omitted is that they delay the denouement. How many in the audience want to hear the solo effusions of two minor characters while everyone is on tenterhooks to see how the intrigue of the two main couples will play itself out? But on a recording one should produce the entire score as composed by Mozart, just as one includes every extant sketch in a critical edition or a comprehensive catalogue of a great painter's life's work.

From my apprenticeship as a coach at the Vienna Opera I remember several cuts in *Der Rosenkavalier* made under the directorship of Clemens Krauss, a musician who would never have done anything without the composer's consent. There was also a sagacious cut in *Salome* (when the title character impatiently awaits the execution of the prophet). When one attends either of these works today in a major opera house, one hears the lot, unabridged and, in my opinion, *against* the composer's better judgment.

These Strauss cuts remind me of another cut, not only proposed but actually composed by Mozart. In the final ensemble of *Don Giovanni*, after Don Giovanni's death, the other characters sing a three-section ensemble: Allegro assai ($\frac{3}{4}$), Larghetto (duet Anna-Ottavio), and Presto alla breve. Mozart composed a transition leading directly from the lively $\frac{3}{4}$ section to the presto, omitting the Anna-Ottavio duet. Although I cannot divine his reasoning here, I think he calculated correctly. We have already heard Donna Anna in two superb arias. Ottavio, also, has had his innings. There is no good dramatic reason for delaying the final curtain.

Mozart knew all that, but obsequious and unimaginative posterity presumes to know better and refuses, with few exceptions, to honor this transition music, which should, as I have previously observed, be included in a recording. This attitude also countenances the practice of having both the tenor arias performed. This is wrong. Why?

Because the florid passages of "Il mio tesoro," sung by the tenor of the Prague premiere in 1787, were too much for the tenor of the Vienna premiere of 1788. So Mozart replaced it with "Dalla sua pace." He did not add a second aria. It was a substitute. He presumably felt that one lyric utterance for Don Ottavio was sufficient, and that another would interrupt the action unnecessarily. No help here from singers! No decent tenor will take on Don Ottavio if one of his two arias is cut. I have never been able to stay with either the Prague or the Vienna version pure and simple.

Mahler, always free with his own ideas when they didn't match those of the composer, ended *Don Giovanni* with the Don's death, omitting the concluding ensemble. This was a musical error of the first order, because the Don's death does not provide a cadence. To end a Mozart composition without a cadence is, musically, nothing less than treason.

There was treason, too, in Chicago, when *Der Rosenkavalier* was given its local premiere to launch the season of 1925–26. The conductor (and music director from 1922 to 1930) was Giorgio Polacco. Looking at a piano-vocal score of 442 pages (Verdi's *Aida* has 278), he took his musical switchblade and went to work marking the pages to be omitted with the usual VI-DE. His method was based on the "lovely" Italian notion that pages without vocal lines were superfluous. Thus his switchbladed pencil marked VI-DE over page 292, which happens to be the great waltz at the end of act 2 and rivals the act 3 trio in popularity.

I do not know if the Met adopted any of Polacco's surgery, but I do know that the prelude to act 3 was not played there in 1937. That was my first season at the house, and, fortunately, my involvement with *Der Rosenkavalier* was limited to playing piano at stage rehearsals.

There has been no pattern—and no malice—in the history of cutting. Needless to say, the cheaper and more cynical impresarios have done anything to save money—and damn the torpedoes! But that is not part of my subject here. Returning to the Met and its bizarre history in the 1930s of having one complete, uncut *Ring* cycle every season, but only on four afternoon performances, we arrive at the more pertinent question: What was omitted in the evening performances?

Looking at one of my much used piano-vocal scores of *Die Walküre*, I spot immediately the big cut in act 2, of about two hundred measures. This cut began after Fricka forces Wotan to agree to have Siegmund killed for incest and included Wotan's narrative to Brünnhilde detailing the events that occurred in *Das Rheingold*. This cut was made not only to save twenty minutes, but also—and I do not mince words—to spare an English-speaking audience lengthy recitative where the words themselves are far more important than the quality and inventiveness of the music.

To speak of Wotan's long expository monologue as recitative may be offensive to Wagnerian fundamentalists (of whom there are still many), but the term is accurate. To omit such a hefty chunk of Wotan's text was—intentionally or not—a radical move toward bringing to the fore the entire question of language. It is intimately connected with the question of my title, "To Cut or Not to Cut?"

One must also consider the truly vicious ways in which spoken dialogue is cut in German *Singspiele* such as *Die Entführung aus dem Serail*, *The Magic Flute* (*Die Zauberflöte*), *Fidelio*, and *Die Fledermaus*. In conducting *Fidelio* at the Vienna Opera, I was deeply disturbed by what had been done to the dialogue. Not only was it cruelly abbreviated, but more than that, adding insult to injury, some essential dialogue was omitted in those vital textual transitions from dry spoken sound to the next musical entry. For example, in the original prose, the words leading to the canon quartet of scene I have Rocco saying to Fidelio/Leonore: "Meinst du, ich könne dir nicht ins Herz sehen?" [Do you think that I can't see into your heart?] This line and a lot of the preceding dialogue were omitted. After the cut, this is what was left: Fidelio enters, he and Rocco exchange perhaps two short sentences and just look at each other. The strings begin the divine prelude to the canon, but the enrichment flowing from the original words when feelingly spoken is absent.

That type of cut is made neither for reasons of time nor for economy. In this instance, it was made on the assumption that foreign tourists, who fill many seats at the Vienna State Opera, would be put off by too much unintelligible prose. In several performances I had good singers (the first scene has no special vocal problems for anybody), but the telegraph-prose snippets between musical numbers could not establish that indispensable poetic transition from one musical number to another.

(There is an inescapable problem, of course, with the lot of foreign singers who learn prose text by rote, speak it with effort, and don't know how words convey meaning. *The Magic Flute* is an even sadder victim of this babel, usually with too much spoken dialogue omitted.)

Yet, when one reads of new productions of bel canto works, or a six-hour *St. Francis* by Messiaen, or a seven-day opera by Stockhausen or no-nonsense *obiter dicta* about uncut versions of Handel operas, with every da capo in place, we can only conclude that we are back in the 1870s when great meant big, long, and massive—nothing short of storming the heavens for the Second Coming! Urtext, second-guessed notions about the composer's intentions, every note that can be located, including discarded sketches saved from the wastebasket!

But let's begin with Wagner, whose works are surely the most difficult of all to cast well or even adequately. The Met was putting on a new *Tristan und Isolde*, and its young, ambitious conductor decided to open, I think for the first time in Met history, an established cut known colloquially as the *Tag-und-Nacht Sprung*, a pun on the text of the great act 2 love scene. I am sure that I never conducted an unabridged act 2, nor do I recall ever hearing one during my student days in Vienna, when I never missed a *Tristan*.

The reason for the cut (traditional for more than a century) is that there are hardly any singers who dare to sing the complete dramatic duet, or who can calm down for the tender, sustained slow center portion ("O sink' hernieder, Nacht der Liebe"). I don't doubt that both Flagstad and Nilsson could manage it all, but adequate tenors were hard to find. Although Lauritz Melchior may have done it in Bayreuth, he could not be persuaded to sing the complete duet in America, where "the livin' is easy" and the fees high.

Well, our intrepid young maestro announced it and did it. His one problem was that he had a pair of singers insufficiently equipped to do even the version *with* the large cut. The critic of the *New York Times* began his review with words to the effect that a performance of *Tristan* where the greatest success is scored by King Marke speaks for itself. In my book of ethics this kind of "fidelity to the score" constitutes cruelty to the listener and is not in the best interests of the score, which must be sung, no matter how fine the orchestra. Even Arnold Schoenberg writes in all his scores with vocal parts, "The voice is always the Hauptstimme [dominant melodic line]."

This leads to the question, Why does a superb musician who knows all this, and has a good ear for the potential of a singing voice, insist on the marathon when he has no more than a couple of ten-thousand-meter athletes to work with? Here I leave the answer to a singer of the Vienna ensemble who has, in his own experience, found that most conductors as directors have been "intent on building their own monument" rather than being concerned with how they might make the most valuable contribution.

Monuments are built by publicity and with entries into encyclopedias and other works of reference. Once this process has started, the monument builder becomes a name for the history books. A pertinent entry might read: "He performed every composition in its longest, most complete version, regardless of intrinsic worth. He held every operatic resurrection to be a masterpiece, and believed the longer it took to perform, the greater it was."

The fashion of performing every note and all the da capos does not contribute to a better appreciation of opera masterpieces. It is rather an attempt to establish standards in an era that has none. It was Henry Pleasants, I think, who wrote: "When anything goes, nothing matters."

Let's take, for example, Richard Strauss's *Die Frau ohne Schatten*. It is, according to diverse opinions, either the composer's magnum opus or an inflated misunderstanding of *The Magic Flute*. It certainly has a super brilliant score and five marvelous roles for which one can find, even today, more than just satisfactory interpreters. But, as with other Strauss operas, it has made its way with a number of wise and necessary cuts. I conducted it at the Met in 1981 with a splendid cast and with all the cuts that had been in the Met library since Karl Böhm premiered it in the new house's first season. Not only was Böhm deeply devoted to Strauss; he, next to Krauss, had the composer's ear and confidence, and there is no doubt that the version mentioned here was authorized without qualms by the composer.

Strauss was a wise and highly practical person, but as a musician he had so much facility that he could become prolix to the point where an intriguing and attractive scene became too much of a good thing. When the spirit moved him, he could—so it seems to me—go on and on, especially when a particular soprano voice stimulated his imagination. But once the scores were finished, and an admiring and friendly conductor dared to plead for a little mercy, either to spare a soprano some overly trying passages or to eliminate some redundancies, he would see the merits of the case and either approve suggested cuts or propose some himself. This can be documented, of course, by comparing the first and second versions of *Ariadne auf Naxos*.

In the case of *Ariadne*, to be sure, the entire first version (a one-act opera originally conceived to follow a full-length comedy by Molière) is a story by itself. But the fact remains that for the second version he used a busy blue pencil infinitely sharper than Maestro Polacco's in Chicago— and shrewder by far!

All this is known to experienced conductors of opera. Most of them would agree that there is much prolixity and superfluous stuffing in the printed scores. Why, then, the current rage to open not only traditional and established cuts but even cuts known to have been made by the composer or to have had the composer's approval? I can think of several reasons: (1) the lack of attractive new works, prompting an attempt to provide an old car with new gadgets; (2) the offer of a recording contract, for which, as I have suggested above, an uncut performance may provide a legitimate justification; (3) the desire to raise a monument to the "great interpreter who does not believe in cutting."

In interviews, or in prepared bios, it is so much easier to say proudly, "I am against cutting," or "I leave cutting to surgeons," or something similarly politically correct. It distances the speaker or writer immediately from the operatic *routiniers* serving anti-artistic, cheap impresarios. There is something in this of the puritan revolutionary who stands up to greedy box-office idolaters. It is an unassailable position, even when one is confronted with the probability that an unabridged production may decimate the stalls after three hours, or when intermittent periods of boredom envelop the dozing audience. People are patient—and awed. I remember from my student days an observation attributed to Wilhelm Furtwängler: "The French reckon that they are at a first-rate performance of Bach only when they are bored."

My own assessment of the situation?

Every work has its own law of length and strength, which must be weighed before deciding whether or not the full text is the best way to serve the work and the audience. The date of origin is an important consideration.

The most significant of operas of the twentieth century are short. I include in this category one that is technically in the nineteenth century but is prophetic: Verdi's *Falstaff*. In the first decade we have *Salome* and *Elektra*. In the third there is *Wozzeck*. All these play, if given without intermission, under 120 minutes.

Philip Glass's *Einstein on the Beach* runs for four and a half hours, and, as previously observed, there are other new stage works of enormous, even inordinate length. In this context it is pertinent to note a similar polarity in the field of instrumental concert music. Scores for large orchestras running to eighty or more minutes may be favorite party pieces for flamboyant baton wielders, but they are, in my view, essentially *vieux jeu*, old-fashioned, and, to all intents and purposes, a reflection of *fin de siècle* misapprehensions regarding the new twentieth century.

My own sound bite is, Big and long is old-fashioned; small and short is modern. *Gurre-Lieder* is old-fashioned; Stravinsky's "Dumbarton Oaks" is modern. In the case of opera, Messiaen's *St. Francis* is old-fashioned; Benjamin Britten's chamber stage works are modern. In my opinion, adherence to tonality or cultivation of atonality plays a minor part.

When I read or hear reports of four- or five-hour revivals of eighteenth-century operas, I am always reminded of the Detroit auto manufacturers who, a few years ago, continued to produce large cars when most of the driving world had shown a clear preference for small vehicles. The trend toward the longer and bigger in opera (nourished, in my view, by deluded impresarios and self-aggrandizing artists) runs counter to the mainstream of our era.

The times demand smaller budgets. Translate that into the technicalities of opera production, and it means shorter rehearsals, smaller casts, and fewer chorus members; in other words, less on every front. To return to *Falstaff*, *Salome*, *Elektra*, and *Wozzeck*, except for the fact that the orchestra scoring is for large forces, they meet all these requirements. Any one of them is simpler and cheaper than an uncut Rossini.

As for cutting? When Mahler ended *Don Giovanni* as he did, eliminating the entire final ensemble, he was wrong. But aside from the sin of robbing Mozart of a cadence, I can imagine that in Mahler's time as opera director—a time when Wagner's dramatic ideas reigned supreme—he did not want to seem archaic by following the explosive end of the drama with an amiable, moralizing ensemble.

There is ample additional evidence that there was more freedom then in dealing with works of the past than we find acceptable today. (I do not include myself in the "we," since I *do* take liberties, but only when satisfied that I have been fully considerate of the composer's intent and his work.) I believe that decisions based on critical perception and assessment are essential for faithful interpretation. The freedom I note in earlier times originated in an apparent paradox. There were surely standards, and the artist, as a nonconformist, could therefore decide to disregard whatever standard was to be violated or simply ignored.

The Mozart bicentennial offered eloquent testimony to our total lack of standards. When the best the planners of great festivals can do is announce that *every note will be heard,* it is an admission that they do not wish to decide which works should be left on their shelves, so they duck the arbitration and perform every blessed note. The same goes for cuts, which are sometimes not only advisable, but even essential for keeping an otherwise good score from bursting out of its frame.

The subject of cutting and abridging is inseparable from the larger subject of score reading. Many scores, depending on the time of composition, are blueprints waiting for the "reader" (performer, interpreter) to erect the building the composer had in mind. Prior to circa 1800 that type of score was written by one and all, by ever fewer thereafter. As we traverse the nineteenth century the score as blueprint is fleshed out with more and more specifics for the performer but without really making things explicit. In the end, the truly explicit score would perform itself, causing the human interpreter to become superfluous. The long and short is that any score, old or new, depends upon an interpreter with a free-floating imagination. Without it, even the best-schooled musician will be groping for the light switch while in a dark cellar.

Pious disclaimers such as "I am only for urtext" or "I am against cuts" are self-promoting alibis for not making decisions. It is the same with the critic, who also must make decisions based on perception and imagination and not merely clock stopwatch differences in timing between Maestro A and Maestro B.

When one thinks through this question of musical text, of fidelity to the score, one concludes that there can be no rules. The diversity of problems is too great. The one and only law of decision is that decisions should be made ad hoc. For this performance we have two singers who can do it, so we open the cut in act 2 of *Tristan und Isolde*. Two weeks from now, when we have other singers who can't cope with the marathon, we restore the cut.

Conviction tempered by professionalism.

Tempo[2]

Musicians these days seem to be very preoccupied with the question of timing. This reflects (at least to me) the extent to which the spirit of sporting competition has permeated musical interpretation and musical criticism. What is more important, the meaning of timing in the musical context is also much misunderstood. Timing is a matter of primary concern for the performer, not for the composer, and it is not the same as tempo.

There are perhaps three main points to consider about tempos. First, they are unquestionably of central importance for composers. Second, musicians feel intense frustration whenever they are given only vague indications of tempo. Third, certain conductors will always show a stubborn disregard for even the most precise tempos.

It may seem a little odd to suggest that tempo and timing are not related, but this is only because the terms *tempo* and *timing* are often used carelessly. Tempo means pulse. As Richard Wagner states at the beginning of his essay *On Conducting* (1897), the right pulse can be found only if one understands the Greek concept of *melos*. Defined as a characteristic tone succession that is distinct from rhythm, the term *melos* is used for melodies, tunes, themes, motives, and any piece of music that may be sung. The differences between well-known anthems provide a simple illustration of its meaning.

Whereas the British national anthem has a range of seven notes within the conventional scale, the German has eight, and "The Star-

---

[2] Leinsdorf's *The Composer's Advocate: A Radical Orthodoxy for Musicians* (New Haven: Yale University Press, 1981) includes a detailed discussion of tempos and metronome markings.

Spangled Banner" twelve. The latter is barely singable because it traverses too large a range for untrained (and even somewhat-trained) voices. Once one has understood the sense of the "leading voice" of a piece—whether it be an anthem, a hymn, the theme of a sonata, a variation, or indeed anything that "moves" musically speaking—one has understood the meaning of the word *tempo*.

Around 1814, Johann Maelzel and others invented the metronome. Many composers (Ludwig van Beethoven being first among them) at first had high expectations of this machine (which Maelzel had patented), but the general enthusiasm gradually turned to disenchantment. Brahms, Strauss, and Debussy are among the many composers who have expressed reservations about its effectiveness.

There is a story about Brahms's *A German Requiem* that provides an excellent illustration of my general theme, since it involves both tempos and timing. Because the work is primarily on the slow side, the least modification of the tempo has a major impact on the overall timing, in performance or in a recording. George Henschel, a British baritone, composer, and at one time conductor of the then new Boston Symphony, once asked Brahms in a letter "whether the metronome markings in his *Requiem* were to be strictly observed." Brahms's reply was evasive, casting general skeptical aspersions on the value of the metronome but insisting that he had nonetheless marked his scores only after the most careful consideration. The composer then promptly removed the metronome figures from the second and subsequent editions. The first edition can, however, still be found in libraries, and is also included in the thematic catalogue of the composer's works. It lists all the *Requiem*'s original metronome figures. The quarter-notes of the first piece are indicated with 80 (which means, in a $\frac{4}{4}$ configuration, that 80 beats (which equal 20 measures) will take one minute). The second movement, in triple time ($\frac{3}{4}$), has a figure of 60 for the quarter-note (thus indicating that the second movement should be slower than the first).

Nonetheless, many leading conductors pace the first movement much more slowly than they do the second, although the composer intended quite the opposite. It seems they do so either because it is the custom, or because they did not obtain a copy of the first edition, or because they simply choose a different route in the full knowledge of how it should be done. In this particular instance the difference in tempo can affect the overall time. Since the seventh movement shares the tempo of the first, the two movements together should last between sixteen and eighteen minutes ("traditional" versions stretch them out to a combined twenty-six minutes or more).

I recall one occasion when I conducted the *Requiem* in Paris. The chorus master was English, so I fully expected that he would be better acquainted with choral music (and with Brahms in particular) than a Frenchman might. As it turned out, however, he had ingested all the customary tempo perversions. At the first rehearsal (during which I always take a seat and ask the honorable gentleman to show me what he has accomplished) he duly gave us the insanely sluggish first section. Praising everybody to the skies, I promptly, diplomatically (and hypocritically), took over. After treating them to exhaustive explanations about the relationship between text and music (apparently one of my specialties during chorus rehearsals) I took them through the first section again—this time at a more Brahmsian clip. When we had finished, the large assembly of French amateur musicians gave me a spontaneous round of applause, for something that I considered to be quite elementary, something that allowed them to understand what the whole thing was about.

Timing and tempos are rarely problematical in the field of vocal music, in which a few natural laws dictate what is and what is not possible. The question of breathing is the prime example. A phrase in a composition for voice (whether sacred, operatic, or lied) is intended to be delivered in one breath. If the composer was competent and the singer's lungs and diaphragm in working condition, there should never be a problem. Wagner, in *On Conducting*, emphasized: "As a proof of my assertion that the majority of instrumental performances are faulty, it is sufficient to point out that our conductors so frequently fail to find the true tempo because they are ignorant of singing."

Tempos were apparently not a problem in 1720, since there are hardly any words pertaining to tempos in the works of Johann Sebastian Bach. Whenever the words *adagio* or *allegro* appear, it is a clear indication to the reader and to the player that the notes are not self-explanatory (which they are for 90 percent of Bach's music). In the first volume of *The Well-Tempered Clavier*, for example, there are twenty-four preludes and twenty-four fugues. Of these forty-eight pieces, only the last two have tempo markings (andante for the final prelude and largo for the final fugue). It is the same with his cantatas, oratorios, and various suites and partitas. There are two main reasons why it was unnecessary to specify tempo. First, composers in those days played or supervised renditions of their works, with little thought of exporting, publishing, or distributing those works to unknown performers. Second, there was at that time only one style of composition: that of the day. This is in marked contrast to our era, in which musicians have to do justice to various musical styles ranging from those of the late seventeenth century to those of the present, usually without having the benefit of the composer's supervision.

Mozart once said in a letter that fugues should always be played at moderate tempos, because otherwise one cannot hear the entries of the theme. Mozart's works are headed by Italian words indicating "slow" or "fast"; he did not make too fine a distinction between Allegro assai (very fast) or Presto (very fast). Thus, his remark that fugues needed to be treated with moderate tempos suggests to me that even as early as 1784 the tempos of Bach (who died in 1750) may have been subject to misinterpretation.

If a conductor mistakes the tempo over a substantial portion of a musical score, he can completely ruin a performance of a known repertory work. I recall listening to a performance of Beethoven's "Pastoral" Symphony by a world-famous conductor directing a reputable orchestra. The maestro treated the first and second movements as one unit, taking the first section somewhat slower than either custom or metronome might dictate, and following with a second section played in a flowing tempo (considerably faster than the metronome, but not much different from the established speed of the famous "little brook" of the movement's title).

The result was an Andante lasting half an hour, without differentiation, and so excruciatingly dull that one lost all interest in the next three movements. The several tempos of this symphony should pose no problem, but for some obscure reason it has been decided that the brook does not rush its "sixteenths" at fifty for the dotted quarter-note. The scene at the brook thus becomes a lively allegretto—a dramatic misreading of Beethoven's tempo indication of *Andante molto moto*. In my reading of the words *molto moto* I have always tried to figure out why this qualification of Andante seemed necessary to the composer.

In Beethoven's day, the business of conducting was still in its infancy and must often have been a rather clumsy affair. I would venture the guess that Beethoven was trying to prevent the movement from being chopped up by someone beating twelve eighth-notes rather than the four beats to the measure he would have preferred. It may sound absurd that anyone of sound musical mind would ever have considered beating out the eighth-notes, but odder things I assure you I have seen and heard. This alarming propensity for dividing the beats is not the result of any intellectual flaws, but simply of faulty coordination between brain and arm motion. It is a propensity often produced, alas, by exposure to unwilling conservatory orchestras composed of musicians who do not wish to become orchestral players and so do not play together! This obliges the unhappy baton-swinger to beat eight when he should beat four, to beat six when he should beat two, and so on.

From his early sonatas onward, Beethoven preferred slow movements with meters in $\frac{9}{8}$ time. Opuses 18 (No. 1), 22, and 31 (No. 1) are fine examples. Among his late works I would also note the slow movement of the Ninth Symphony, in $\frac{12}{8}$ (which can die a quick death if chopped up into eighth-notes) and the slow movement of Op. 127, also in $\frac{12}{8}$. If you ask any sensitive musicians how one should phrase certain passages in Beethoven's piano or chamber works, I guarantee that they will reply "in 3" and "in 4" respectively (never in 9 or in 12). It is not easy to reach the point where sixty, seventy, or more musicians are all playing four times six notes rather than twelve times two notes. To reach that stage one certainly must have a permanent ensemble, but more than that, one must have a steady heartbeat and a conductor who has full confidence in his ability.

If all these conditions are met, the only correct tempo will be very close to the fifty for the dotted quarter-note. The movement is then transformed into something so much more profound and spiritual than a mere description of a brook, thus preparing the way for the divine splendor of the final movement. Once one has achieved the right tempo for the second movement, the pace of the opening becomes clear. One traces first the four beats of the second movement, then (in a somewhat quicker beat) the *whole* $\frac{2}{4}$ measure of the opening (in figures, from fifty to sixty-six). This method should produce satisfactory and convincing results for a well-prepared conductor, and it will also become apparent that the specific figures are not as important as the relative relationship between the composer's various numerals.

In Central Europe, Richard Wagner's method of playing Beethoven inspired a tradition of playing the symphonies (at least the Third, Fifth, Sixth, Seventh, and Ninth) with doubled woodwinds. In both Europe and America his method favored the use of very large string sections and tempo ideas that even the eminent musicologist Eduard Hanslick recognized as bizarre, but which prevailed until the wave of authenticators took over the podiums. Yet, in *On Conducting* Wagner's remarks about performing the prelude to his opera, *Die Meistersinger von Nürnberg*, are very similar to my advice regarding the "Pastoral" Symphony.

Wagner's essay has been translated into English, but for those who might not be able to find it I would briefly summarize his comments on *Meistersinger* thus: he explains in the simplest terms how to bring the various elements of the prelude together under a large umbrella labeled "Same Tempo." Let me briefly describe the various sections. First, there is the March of the Masters, with a short interlude anticipating the first scene in the church; then there is the lyric love music of the young pair Eva and Walther (E major); followed by a Scherzando section that anticipates Beckmesser (the fall guy of the comedy); and this leads into a polyphonic climax in which the Prize Song, the March of the Masters, and the Theme of the Apprentices are combined in a singularly artful and effective coda.

In his score Wagner begins with the directive "Sehr mässig bewegt," a tempo indication that over the course of the score's various editions has inspired all sorts of interpretation. The transition to the love music is marked "Bewegt, doch immer noch etwas breit" (moving, but still somewhat broad), and the love music "Mässig, im Hauptzeitmass" (moderato, in the main tempo). Toward the Scherzando part there is a "noch bewegter" (moving faster) with the entry of the Scherzo music we read "Im mässigen Hauptzeitmass" (in the main tempo, moderato) and for the Coda, where the thirty-second-notes begin, he adds a "sehr gewichtig." (very weighty). Avoiding the common Italian tempo indications was a manifestation of Wagner's nationalism; while Italian indications are open to wide interpretation, the German terminology is no less vague.

Aside from translating Wagner's marks I would mention two additions made by the conductor Hans von Bülow in his arrangement of the score for piano two-hands. After "sehr mässig bewegt" he adds "durchweg breit und gewichtig" (broad and weighty throughout). This is clearly not Wagner's indication, and since Wagner uses the term *weighty* for the coda (to get the thirty-second-notes out fluently) this is obviously an error on von Bülow's part. For the love music von Bülow totally contradicts the composer in changing the composer's moderate primo tempo to "A bit more moderate still" than the primo (main) tempo. All this may seem like mere hair-splitting, but it does matter. Richard Strauss cursed von Bülow for his arbitrary treatment of *Don Juan*, and there are some wonderfully obscure comments written into von Bülow's edition of the Beethoven piano sonatas (published by Cotta). If the German von Bülow could not resist making additions in copying Wagner's tempos, imagine what others did, especially in translation.

Wagner's opening directive is simply "Molto moderato mosso," which is as ambiguous as it could be. Following Wagner's advice that the entire prelude should proceed in one single tempo, a conductor might prepare himself for rehearsal by tracing the tempos of the other sections (just as he would trace the six tempo-metronome relationships in the "Pastoral" Symphony). Since the prelude to the *Meistersinger* is a classically constructed piece, Wagner's methods for achieving proper pacing, timing, symmetry, proportion, and so forth are similar to those best suited to a symphonic interpretation.

One should not, however, forget that Wagner's guidance is binding for his music alone. He also misrepresented Beethoven (for profound reasons of his own) and admitted having undervalued Mozart's instrumental compositions. Wagner was more eloquent than most composers about the importance of tempo to a correct interpretation. If one can believe the testimonies of his contemporaries (I, for one, am frankly skeptical about them), Wagner's tempos were faster (to judge by the overall time elapsed), than the standard common nowadays around the world. My skepticism is based on the (admittedly inconclusive) evidence of an overall elapsed time for *Rheingold* that is shorter than that heard these days, either in Bayreuth or at the Met. This must be inconclusive since a very fast approach to fast sections combined with a slower-than-customary approach to slow sections may create new total times that are irrelevant to the study of a composer's original intentions.

In this connection it is crucial to consider the decisive difference between vocal music and instrumental music. Nowhere is this more lucidly demonstrated than in performances of Verdi's *Requiem Mass*. At the start of the first section the strings (for twenty-seven measures) play an important theme, with the chorus interjecting whispered responses such as those heard in Catholic services. The identical music, one half-tone higher, is sung in the last section of the work by the unaccompanied chorus, led by the solo soprano. Verdi had marked both sections with the identical metronome marking for tempo. Most performances I have heard (perhaps including my own many years back) are so intent on creating a mysterious atmosphere that there is a loss of tempo control at the start, to the point where the hushed sounds are all-important and the relationship with the later recapitulation is almost completely lost.

The conductor is compelled to take the a cappella section in the final movement at the right tempo, because he is not dealing with a group of string players who can change bow whenever there is a dragged tempo. He is dealing instead with a group of singers led by a prima donna who has absolutely no intention of getting blue in the face simply because the distinguished maestro happens to think both spots should be taken slower than Verdi did. In the broadest sense, conducting opera is so much more simple for this very reason; there is, as it were, a built-in, fail-safe system in the vocalists' limited lungs and diaphragms.

A favorite indoor sport of mine is to switch on a radio in the middle of a piece of music and guess who is performing. I once chanced upon the last movement of Mozart's *Requiem* and, realizing that it was not the Süssmayr edition, stayed with it long enough to hear the final fugato. The performance had been billed, it transpired, as "authentic," by "early music" standards. One of the great tenets of the early music enthusiasts is that tempos used to be much faster than they are now, yet is it authentic and realistic to imply that the immortal souls are in a jolly mood after hearing the words "Lux eterna luceat eis Domine"? The original fugato text (in the first movement that Mozart finished completely) is "Kyrie eleison" and "Christe eleison." Even in 1791 (assuming that tempos really were faster then) the three trombones playing the three lower voices would certainly not have galloped through this passage in the manner of Tommy Dorsey. This is why it is so dangerous to claim (as some early music experts are wont to do) that rigid rules should be applied to musical performance. This particular rendition of the Mozart fugato was simply wrong. Even if tempos were faster in those days, one simply cannot do this to a fugato in a mass for the dead.

It is true that my tastes were formed many decades ago. Whereas I hope I am flexible and open to new discoveries, and whereas I certainly detest the habit of glorying in the past, I am fully aware that my objection to radical interpretations of old music is born partly out of unfamiliarity with things outside my experience. I recall, for instance, listening on one occasion to Bach's Suite No. 2 in B minor. It was played by a thoroughly trustworthy ensemble, and that is just the way it sounded to me—trustworthy. What I heard, I liked—old instruments, a fine continuo, and so forth—and yet when it was over it was as if the piece could have been composed by any one of many thoroughly professional, serviceable, and undistinguished composers. To have heard Bach's music in this way was simply painful to me.

I have included that story among my remarks on tempo because, like many thousands of other musical students, I was taught that tempos can have a significant influence on expression and meaning. A musical composition is, in this sense, similar to a speech. It is quite clear that a speaker who is delivering conventional formalities of no great consequence will always be well advised to get on with it, while anyone delivering a major speech should take his time and perhaps even slow down when relating a complex idea.

In the music profession (as in any other profession) there is never any shortage of people happy to dispense general advice. They are to be found in conservatories, opera house lobbies, theater green rooms, or master classes, and their advice is often extremely useful. Nevertheless, no professional musician should depend upon others to tell him which is the "right" tempo. I always felt proud to be asked for professional advice and invariably agreed to help younger conductors, but I never answered for them the question of how fast or how slowly a piece should go, because the question is based on fundamental misconceptions about the nature of tempo.

There are many types of music that are written to fulfill a particular function. The march is a classic example. The famous funeral marches from the piano sonatas of Beethoven and Chopin, the "Eroica" Symphony, Mahler's Fifth, and numerous other concert and operatic pieces were originally composed and played to heighten the solemnity of a funeral parade. Wagner's splendid "Entrance of the guests at the Wartburg," from act 2 of *Tannhäuser*, is a festive march, not quite of military character but with the discipline associated with a formal, stuffy festivity. There is also a festive quality to the *Radetzky March* by Johann Strauss, Sr. Whereas the latter is in alla breve, the former is "in four" but in the same tempo. There are also marches, such as Sousa's "Stars and Stripes," that have almost become national hymns, while Elgar's processional *Pomp and Circumstance* has become a quasi-official commencement tune. Military marches have various speeds because the different cadences of each nation's armed forces must be reflected in the musical tempo.

There are countless examples of how tempos vary within each type of music. In the eighteenth century, the popularity of dance music led to the establishment of the minuet in the symphonic structure. In dance music, tempo is traditionally established by the formal motions of the dancers, yet the symphonic minuet often carries a qualifying word to change the tempo. Oddly, even the Scherzo of Beethoven's First Symphony is marked "Menuetto," but I doubt anybody would be foolish enough to apply even a fast minuet speed to that particular movement.

Most major compositions played today by small, medium-sized, and large orchestras have their origins in functional music. Eighteenth-century music was mostly functional, and church music influenced many great works (such as Beethoven's *Missa Solemnis*) that are no longer part of the sacred service. The idea of putting a wide variety of styles from different countries into a strait-jacket must seem absurd to anyone who tries to line up dozens of dance and march forms in their original and in their transferred garb as symphonic pieces. I do not know whether the minuet played by the first of the three stage-bands in *Don Giovanni* is an original minuet tempo, but I do know that the tempo of that minuet must be such that the Contre-Danse and the German Tanz, played simultaneously by bands two and three respectively, fit naturally into the overall unity of the stage music. All functional music—whether it be composed for dances, church services, or background music for tea-time at a genteel hotel—slips automatically into traditional tempos, but those tempos change when they are employed in a symphony.

Music composed by the great masters for purposes of study has undergone a similar process of change. Bach's *The Well-Tempered Clavier* is the first and greatest example of this genre, and its most famous successors in the nineteenth and twentieth centuries are the etudes by Chopin and Debussy. Among works by lesser composers are Paganini's *Caprices* for violin. All these great study exercises "made it" to the concert stage, and in their exploration of the limits of a particular instrument helped to promote the phenomenon of "virtuoso" composers, such as Sergei Rachmaninov, whose inspiration essentially stemmed from the instrument. In these works, tempo is less important, because the central concern is to test the limits of technical proficiency. In the realm of the ensemble there is very little such music; in symphonic literature, virtuoso music as such is represented most prominently by Ravel's *Boléro* (a dreadful bore after the first hearing and after the initial shock has worn off). This work did provoke a lively discussion about tempo, however, when the conductor Arturo Toscanini, much to Ravel's displeasure, sped up the tempo at one point in the later variations.

In recent years the great symphonic tone poems by Richard Strauss (*Don Juan* and *Till Eulenspiegel* in particular) have wrongly been transformed into empty virtuoso displays. In his letters to his parents, Strauss complained bitterly that the conductors Arthur Nikisch and Hans von Bülow played "merely well-orchestrated pieces" without paying attention to their poetic content. A couple of years ago I rehearsed, with a German orchestra, a program that included *Till*. Musicians in good ensembles are always alert to conductors' choices of tempo, because they realize that those choices are critical to their playing. On this occasion I was regaled between rehearsals with woeful tales of how they had been obliged to race through *Till* a few weeks earlier when a young man from abroad treated the work as a virtuoso bravura display piece. I regret to say that I once witnessed a similar race, involving the same piece, on my television screen. The added brutality of sound made *Till* into a nasty criminal instead of the legendary prankster.

One very important question regarding tempos is their interrelationship with musical content. The easy answer to this question is simply to deny that there is content, but even if one considers works that are not designated as program pieces, there has been content ever since the middle symphonies of Haydn. Early music experts are not alone, however, in their wholesale denial of content. In fact, it was Arnold Schoenberg, in his famous lecture about Johannes Brahms, who provided the most radical denial of the relationship between content and musical setting. He attempts to prove this point by demonstrating how Brahms, in his lied "Feldeinsamkeit," paid no special attention to the word *lange* (for a long time). Schoenberg was a very sophisticated analyst of music, so I am sure he convinced many people with this argument, but I believe his analysis was more politically than musically motivated, in that Schoenberg was trying to establish Brahms as a modernist.

It is now generally accepted that even the music of Bach's predecessors had content. As for Bach, his vocal works abound with illustrations in the instrumental accompaniments, and the same formulae are often found in the vocal parts. I believe that every movement of the late Mozart symphonies can also be interpreted in poetic terms, and even if those terms need not be explicitly stated they are very helpful in finding the right tempo. To take just one of many examples, the final movement of the Symphony No. 39 in E-flat has an underlying idea that demands a somewhat heavy-footed allegro and not the usual, driven virtuoso brio of the simpler finales of Nos. 35 and 36. The tempo indications over Mozart's final movements are instructive in this respect. Those of symphonies No. 35, 36, 38, 40, 41, and 39 are, respectively, Presto, Presto, Presto, Allegro assai, Allegro molto, and Allegro.

Beethoven's debts to Mozart are obvious and well documented. Perhaps most famously, he modeled his "Eroica" Symphony upon Mozart's symphony No. 39—first movement in $\frac{3}{4}$, second movement in $\frac{4}{8}$, third movement's trio with concertizing solo instruments, and the fourth movement in $\frac{2}{4}$. The question arises, though, whether Beethoven would have been so eager to follow the metric pattern if the finale had been the classic Haydn-style romp. It is a speculative inquiry, but even idle speculation is often more fruitful than research based on erroneous comments passed on from generation to generation (in the case of Beethoven, such research seems to know no bounds). There are problems involved in bringing the final movement to the tempo and inflection that I propose, because most orchestras have the Haydn-type final $\frac{2}{4}$ Presto in their fingers, and furthermore the violins automatically play with a flying spiccato (for which the right tempo is faster than the one I try to convey).

Musicians are often compelled to play tempos with which they do not agree. Important leaders of string or woodwind sections have a built-in tempo that they have practiced and stayed with since their days at the conservatory. If a conductor directs them at a noticeably different tempo they often feel uncomfortable and do not forget it easily. A few years ago I arrived at the first rehearsal for a performance of Mahler's Fifth Symphony by a top orchestra. Even before I reached center stage, the harpist, the two concertmasters, and the principal violist and cellist were all at my side. "How slowly do you take the Adagietto?" they asked. I assured them that it would be playable, and asked why they were so anxious. It appeared that one particular conductor from their past had been so slow that the harpist had not known where and when the next note should be played and the strings had not known how often they would have to change bows. The remarkable thing was that those traumatic events had taken place almost two decades before. Even though the orchestra had in the intervening years performed the same symphony several times with excellent people, that wrong tempo had remained a vivid memory.

Mahler's music, being rhapsodic rather than classically proportioned, leaves more room for flexibility in tempos than, for example, that of Mozart, in which the slightest error changes the tenor of a piece dramatically. In consequence of this, Mahler's music has been recorded at such a variety of speeds and nuances that any valiant journeyman now feels perfectly entitled to sail briskly into a cycle of his symphonies. Their assumption seems to be that to attack these large and often unwieldy scores, all that is required to bring out the music's expressions of conflict and yearning is a thoroughly neurotic disposition.

There are countless similar examples of how tempos have been subjected to widely differing interpretations. Those examples should be sufficient to convince people that there can be no such thing as a "model" pre-recorded version of a major repertory work. In this regard, however, it is unfortunate that many major conductors have chosen to compete with each other to produce the slowest tempo. This particular international contest may have started with the same very serious man whose "Pastoral" Symphony I found so utterly dull. In his later years he clung to the notion that greater profundity could be gained by slower tempos. Other conductors who hit their prime in the 1960s and 1970s may simply have been reacting to the pre-war years (1918–33), when "ever faster" became almost a motto. The Schoenberg school may also have been influential in promoting tempos, and that provided a way to show off the superior technique of American top orchestras.

At this point the distraught reader might well ask whether there is any way of knowing what the composer really wanted, and thus of establishing an ultimate authority for each tempo. The answer is no, and the case of the composer's amanuensis is another classic example. There are Wagner piano-vocal scores, in the Peters edition, that contain annotations by the conductor Felix Mottl (who, along with Hans Richter, was one of Wagner's original helpers). The scores contain Mottl's quotes of Wagner's directives during rehearsals. Anyone who has read about Beethoven will know that Schindler was a notoriously unreliable witness and reporter of what he saw and heard from Beethoven, or in Beethoven's company. Similarly, many who have read about Stravinsky will have little or no confidence in the reports of Robert Craft. It is more than probable that one should treat Mottl's observations with a similar degree of caution. Even the most faithful amanuenses are bound to distort the truth in some way, so we must treat their testimonies as essentially unreliable.

There is, then, no ultimate authority in the matter of tempos. If this apparently alarming fact causes the conducting student to feel unsure, it is nonetheless a welcome one, because music is always changing. By reading widely and developing a greater ability to read music, the student will learn how to judge whether changes must be made to make a problematic composition fit the circumstances or whether it would be wiser simply to drop the piece. In recent years conductors have also had to adjust tempos to account for larger concert halls. Older European opera houses rarely have a capacity of over two thousand people. Their "horseshoe" design forms a shell that favors the sound for those on stage, while the lowered pit sends the sounds of the instruments straight up toward the ceiling, allowing the music to cross the direction of the voices at a ninety-degree angle (and thereby benefiting everyone in the hall). The larger modern halls (both in Europe and in America), with their capacities of three or even four thousand, put a premium on large voices and loud singing. This in turn compels singers to sing faster, and that is less tiring. The problems faced by the modern performer are simply different from those of performers in earlier centuries.

Since change seems to be such a permanent feature, how odd it is that so many young musicians and early music specialists should seek to apply so many rules to the interpretation of pre-1750 or pre-1800 music (one even begins to fear for music up to 1850 and beyond). The only true test is performance, and all their claims about old instruments, tempos, balances, and acoustics become largely irrelevant when it is time to mount the podium. The beautiful notion of the authentic, or authoritative, performance is simply an illusion.

The Metronome

In 1927 the centennial of Beethoven's death was observed in Europe as extravagantly as the bicentennial of Mozart's death was observed in 1991. I well recall how my Viennese piano teacher, who held regular musical evenings in his apartment to prepare his students for public performance, scheduled for that season all Beethoven's compositions for and with piano. Then, as now, there was great debate over the reliability and accuracy of his metronome markings. Then, as now, the debate pitted the purists against the pragmatists.

Purists such as Rudolf Kolisch considered the numerals in Beethoven's works as binding as the Ten Commandments, while the pragmatists questioned several metronome markings (most of which they considered too fast). If a Viennese music lover of 1927 were asked, Too fast compared to what? he or she would doubtless have retorted, Too fast compared to Furtwängler.

Now we are all at it again. This time the debate has been stimulated by a group of conductors who choose to present Beethoven's music with what they regard as "original" instruments and tempos. The critics, always eager to comment on musical fashions, are delighted to have a lively topic for debate. I doubt, however, that there is much to be learned from such debate. The metronome markings of Schoenberg are just as controversial as those of Beethoven, with the difference that in Schoenberg's case no claims of deafness or mechanical inaccuracy of the ticker can be made. The metronome markings of Igor Stravinsky do not seem in the least controversial to me, and I believe that those of Beethoven are just as explicable.

It was in 1970 that I first hit upon a solution to the puzzle of these controversial metronome settings. My wife Vera and I were staying at a hotel in Ouchy while we looked for an apartment in the French-speaking part of Switzerland. One afternoon I found the lounge television tuned to a channel that was showing Otto Klemperer conducting his London orchestra in Beethoven's "Pastoral" Symphony. The conductor sat on a high stool, immersed in the score, which was open on the music stand before him. When the "rainstorm" movement began with a tempo approximately half that which is customary, I realized that Klemperer, in his absorption, had quite forgotten that he was before a public audience. He appeared to be reading the score as if he were alone with it in his den. To one who is in such a contemplative, almost trancelike state, any tempo might be appropriate. The resultant music is essentially a re-reading of the finished score that may differ significantly from the previous readings or performances by the same person.

Beethoven, too, had been deeply immersed in his reading, concerned not with playable tempos or hearable tempos (two distinct things), but rather with what he saw and heard as he read. Any musician doing the same would be perfectly content, for example, with the metronome marking of the last movement of the Eighth Symphony, which in practice should not be tried at the speed of the numeral (the whole measure at eighty-four). In my opinion the six repeated notes of the main subject can be played, but cannot be heard, at 168.

Whenever passages are cruelly difficult (one thinks, for example, of the "Magic Fire" music for strings, in Wagner's *Die Walküre*) some conductors prefer to think that the composer wanted an *al fresco* overall effect and that consequently the notes do not have to be played exactly as they appear. This is nonsense. The notes must be played, and the only necessary directive is to find the tempo in which these notes can be heard and played for the proper effect. This is also the only sound guidance for passages such as the final movement of Beethoven's Eighth. The best effect is obtained when every repeated note can be heard as one hears the roll of a snare drum.

Beethoven's metronome marking of eighty-four for the whole measure is entirely correct—for *his* reading of the finished score—but there are also numerous other metronome markings that are right for the best instrumental rendition. The key here is the perception, imagination, and insight of the conductor (or soloist), who must be able to choose the most suitable tempo from several possibilities, ranging from that which is right for reading, at one extreme, and that which is right for playing, at the other. In my view there are four main criteria involved in this choice: Does the tempo emphasize the character of the piece? Can it be played to best effect? Can it be heard without asking too much (or too little) of the listener? Is it right for the particular circumstances?

The first criterion reflects that there are always differences about the expressive meaning of a piece of music. Let us look at a well-known example from the European post-Wagner tradition: the second (A minor) movement of Beethoven's Seventh Symphony. This movement had been performed for many decades as a *marcia funebre* (a fact discussed in many program notes, interviews, and other works of musical interpretation). I assume, without having any documentary proof, that this interpretation was first made popular by Richard Wagner who, in his essay *On Conducting* (1897), wrote: "a slow tempo cannot be slow enough (to make its impact) and a fast tempo cannot be fast enough to accomplish the same purpose."

In saying this, Wagner may have wanted merely to ensure that his music was treated accordingly. He also became a famous Beethoven interpreter, and one who wrote acid polemics against other accepted authorities on that composer, so this may be the reason this slow movement by Beethoven, in minor key and in $\frac{2}{4}$ meter (as is the slow movement of the "Eroica" symphony) was turned into a dirge. That the heading of the A minor movement was *Allegretto* and that of the "Eroica" *Adagio* was conveniently overlooked and, I suppose, justified by some suitably metaphysical wisdom (an ever-present philosophical auxiliary for many German musicians). I can attest to the fact that the great conductors were still presenting this movement in funereal tempo in the 1920s. It was not until near the end of that decade that Toscanini, touring with the New York Philharmonic, revolutionized the way it was conducted by introducing a Tempo Allegretto that has been standard ever since.

As bizarre as the argument for the funereal tempo may seem, it is not entirely without foundation. If one asks oneself "What does the movement express?" then the tempo marking (seventy-six for the quarter-note) is certainly too fast. If one disregards the notion of the dirge, then seventy-six is the right tempo. Since Beethoven's metronome figures have been used as a political football for anyone who wanted to kick them around the yard, it is hardly surprising that total disregard of the composer's figures became the rule rather than the exception.

As for the second criterion, it is not until the first rehearsal that a conductor can know for sure whether the chosen tempos are playable to the best effect. This is because the achievement of this effect depends very much upon the skills of the musicians at hand—their skill at judging not only the speed but also the weight of sound (which may be fine for the city of Cottbus but not so fine for Heidelberg). All that one needs for such significant differences to emerge are two concertmasters of different schooling and with different ideas about bowing.

Turning now to the third and fourth criteria, the size and the acoustics of a given auditorium will have an enormous influence on what can be heard and what is appropriate for the circumstances of the occasion. Modern musicians, trained usually for solo or chamber music careers by ambitious conservatories (such as Juilliard and Curtis), generally possess more acquired facility than those of the past. There have been occasions in the past when I have not been able to follow even music that I knew well, because the first violinist went so fast. These were performances of chamber music works by classical composers, performed by brilliant virtuoso soloists. It is possible that I was sitting so far away that the sound did not decay fast enough to permit clarity of passages, because I always knew that the soloist was playing everything correctly, without cheating or faking.

Whereas the first criterion can be met by the conductor alone (since he is quite capable of determining for himself in advance the meaning of the piece), the other three can be met only in actual rehearsal and where the performance will take place. This is extremely difficult for the beginner, since the differences between performing in the Royal Festival Hall, London, and the Concertgebouw, Amsterdam, are not written down in any textbook. How much easier it is (and how much more certain to produce errors of judgment) simply to fall in line with those who maintain that all music was played faster before 1800! Musicologists' theories about tempos and metronome markings in Beethoven's works often seem to be little more than idle speculation; yet those theories are welcomed by many record companies who feel that the music world needs something different and "authentic." Who, however, is checking whether this interpretation is authentic?

There are many famous examples of how composers have interpreted their metronome markings. One example concerns the young Richard Strauss, who in the 1890s lived in Berlin and witnessed performances of his *Tod und Verklärung* by Arthur Nikisch and of *Don Juan* by Hans von Bülow. In a furious letter to his parents about the latter performance he wrote the memorable words, "and I sent him the approximately most exact metronome figures." The paradox of those words *approximately most exact* goes a long way toward explaining why a composer's metronome indications should be regarded as binding. Strauss was a pragmatist, in the sense that he was a professional conductor before he made his mark as a young composer of genius. His early compositions were as smooth and competent as Mendelssohn's lesser masterpieces, but his real breakthrough did not come until he was around twenty-four years old, with *Guntram*, the Symphony, the Violin Sonata, and the other juvenilia of the early 1880s. Because he was a professional conductor for some time, his metronome markings are not, I think, of the "Beethoven" variety. He was the son of a horn player, schooled in the tradition of his father, and always an insider of that complex organism known as the orchestra. So when he wrote that he sent "approximately exact" metronome markings, we can take him at this word.

Debussy was another great composer who made an overt statement about the metronome, declaring that it was "fine for the first five measures." This apparently innocuous statement tells us a great deal, and certainly begs the question, Why does hardly anybody observe the 116 for the opening of *La Mer*? Since Debussy was such an extraordinary performer on the keyboard, a conductor should certainly feel able to trust his metronome markings (especially considering his disclaimer that they are good only over the first few measures).

I am rather afraid that the foregoing sketches may have deepened, rather than lessened, the confusion about the intrinsic value of metronome figures. Let me put it in very simple terms. Throughout my career I always looked carefully at the metronome figures of any composition that contained them. Since the basic sixty speed can be checked on the second hand of a watch, one does not even need to buy a metronome. I therefore generally advise students to become aware of the sixty speed and to study the metronome marks of those composers who use them, but not to buy a metronome. A stopwatch will give you the metronome mark you are singing, humming, or thinking while the hand races (or drags) around the dial. The trick is to measure six units that establish your tempo in metronome figures.

I noted earlier that I found Stravinsky's metronome markings to be entirely convincing. This is because when I carried out the above test with my stopwatch I came so close to the printed figures that by force of sheer vanity I considered them right. The most effective way of achieving the correct tempo is to compare metronome figures within the same work and between works of similar character by the same composer. In this respect I would cite the Scherzo movements in Beethoven's symphonies, which are rarely heard at their respective speeds. One often hears, for example, the Scherzo of the Ninth played faster than that of the Third, even though the composer gave the identical figure for both.

Whenever I teach a series of seminars on this subject, I usually begin by asking students to tell me (without reference to scores) which of the eight Beethoven symphonic Scherzos is the fastest and which is the slowest and to give the other six in their order of speed. The replies invariably indicate that students who claim to know Beethoven's symphonies well have not even deemed it important to look at the metronome figures. Those who ignore Beethoven like this while simultaneously denouncing his errors are rather like New York cab drivers who have no idea where "uptown" might be, yet are extremely adept at running traffic lights.

I have read two accounts (one in a German, the other in an English-language publication) of a particularly crass violation of Beethoven's metronome equations. At the end of the Ninth, the relationship between the measure 916 Maestoso and the preceding Prestissimo must be such that the quarter-note of the Maestoso equals the entire measure of the Prestissimo. This must be so because the sequences of thirty-second-notes, from 917 on, lead without any break into the eighth-notes of the final Prestissimo. This relationship among the three subsections Prestissimo, Maestoso, and Prestissimo is binding, even if one disagrees with the specific metronome figures (132/60/−). All recordings issued by the big record companies turn the Maestoso into an Adagio with six beats to the measure and eliminate this essential ratio, thus failing to express the continuity of this final variation. How this became accepted remains extremely puzzling to me.

If the issue of Beethoven's metronome marks were not sufficiently trying in itself, there is also the fact that the various editions of his works contain considerable variants. The so-called latest edition of the string quartets contains no metronomes, while older editions do. In these days of positivist musicology it is unacceptable for an editor to withhold any sign that might conceivably be attributed to Beethoven. If there is doubt about the provenance of any marking, it should be mentioned in a footnote.

It is vital that we come to terms with Beethoven's metronome markings, because the wholesale discrediting of his figures must also affect our understanding of metronome markings by other eminent composers, including Bartók, Debussy, and Stravinsky.

Three

Of Miracles, Magicians, and Myths: Essays on Composers

The Myth of the Unsung Genius

Whenever a new composition is greeted with critical indifference or hostility, well-meaning supporters emerge to reassert the popularly held view that geniuses are always misunderstood in their lifetimes. The clear implication of this assertion is that we, in our age, should take care lest we fail to detect the new immortals hiding in our midst. This is a tempting idea, but also a largely mythical one. All the great composers were successful in their lifetimes and fully recognized by their contemporaries.

I suspect that nobody really understands the meaning of the word *genius*. It is used too freely, as if it were the equivalent of a minor military decoration. Neither psychohistory nor the most assiduous perusal of the composer's sketch books will ever reveal the true nature of Beethoven's genius. The tragedy of his deafness has been used by dilettante historians to imply that his contemporaries did not appreciate him, whereas he was adored during his lifetime and compensated both morally and financially. A New York critic once told his readers that the conductor and composer Gaspare Spontini (1774–1851) was more famous and more successful than Franz Schubert. Intrigued by this astonishing declaration, I has-tened to consult the *New Grove Dictionary of Music and Musicians*. There I found a delightful footnote that explained that *La Vestale*, Spontini's principal work was a "marvel of noise," was given 213 times, and was pro-duced all over Europe in its heyday. The dictionary then went on to recount a humorous tale current in Paris in Spontini's day. The tale concerned a well-known physician who, having advised a friend to go and listen to *La Vestale* as a remedy for his deafness, accompanied the friend to the theater. "Doctor," cried the friend after a particularly loud passage, "I can hear!" Alas, however, the doctor made no response, since what had cured the patient had deafened the physician. This story (whether true or invented) illustrates that *La Vestale* was recognized for what it is: a noise-maker. Such a work is always a sure-fire hit with a noise-loving crowd, but to compare Spontini with Schubert is as absurd as comparing Hermann Hesse with Judith Krantz.

The year 1986 offers a further poignant example of the vagaries of success. Whereas the centenary of Franz Liszt's death was observed with considerable pomp and ceremony around the globe, the two-hundredth anniversary of Carl Maria Weber's birth was virtually ignored. It is arguable whether Liszt as a composer ever had a success comparable to Weber's opera *Der Freischütz*. After its premiere in Berlin in 1821, the opera was accepted for production by thirty-three German opera compa-nies within eighteen months. Imagine a 1980 New York hit running in thirty-three productions simultaneously by 1982! Such a reception would clearly be impossible today, because the conditions of the modern show business world simply would not allow it. My point is that Weber was patently successful in his lifetime (and his opera is still in the repertory of virtually every German opera house). As the years passed, the opera's success remained essentially limited to the German-language orbit in which his libretto found an understanding public. The worldwide success of Liszt the composer—success that was greatly encouraged by his per-sonality and by his bravura as a performer—has been perpetuated since his death by generations of virtuoso pianists. This international acclaim did not, however, extend to Liszt's larger compositions for orchestra and chorus. Besides the coincidence of their 1986 anniversary celebrations, these two masters, Liszt and Weber, have little else in common. Both, though, lived to taste the fullest measure of triumph within their respective contemporary environments. Even Johann Sebastian Bach has been subjected to the horrors of sloppy historical scholarship. Since his life seemed to have been peaceful and free from hardship, the historians decided that he had to suffer posthumously. He was forgotten, they said, from his death in 1750 until 1829 when Felix Mendelssohn suddenly "rediscovered" him by performing the *St. Matthew Passion*. Bach's music was never forgotten. The German musicologist Johann Forkel, for example, called Bach a "national treasure" in 1802. The two main reasons why his works were played less frequently in the years after his death were the obsolescence of many instrumental techniques of Bach's age and the lack of organizations equipped to produce the choral works. For the same reasons, we now consider the nineteenth-century interpretations of Bach's instrumental music stylistically wrong. Musicians in that period had to adapt his music to existing playing practices.

To assess the career of a composer/organist/choirmaster/teacher employed by church councils during the first half of the eighteenth century, we need to remember the differences between that age and our own. In Bach's day there were no printed reviews after each Sunday's new cantata, and there was very little public notice of his life and work. Yet he must have been greatly honored and appreciated. His fame must have been spread by the guild of organists and singers who benefited from his teaching and from his guidance. Is it conceivable that a mere choirmaster of the Lutheran Church would be received by the King of Prussia if he were not considered great?

Mozart's success has often been misrepresented by biographers who equated his unresolved financial crises with lack of success. Even Theodor Adorno, who should have known better, chides Mozart's (and other composers') contemporaries for letting composers starve, only to elevate them posthumously to the status of revered masters. Adorno was a social philosopher and should have known that a free composer, without a court or church appointment, was effectively a peddler in an age when any copyist might steal a composition to resell it as his own. There was no protection or copyright for creative work, there was no repertoire, and nearly every musical event offered new pieces—either composed for the occasion or heard for the first time locally. Since Mozart's life is well documented there is no difficulty in setting the record straight, and yet in reading about his life one must be constantly skeptical and wary of sources. Perhaps it has proven too difficult to reconstruct the circumstances that prevented Mozart from translating his unparalleled triumphs into a comfortable financial existence; perhaps it has simply been easier to avoid this issue altogether and blame the indifference of contemporary society.

The free artist—whether composer, painter, novelist, or dramatist—has always needed a source of income. Even with our modern system of royalties, performance fees, and residuals, only a small number of best-selling authors can live without a teaching position or some other permanent salary. Prior to the French Revolution a composer had to have a court or church appointment to survive (the twentieth-century equivalent might be a university or conservatory appointment). In the early nineteenth century the free artist depended on sales of his music to publishers. Beethoven's career was successful in both artistic and financial terms. He was aware of his success and he knew how to ensure that his success be reflected in adequate remuneration.

Those who cling to the myth of unrecognized genius decided that the "late Beethoven" was incomprehensible to his contemporaries. This particular little canard has been touted by dilettante scholars and reputable musicians alike. In the preface to the Philharmonic edition of the late quartets, we read that the public's appreciation of the works has benefited from the "tremendous musical development of the past hundred years." This text is printed in all five scores. Whereas I would dispute whether the past hundred years of "tremendous musical development" have heightened our understanding of Beethoven's works, I would say that the considerable appreciation and understanding those works found in the 1820s is simply a matter of fact. The Kinsky catalogue is considered the standard reference work for Beethoven's compositions. On page 384 of the catalogue one finds the following entry (my translation):

Announcement of the publishers Schott in the intelligence section of *Caecilia* in number 11, August 1825: Advertised in score, in parts, for piano four hands and two hands . . . It is the much admired newest quartet [Op. 127] of our contemporary master, deemed the acme of instrumental music . . . the best quartet in Vienna, frightened by its difficulties, had laid it aside for a while, but later, after several rehearsals, recognized that it was the best work of Beethoven. The whole thing will be published before the year's end.

Even if one discounts the commercial hyperbole, one learns from this paragraph that Schott printed piano arrangements for two and four hands. Why would anyone do this if the compositions were neither understood, nor respected, nor considered fit for home playing? A certain Christian Rummel made the four-hand arrangement. This was favorably reviewed and must also have sold well for some time, because in 1860 another musician, F. X. Gleichauf, was commissioned to make a new four-hand version. Is this the lack of comprehension referred to by H. G. in the Philharmonic score? I scarcely think so. I rather believe that H. G. and other, similarly disposed, historians are in error. After Beethoven's death in 1827, the slow movement of Op. 127 (or at least its theme) was made into a song with a text by a local poet. The resulting work was doubtless kitsch of the most criminal variety, but one must ask oneself whether this would have happened to a composition that was unappreciated.

Three of the five late Beethoven quartets were dedicated to Prince Galitzin, an amateur cellist who had transcribed several of Beethoven's piano sonatas for string quartet. After receiving them the prince wrote to the composer on 29 April 1825: "Thank you so much for the precious gift of the sublime quartet . . . I had it played for me several times and recognize the full genius of the master." A year and a half later he wrote again, this time about Op. 130 and Op. 132, "I received from you two new masterpieces of your immortal and boundless genius." In yet another letter he wrote, "The paper in Leipzig is so laudatory of your new quartet that I am beside myself with impatience to find out about it."

The *Grosse Fuge* (Op. 133) was also commissioned by the publisher Artaria in a four-hand transcription, but Beethoven did not approve of the first arrangement and proceeded to do the job himself. Artaria had already paid the first arranger, but was happy to pay Beethoven also, because the four-hand version was in demand. We know this because we have written evidence. Nonetheless, evidently such documents did not convince our wise historians that the late works were instantly accepted and, one assumes, understood. If it were just the sloppy scholars who insisted on the myth of unrecognized genius, things would not be so bad. The insistence is widespread, however, and has been applied to most of the great composers since Beethoven. An acquaintance of mine (a history major with a keen interest in music) argued, for example, that audiences in the 1820s were simply too small to be called a "public" in the sense we understand today. I find this view shortsighted, but it is supported by many biographers and other commentators.

Our modern idea of what constitutes the public is now defined largely by TV ratings and reported attendances at free concerts in the park. I recall one occasion in 1966, at Tanglewood (the summer home of the Boston Symphony) when a particular event was carried live by one of the commercial networks. We were later assured that, at one point in the broadcast of that two-hour concert, the audience was larger than the combined total of all the capacity houses seen at Huntington Avenue (the Boston Symphony Orchestra's symphony hall) since its opening year, 1880. Success indeed!—and yet I wonder whether we really can feel that we triumphed with those families who were eating dinner, talking, and washing the dishes while we performed in the TV set? Success is a complex and relative idea, and clearly the size of audiences in the 1820s should also be understood in relative terms.

As a result of the massive social upheaval wrought by the French Revolution, great music was accorded a new and higher status that it still retains today in the older urban communities of Europe. Among citizens of the upper middle classes, the highest priority was given to the acquisition of *Bildung*. This is really an untranslatable word, not fully rendered by the words *education* or *culture*. It might be explained as a state of mind leading to a better life: one "built" in oneself a keener awareness of the world. One learns an awareness of the great human accomplishments in antiquity, art, philosophy, mythology, history, and the performing arts.

Bildung also included a close companionship with nature, which to urban dwellers meant hiking, mountain climbing, butterfly collecting, and gardening. The collection of *objets d'art*, coins, stamps, and other similar hobbies were part of this attempt to construct a separate life for oneself to erase the memory of the day's prosaic endeavors and elevate oneself to a "higher" psychological realm. When music of the great composers began to be considered part of this separate life, something happened to the status of all classical composition.

Whereas the chamber music of Haydn and Mozart has remained the core repertoire of quartet players, it was the unparalleled impact of Beethoven's music that led to the formation of the great musical institutions we still know today: regular symphony orchestras and their traditional program patterns of overture, concerto, and symphony. One can study the programs of the Berlin Philharmonic during the twenty-five years of Arthur Nikisch's tenure, the annual subscription cycle of the Vienna Philharmonic, or any seasonal brochures issued in Scandinavia, Germany, or the United States. Repeatedly one finds the symphonies and concertos of Beethoven, Schumann, Mendelssohn, Tchaikovsky, Brahms, and Dvorák. Like the mighty pillars of a cathedral apse, the works of these composers are essential to the great edifice of classical music.

Ever since *Bildung* was first embraced by the world of music, it has been a concept intimately connected with the figure of Beethoven. One is led to wonder what precise quality has placed him on his unique pedestal. His magic cannot be defined with music alone; other frames of reference, sociology foremost among them, are also needed. Beethoven is rooted in the humanistic spirit of the eighteenth century, the age that produced *The Magic Flute* and Goethe's *Wilhelm Meisters Lehrjahre* (in broader terms: the liberation of the individual from religious bondage). In his early works (up to and including the Sonata No. 12, Op. 26), Beethoven combined the peaceful, light spirit of Haydn with the fires of *Sturm und Drang*. From the "Kreutzer" Sonata, Op. 47, onward he wrote a series of miraculously perfect works before appearing to leave the terrestrial realm altogether, from the Sonata No. 28, Op. 101 until the end. Beethoven's works were progressively elevated by the public to the realms of the gods. This development was not Beethoven's fault, and fortunately there are many people who realize that musical works of the great masters need not be treated with pious reverence.

Music audiences have developed gradually into a mixed crowd of true music lovers and snobs who feel they have to be seen. Certain codes of behavior have been gradually imposed, perhaps originally to show genuine reverence, but later to ensure that nobody was shown up by incorrect behavior. This development accounts for the many superficial rules governing concert manners both on stage and among the audience. Most of those rules make no sense today, and probably never did. For example, we know from Mozart's letters that in his day it was proper and pleasing to the composer if the audience applauded in the middle of a piece. Today, however, most performers will stifle any attempt to applaud until right at the very end of the performance.

There is a great unanswered question that goes to the heart of the crisis facing modern music, namely, How did the public become indifferent to contemporary classical music? To blame the public for the present state of affairs is, in my view, simply meaningless. Beethoven clearly did consider both the audience and the potential success of his works. No work has more right to be called a masterpiece than his "Eroica" symphony, and the composer's preface suggests that the symphony be placed at the beginning or toward the beginning of a concert lest a fatigued audience be unable to appreciate a work of unusual length. When the first version of his opera, *Fidelio*, was given without much acclaim, Beethoven made some changes for the second run a few months later. When those revisions did not do the trick, he waited for eight years before rewriting it in the form familiar to us today.

Schoenberg, with his apparent indifference to the public's wishes, seems to have become the role model for many modern musicians, who genuinely believe that a score, like a painting, is justified when it has found a single buyer. If, as I believe is the case, a certain sector of the public feels alienated by modern compositions, I regret that the composers have only themselves to blame. As I said at the outset: all the great composers were successful in their lifetimes and fully recognized by their contemporaries. The unsung genius is little more than a myth.

A Tale of Three Composers

I seem to recall that the author Stefan Zweig once wrote a triptych about those three literary masters, Honoré de Balzac, Charles Dickens, and Feodor Dostoevski. I should like to follow suit by taking a brief look at three great masters of twentieth-century music: Richard Strauss, Arnold Schoenberg, and Igor Stravinsky. In doing so I hope to shed some light on the murky subjects of artistic integrity and bourgeois morality.

RICHARD STRAUSS

Let us begin with Richard Strauss, who was born in 1864 to well-to-do parents. The thematic catalogue of writings by and about the composer tells us that, for the publication of his Symphony in F minor (1884), his father had to pay one thousand marks as a contribution to the printing costs. His next work, the Piano Quartet, was submitted for a competition and won three hundred marks for the composer. Then came the symphonic poem *Aus Italien*, for which Strauss received a fee of five hundred marks.

Like Felix Mendelssohn, Strauss never knew the poverty experienced by composers such as Mozart and Schubert. Mendelssohn died at the age of thirty-eight, Strauss at eighty-five. In their smoothness of finish and in their overall technique both composers were as skilled as Mozart, but neither developed musically like Mozart, who went on maturing from his first composition until his death. As the critic and composer Virgil Thomson once noted in one of his best short summaries, Mendelssohn, after his early, sensational *A Midsummer Night's Dream*, spent the remainder of his creative life "looking backward." Similarly, the *New Grove Dictionary of Music and Musicians* begins its entry on Mendelssohn thus: "Although he grew up surrounded by romantic influences, his inspiration was essentially classical and his musical ideals were embodied in the works of Bach, Handel, and Mozart rather than those of his contemporaries."

Richard Strauss composed some of his greatest works, beginning with *Salome* (1905) and *Elektra* (1909), after the age of forty. I believe that if he had continued in the style of those two operas he would have crowned his artistic output with a *Wozzeck*-type dramatic masterpiece. Unfortunately, this was not to be. Strauss was influenced, after all, by the forward-thinking artists of *fin de siècle* Vienna and by his long correspondence with Gustav Mahler. His abrupt change of course after *Elektra* demonstrates his rejection of those influences. No matter how much one admires *Der Rosenkavalier*, one cannot but see it as a giant step back, in terms of subject matter and score, from *Elektra*.

Neurosis and Weltschmerz were clearly alien to Strauss's bourgeois personality. In art, as in politics, it has always seemed that the well-to-do are less likely to be progressive than the poor. This is as true of the world of composers as it is of the simplest family configuration in which a child shows talent for the piano or the violin. The poor will encourage the child, but the affluent will discourage any indulgence beyond the hobby stage; the poor see, in a modest musical career, social and general advance, while the affluent see only the risk that their child will not reach the very top, both socially and financially. Strauss, known since the age of twenty-two as a wizard of composition, decided to do more and greater things within an established Germanic pattern.

The resultant works appealed to a public that survived the 1914 war, the Weimar Republic, the Third Reich, and the Marshall plan. All fifteen operas by Strauss are still favorites of Munich's operatic establishment (sometimes given in a complete festival cycle) and by most provincial houses they are performed piecemeal and intermittently. Even foreign-language opera companies in Belgium, Italy, and the United States still cultivate the lesser works of the Strauss canon, and his three or four early symphonic poems have become firm favorites worldwide.

Strauss commented in his memoirs: "Both operas [*Salome* and *Elektra*] have a singular position in my life. In these scores I tested the extremes of harmony, psychic polyphony ('Dream of Clytemnestra'), and receptivity of contemporary ears." His music was received—and is still received today—with genuine enthusiasm and genuine participation and attention, while any audience sitting through *Daphne* (gorgeous moments and all) or *Capriccio* needs to be rather more indulgent. *Salome*, *Elektra*, and (in my view) *Don Quixote* are among those works that "define" the twentieth century, and even the banality of their themes cannot detract from this fact. *Don Quixote* has the same "psychic polyphony" that the composer associates with "Clytemnestra," and it is also similar to that work in its being a fantastic musical portrait of a deranged human mind. It is noteworthy that only a non-German, Romain Rolland, recognized that after *Der Rosenkavalier*, Hugo von

Hofmannsthal's librettos were, to say the least, not particularly helpful to the composer.

According to the thematic catalogue, which includes many references from Strauss's letters and diaries, the composer felt that throughout the first half of the twentieth century he never compromised his 1911 style and never stooped to making things easy for the general public. In creating *Die Frau ohne Schatten*, Strauss and von Hofmannsthal tried to create a latter-day *Magic Flute*. In fact, the work is so convoluted that only a true believer would bother to explain to the public exactly how it is related to Schikaneder and Mozart. I genuinely enjoyed preparing and conducting *Die Frau ohne Schatten*, and no conductor could fail to admire and enjoy the mastery of orchestration and of the female voice that Strauss displayed in that work.

As a musician I admire what Strauss could do with notes and with poetic ideas transferable into sounds. I also believe that he ultimately betrayed the music of the twentieth century in favor of the traditions of the past.

ARNOLD SCHOENBERG

Arnold Schoenberg was ten years younger than Richard Strauss and took a different road from that followed by the older composer. If Strauss chose the road that led backward, Schoenberg's chosen route led to something very different—independence.

To ensure he was seen as a nonrevolutionary who merely allowed music *qua* music to take the lead, Schoenberg wrote a remarkable essay entitled "Brahms the Progressive." In retrospect this essay might be viewed as a twisted version of an apology for his music. For all those readers who have thus far skirted the gloomy forests of twelve-tone scholarship, I should explain that the great Wagnerite-Brahmsian schism originated in the view that if Wagner was the future of music, Brahms represented a latter-day classic composer in the Beethoven mold. One might suggest that Wagner's so-called futurism was rooted less in his methods of composition than in his magical ability to make of music a new kind of emotional and sensual experience. In his essay Schoenberg attempts, with a devilish ingenuity, to show how Brahms, in stretching a four-measure phrase into a five-measure phrase in his lied "Feldeinsamkeit," was guided primarily by structure.

Any analyst other than Schoenberg would conclude that the text was the motive for Brahms's action. I mention this detail because it shows that musical analysis, like any other type of statistical data, can be made to dance to the tune of any piper. Schoenberg's essay effectively served to buttress his assertion that composition with twelve tones was no more revolutionary than Brahms's lied maneuver, and his contention that even Brahms was progressive has since inspired countless young composers to create their music in a spirit of determined autonomy. Furthermore, this notion of autonomy has also caused an unprecedented fragmentation of composition in the second half of this century.

Schoenberg began where Wagner left off, with *Gurre-Lieder*, the symphonic poem *Pelleas und Melisande*, the sextet *Transfigured Night*, and the *Chamber Symphony*. In 1907 he created a string quartet whose subtitle is "in F-sharp minor" and which, in its later movements, finally rejects the notion of the tonal center. After the second movement the four players are joined by a female vocalist. It is perhaps not insignificant that the text of one poem reads, "I breathe the air of other worlds." One might well ask why the laws of tonality had to be rejected as part of an autonomous music development. The answer is that chromatic intensity, which had already been taken to extremes in Wagner's *Tristan und Isolde* (1865), now threatened to go completely out of control. Schoenberg, like Strauss, saw the trouble ahead and abruptly changed course. Unlike Strauss, however, he did not turn back. He abandoned the road altogether.

As Alban Berg once observed, in the first years of atonality only short pieces were successful. The composition with twelve interdependent tones then arrived to provide a badly needed supporting structure. The twelve-tone system, which quickly won as many disciples as it did opponents, was used in Berg's *Lulu* and in Schoenberg's *Moses and Aaron* (both of which works remained fragments). Alban Berg died in 1935, Arnold Schoenberg in 1951. Although the flame of the twelve-tone system would flicker intermittently over the ensuing years (notably through the late intervention of Stravinsky), by the 1980s one could state with some assurance that the system had replaced nothing. The great masterpiece that will always remain in the repertoire of orchestras and violinists is Berg's Violin Concerto, which is ingeniously constructed on a row of twelve notes that almost force the composer into very familiar harmonic combinations in sound.

The most consistent and influential practitioner of twelve-tone music was Anton Webern, who confined himself to very short compositions. The failure of twelve-tone music was due to composers' relentless pursuit of autonomy. The public was neglected, producing music that was wonderful to look at but not to listen to. As someone (I forget who) once remarked: "I'll believe in that system just as soon as I've heard the first twelve-tone operetta."

IGOR STRAVINSKY

Igor Stravinsky was the greatest figure in the history of twentieth-century music, and yet he also encountered more than his fair share of bad publicity.

Among the most damaging influences in his life and career was his close association with Robert Craft. Stravinsky's late excursion into the realms of the twelve-tone system, undoubtedly much promoted by Craft, was rather like the act of the aging king who increasingly places his trust in a clever young courtier. Perhaps Craft filled a void for this ultra-sophisticated artist, who was living in the desert of the Hollywood hills after a lifetime of the most fertile collaboration with Paris, New York, the impresario Sergei Diaghilev, and the choreographer George Balanchine.

Stravinsky was roundly condemned by Theodor Adorno and, in more than implied terms, by all the disciples of Schoenberg. Their condemnation was born out of their conviction that only one school of composition was worthy of the name: the so-called German main line that runs from Bach through to Schoenberg. Stravinsky, they said, had no place there, and yet Stravinsky was one of three composers who wrote masterpieces in the years just before the First World War. Those works were Schoenberg's *Gurre-Lieder* (1900), Strauss's *Elektra* (1909), and Stravinsky's *The Rite of Spring* (1913). I fancy I almost see in the orchestral setting of Stravinsky's score a symbolic, perhaps partly subconscious, calling card engraved with the year 1876. Stravinsky's score calls for four tubas, the same quartet of instruments made famous through Wagner's *Ring* (first performed in 1876), in which the tubas first appear, in D-flat, to announce that Valhalla has been built. Perhaps Stravinsky also recalled that Wagner's tubas are the motif of Hunding, producing associations with mythic forces and barbarian habits that are not too far removed from the subject of *The Rite of Spring*. Strauss's *Elektra* also uses tubas, by the way.

The Rite of Spring represents the end and the crowning glory of romanticism, and is comparable in its fashion to Beethoven's Ninth, to Wagner's *Tristan*, or to Verdi's *Falstaff*. It is not a harbinger of things to come; there has been nothing like it since—Sergei Prokofiev's *Scythian Suite* is not even a good imitation. *The Rite of Spring* was a work that could only be the end of a line, and I believe that the demonstration that greeted its first performance was prearranged. In 1860 the Jockey Club had tried to punish Wagner for placing the ballet divertissement in the first act of *Tannhäuser* instead of the customary second. We should have learned by now that demonstrations are generally organized and well timed. Nowadays demonstrators are kept quiet until the television cameras have arrived, and everything must be timed just right to make the evening news. There must have been a 1913 group like the 1860 Jockey Club, coached by some hostile elements to stage a protest.

Theodor Adorno's quip, to the effect that Stravinsky presided over a cozy cenacle for whom he decided the coming season's musical fashions, is not entirely without foundation (even if it is mean-spirited). Nonetheless, anybody but a fervent disciple of Schoenberg can understand Stravinsky's so-called trend-setting as part of a composing tradition exemplified by Mozart (who once declared in a letter from Paris that he had studied "what people liked" before putting certain things into his "Paris" Symphony). If Mozart was allowed to keep his ear to the ground in the Paris of 1778, one sees no reason to deny Stravinsky the same right in the Paris of 1920. Ultimately, Stravinsky's historic importance resides in the fact that he never neglected the public, and yet never stooped toward them.

Stravinsky's enemies also charged that he relied on others for thematic material. To paraphrase the words of the film director Jean Renoir, art suffered a fatal blow on the day we invented plagiarism as an idea.

Plagiarism, he suggested, should be recommended; the plagiarist rewarded and decorated. The use of somebody else's tune, theme, or song has long been an unquestioned practice—consider the countless works entitled "Variations on a theme of" followed by the name of the originator. Many themes have been invented, and yet inventing a new theme is much less of a rarity than making something of an existing theme. The latter skill requires a truly creative composer, and it was one of Stravinsky's many strong points that he borrowed wherever he could find something useable.

One need think only of his very brief, but exquisitely original, treatment of Tchaikovsky's melody "None but the lonely heart." This appears toward the end of Stravinsky's ballet *The Fairy's Kiss*. I once made my sequence of music from this ballet, one of my main reasons for doing so being the opportunity to include that wonderful treatment of the great Tchaikovsky melody. Originality lies in the treatment of raw material. I believe that Adorno's publicly expressed hostility toward Stravinsky was caused by a deep-seated rage and envy. Stravinsky hit on a formula for writing music that was modern, still understandable without having to be read first; original, inventive, and independent of the ultraconservative musical associations and the classic tradition of composition as defined by Vienna.

On Programming Webern

The subject of this essay was suggested to me by a couple of letters printed in 1990 in the *New York Times*. They were written in response to a New York Philharmonic program that opened with several compositions by Anton von Webern and closed with a Beethoven piano concerto played by a very famous soloist. The first letter to the editor, headlined "Surely, Webern Is Something to Sneeze At," suggested that the audience's unrest during the concert was predictable "[s]ince many concertgoers regard performances of Webern as the musical equivalent of a visit to the dentist." The second letter to the editor, headlined "Misery Loves Company," defined a concert hall as "a place where people come to cough and sneeze to the accompaniment of fine music."

These two letters, which were printed by a newspaper whose critic undoubtedly had a healthy respect for Webern, reflected my views so accurately that on reading them I felt as if I had hit the jackpot. I should add that Zubin Mehta, conductor of the New York Philharmonic, has long been a friend of mine and has always been a perfect host to me during the years of his incumbency as music director of the New York Philharmonic. I would state unreservedly that my guest visits with that orchestra are my favorite engagements. Mehta has performed Webern repeatedly with the New York Philharmonic but never so many pieces together as on the occasion referred to in the two letters to the *New York Times*. In constructing that program he said yes to those who would ask whether there is an obligation to perform Webern and yes to those who would ask whether music is an international language. Several record companies have also said yes, by the way, to Webern's status as an international composer. I clearly recall the delight of one Artists and Repertory man who managed to squeeze all Webern's instrumental music onto a long-playing disc.

In playing Webern's music, Mehta evidently feels that he has an obligation not only toward the composer but also toward the ten thousand or so people who would typically attend a four-program run at the Avery Fisher Hall. Unfortunately, most of those ten thousand souls are quite determined not to have Webern's music brought to their *inattention*. This inattention is quite intentional and represents a time-honored habit of subscription audiences used to hearing the old masterpieces again and again without truly listening to them. Of all compositions— old, new, modern, obsolete, light, heavy, experimental, or conservative— none require such intense attention as the compositions of Webern. His musical forms are so concentrated that anyone allowing his mind to wander for fifteen seconds will lose the thread of the entire piece. This is the opposite of Vivaldi, whose forms are such that one can happily wander out of the hall (mentally or literally) for five whole minutes without losing one's way.

I have performed some of those Webern pieces for the very same public, only to abandon any thoughts of programming them again. Performers should be champions of what they believe in, but this does not mean that they should also see themselves as missionaries. They should perform music they believe in, but never for people who are vehemently opposed to it. To choose concert programs rationally, realistically, and effectively, one need not cater to the lowest common denominator. I am reminded of the time when Leonard Bernstein agreed to record a symphony by Sibelius with the Vienna Philharmonic (Sibelius is as unpalatable for the Viennese as Webern for the audiences of Fisher Hall). Bernstein cleverly scheduled the concert that was to be used for the recording as a free matinee. The public duly flocked into the hall and applauded so enthusiastically one might have thought one was in Helsinki.

Webern's music is not "international" (in the sense that it cannot easily transcend national boundaries) and it is also not music for everybody. The unfortunate behavior of the Fisher Hall audience was entirely at variance with the rapt attention of a crowd assembled in September 1986 in the small auditorium of New York's Museum of Modern Art, where an exhibition of *fin-de-siècle* Viennese art opened with a chamber music concert. The program consisted of music by the Second Viennese School, featuring Berg's Piano Sonata, Schoenberg's String Quartet No. 2, and Webern's Five Pieces for Quartet. The rapt attention given to the music was understandable in an audience that had genuinely come to listen to the music, but it was also quite clear that Webern's music was the most enthusiastically received.

To nonmusicians I should explain that the secret of Webern's style is an unprecedented concentration of every compositional element. Like a skillful climber he progressively shed every ounce of the extra weight that so encumbered his first numbered work, the *Passacaglia*. He thus comfortably outpaced those of his contemporaries still loaded down with the heavy instrumentation of late romanticism, and made a rapid ascent to the summit. The atmosphere at this music summit is somewhat rarefied, and the music played there is not to everybody's taste. Arnold Schoenberg criticized Alban Berg's "thick" textures, but those textures did not diminish the international appeal of *Wozzeck* and the Violin Concerto. Berg's much leaner *Chamber Concerto*, by contrast, never progressed beyond the small auditorium.

In music there can be no missionaries, because there is simply no one to be converted. One can quite understand how the priest's robe would appeal to some of the more power-hungry international musicians, but it is out of place in the world of music. America does not need musical converts because, like Vienna, Munich, Berlin, and London, it already has a large public.

Ludwig van Beethoven

Beethoven's *oeuvre* is unique in the annals of music. Few, I am sure, would dispute this statement, but it does nonetheless require some explanation—not least for those who happen to like other music more than they like that of Beethoven. The word *unique* must not be confused with the word *better*. Nobody is diminished by calling Beethoven a composer *sui generis*.

As I have said elsewhere, I believe that composing is a craft more than it is an art. Some composers are more creative in this respect than others, but Beethoven went farther and deeper than any other musician into the essential being of humanity. This has made him the archetypal creator of works of genius, if a work of genius can be regarded as a creation that alters the life of humanity. The composer's catalogue contains 138 opus numbers, and later research added another 205 items (mostly minor compositions, except for some wondrous sets of variations for piano). Historians generally divide Beethoven's works into three distinct periods. According to this perfectly correct and clear categorization, the first period is still recognizably eighteenth century and linked with the world of Haydn and Mozart. There was an interval of around three years separating the third piano concerto—which is an extension of Mozart's concerto in the same key—and the "Waldstein" Sonata, Op. 53. During this interval, which lasted approximately from 1800 to 1803, there was only one major composition, the Violin Sonata, Op. 47. This "Kreutzer" Sonata marks, perhaps better than any other work, the transition between the eighteenth-century Beethoven and the series of masterpieces written between 1803 and 1812. Let us glance at the scores that follow: the "Waldstein," the "Eroica" Symphony, the Piano Sonata No. 23, Op. 57 ("Appassionata"), the Piano Concerto No. 4, the three "Rasumovsky" Quartets, the Fourth Symphony, the Violin Concerto, the

Fifth Symphony, the "Pastoral" Symphony, the Sonata for cello and piano, two trios and, in 1814, the final version of the opera *Fidelio*.

The Piano Concerto No. 5 had been written earlier, as were the Seventh and Eighth Symphonies, the Quartet in F minor, the Violin Sonata No. 10, and the Piano Trio in B-flat Major, Op. 97 ("Archduke"). Other compositions emerged during that incredible decade, most of them perfectly fine works that are still played frequently today. Yet they are not, I believe, quite in the same galaxy as those others. Of course, everyone can dispute the components of this list according to personal taste; I wished only to show why this second period of Beethoven's output might quite rightly be regarded as the last word in creative genius. Indeed, the composer's fame rests essentially on the works of this middle period and on the Ninth Symphony (another quite unique work and, curiously enough, one that belongs to both the middle and third periods).

How theoreticians and analysts explain the distinctions among the three periods I have no idea, since I never took analytical music theory. I do know how I would characterize it. Whereas the major pieces of the second period are essentially extrovert in nature (including some of the slow movements with their unforgettable melodies), those of the third period are, except for the Ninth Symphony, increasingly introverted. Beethoven's last period consists of five piano sonatas, five string quartets, and two gigantic scores for orchestra and chorus, the Ninth, and the *Missa Solemnis*. Discussion of this third phase is generally based on unreliable contemporary sources, but I see in some works of this late period a clear reflection of the composer's earliest ideas and findings. The composer recreates those ideas—never literally, but certainly in character and tonality—and elevates them to a higher plane.

After the middle, Promethean period, the third period of Beethoven's life work returns to more "singing" music—in this respect one need only compare the Finale of the Fifth Symphony with the Finale of the Ninth Symphony. Whereas one can sing the theme of the earlier work, the theme is more fanfare than song. The Ninth *must* be sung, whether by cellos, basses, or the human bass voice. (Is it accidental, by the way, that both these themes are marked by the composer with the same metronome figure?) Similarly, the first theme of the "Eroica" Symphony is a bugle call, whereas the first theme of the late String

Quartet in E-flat, Op. 127 (which has the same meter, approximately the same tempo, and the same key), is a song. There are many similar comparisons to be made between the two periods.

Beethoven's "Eroica" Symphony

I believe that Beethoven purposely conceived his Third ("Eroica") Symphony as an extraordinary, landmark work. For eighteenth-century music lovers, the symphonic musical form was as clearly defined as the forms of Aristotelian tragedy. It achieved its perfect expression in the later symphonies of Joseph Haydn and Wolfgang Amadeus Mozart. The final movement of the "Jupiter" symphony is such a miracle of compositional achievement that at least one complete book has been devoted to that piece alone.

Then came Beethoven's "Eroica" Symphony. I would argue that with this one exceptional work, Beethoven not only left the eighteenth century way behind in style and rhetoric, but also created, so to speak, an entirely new being which, in its first few moments of life established itself as the dominant member of its species. Perhaps a wholly different image might be more appropriate. One might compare this symphony with man's first orbital flight in a spacecraft after many years of being confined within the earth's atmosphere. Some musicologists may not share this view, and I think this is partly because the work's uniqueness does not lend itself to detailed interpretation. It should also be noticed that in describing this work I have chosen not to use the term *better*. Comparison of that nature is inappropriate here. A lover of fugues might argue convincingly that one Bach fugue is better than another, just as a lover of operatic vocal music might argue that this or that Mozart opera is better than another. The "Eroica" symphony, however, is simply one of a kind, and therefore does not bear comparison with other works, either by Beethoven or by other composers.

The composer Carl Friedrich Zelter once remarked to Johann Wolfgang Goethe in a letter that Johann Sebastian Bach was "an incarnation of God: lucid, yet unfathomable." In a book review I once described Mozart as a manifestation of Apollo. In this respect the composer of the "Eroica" Symphony might be seen as an incarnation of Prometheus, who stole fire from the Gods and gave it to humanity in the guise of arts and sciences. Lest the association with Prometheus be misunderstood, I do not refer explicitly to Beethoven's ballet *The Creations of Prometheus*. Few would see the composer's music for that ballet as among his most important scores, even if the theme of the "Eroica" variations does make a brief appearance. Before he wrote the Third Symphony, Beethoven had already used the "Eroica" variation theme on four other occasions: as a simple German dance in the aforementioned ballet, and three times as a theme for virtuoso piano variations. It was almost as if he had subjected the theme to several different treatments before getting it the way he wanted it.

As with many other Beethoven compositions, the key to the "Eroica" is the utter simplicity of its themes and motifs—the first movement's main theme has just three notes. It is as if an unpromising scrap of raw material that had lain unwanted for years had been suddenly taken up and magically transformed into an object of great beauty. It is in this respect that the work was a breakthrough—the material selected was shown to contain hitherto unrecognized properties. For decades the same themes, tunes, and motifs had served to make music that was agreeable enough to the senses in a superficial way but never penetrated to the inner soul of the listener.

The work's second movement, the funeral march, transformed the meaning of the word *adagio* and has been the inspiration of every symphonic composer since Beethoven. Prior to the "Eroica" symphony, the word *adagio* simply meant slow—nothing else. It was traditionally used to describe introductions to overtures or other first movements—as a slow preface with no more than formal significance. Many years later Beethoven gave a further clue to his intentions when he wrote beneath the title of the Kyrie in his *Missa Solemnis* the words "from the heart—may it reach the heart."

After these two sections, which last approximately half an hour, come the shorter, life-enhancing third and fourth movements—one a glorified sublimation of a hunt, the other a set of variations on basic material that illuminate the German Dance until other sounds intervene. The trouble with this revolutionary work is the idea that henceforth every instrumental composition in four movements had to be compared to Beethoven's Third.

My contention that Beethoven knew how different this work was finds support in his preface to the first printed edition of the full score. Written in Italian, the preface recommends that the work be placed toward the beginning of a concert, lest the public be tired after too many other music numbers. The key word in the first sentence is the Italian word *apposta* (on purpose): "This symphony, having been written, on purpose, longer than usual." Of course, considerations of length alone mean little, but in 1805 it was the simplest way to indicate that the work was of a wholly new dimension.

On the Bicentennial of Amadée Motzard

In the days of Amadée Motzard, orthographic conventions were evidently more liberal than they are now. There are several different spellings of Mozart's name, and all may be found in the letters and other documents published as part of the *Neue Mozart Ausgabe*. The critical compendium of all the composer's works, this volume has been published by Bärenreiter since 1955.

There are many other, more significant, differences between the world of the composer in Mozart's times and the world of our contemporary composers. For one thing—orthographic differences notwithstanding—the musical scores of professional composers invariably displayed correct syntax, grammar, and spelling of musical notation. A brief perusal of certain contemporary scores will show the musical reader that this skill is not to be discounted today.

In Mozart's times the professional composer was required to do more than merely write masterpieces. He was also charged with the supervision and direction of his compositions, which would be written either for a prince or for a wealthy individual seeking music for his estate or townhouse. Amadée Motzard, too, was trained to become a servant and a music master at somebody's establishment. His impatience with this tradition—demonstrated in his behavior toward his boss, Prince Colloredo—was more than just a rebellion. Throughout Europe, revolutionary ideas were in the air. The storming of the Bastille took place when Mozart was thirty-three years old and the spirit of that momentous period fills the pages of the correspondence between the composer and his father.

Now the Mozart bicentennial is upon us. The musicologists have emerged from their secret redoubts with sharpened quills (or at least newly programmed computers) to tell the waiting world what they think of Mozart and his music. Some of those sages even double as performers. Notable among these musicians are the members of the early music club—an international jet set of chamber ensembles, old-instrument groups, consorts, academies and other associations with similarly quaint titles.

Whereas their renderings of minor baroque music are amusing and often charming, one cannot, unfortunately, say the same of their versions of Bach and Mozart. The immortal scores of the eighteenth-century giants are for all seasons. They do not belong in antique shops.

Even the *International Herald Tribune* was moved to publish, on 14 September 1990, a long essay by the University of Berkeley's Richard Taruskin. It was headlined "Consumer Mozart: From God-Child to Musical Yuppie." I confess that five days later I had still scarcely recovered from this headline, but was mildly relieved to read, in the letters page of the same newspaper, a reaction to Mr. Taruskin's article. The writer protested that Taruskin's article covered every angle except the one that counted—the beauty of the music and the still inexplicable genius of the composer.

I read Mr. Taruskin's essay several times and found that it contained many clichés and generalities. He begins by giving a negative review of Wolfgang Hildesheimer's biography, *Mozart* (1982), which in my view is easily the most perceptive and profound interpretation of Mozart's life. Hildesheimer identifies the essential pattern of Mozart's later years: as the composer's musical genius became ever more touched by divinity, his daily existence deteriorated in every sense.

If this is indeed historical revisionism, as Taruskin claims, then it is a welcome and necessary kind of revisionism. In my view, however, it is no such thing: for many years the erroneous portrait of Mozart the careless, childlike innocent has been believed only by those who also think that

Blossom Time is intimately linked with Franz Schubert. [Sigmund Romberg's *Blossom Time* (1921) is based upon the 1916 sentimental *Dreimädlerhaus*, by Heinrich Berté, which in turn is based on melodies by Schubert—ED.]

After chiding Hildesheimer for "demystification," Taruskin turns his attentions toward Peter Shaffer's play *Amadeus*, apparently unaware that the play was not about Mozart at all and that the film [by Milos Forman] did less damage to Mozart's image than some of the clichés dispensed by our learned music professors. I met and talked with Peter Shaffer and saw both versions of *Amadeus*. I can assure the reader that Shaffer reveres Mozart the composer as much as the rest of us.

Taruskin goes on to note that Mozart is so familiar that some performers have gone out of their way to "defamiliarize" him.

Mozart's music was not performed in concert as frequently as the music of Beethoven. Radio broadcasts of opera performances began in the mid-1920s, but it was not until the music festivals of Salzburg and Glyndebourne began to feature Mozart's operas that his unique masterpieces for the musical theater gained international recognition. When Bruno Walter conducted *Don Giovanni* in Salzburg in 1934, it was the first time the piece had been performed in the original language in an Austrian city. When I had attended the Vienna Opera's performances in earlier years it was always "Reich mir die Hand, mein Leben," never "La ci darem la mano."

The revival of baroque music, which coincided with the advent of radio, the microphone, and the old-instrument movement, took hold of a younger generation that was tired of heavy emotional romanticism played by large instrumental bodies. The rise of anti-Wagnerism even intensified the hold of the classics upon those who had had their fill of the nineteenth century.

In my estimation the adoption of Mozart's music by the old-instrument movement and similar musical archeologists has gone quite far enough. One can see how Mozart's works might be susceptible to the treatment given to Vivaldi's works, but they should not be so treated (with the possible exception of the compositions written up to his twentieth year).

One can only hope and pray that the commemorations of the bicen-tennial year will not damage the music. The "defamiliarizers" to which Mr. Taruskin refers are mostly operatic stage managers who have endeav-ored not only to defamiliarize the public but also to alienate audiences from the greatest operas. Since these fellows are egged on by a large per-centage of newspaper and magazine critics, a recognizable performance of a Mozart opera may already be an endangered species. This would be a great shame, because any great composer is most readily approached and understood through music set to words. Mahler's symphonies *with* voices became popular decades before his purely instrumental pieces. The same is true of Brahms, with his *Requiem* and his many lieder, and the prime example is Schubert, who became famous with just one lied, "Erlkönig," while his chamber music, piano sonatas, and symphonies were performed less frequently.

Unlike Bach, Haydn, Beethoven, and Wagner whose life work cul-minated in one great work (respectively the B minor Mass, *The Creation*, the Ninth Symphony, and *Tetralogy*) there is no similar acme in Mozart's catalogue. Perhaps it would have been the *Requiem* had he lived to do more than a sketch. Then there is always *The Magic Flute*—these days it seems almost paradoxical to state that a work is at once the composer's most complex and most popular, but this is certainly the case with Mozart's *Magic Flute* (at least in the German-language cultural sphere).

The first performance of *The Magic Flute* was given in the librettist's Theater auf der Wieden on 30 September 1791. It is said that by 1801 there had been 223 performances there, although the figure ought to be taken with a grain of salt since Emanuel Schikaneder, the theater manager, claimed a hundredth showing when the correct figure was eighty-three and the two-hundredth when the true figure was 135.

There is no doubt that the original impetus to write this work came from a performer who needed a hit. Whatever his literary talents, what-ever the puzzling incompatibilities in the libretto (the shifting loyalties of the Genii, the metamorphoses of Pamina's mother), in the end the whole work proved to be a miracle akin to one of William Shakespeare's all-encompassing plays. Mozart's creation was admired by Goethe and has been particularly beloved of generations of children for two hundred years. For many of those children it was their introduction to the mysteries, not only of Isis and Osiris, but of great music and of great opera at its most human. The dramatis personae of the opera runs the gamut from the embodiment of the philosophical and humanitarian summit of the Enlightenment to the frustrated and racially motivated schemer; from the excesses of a bereaved mother to the paternalism of a priest; and from the fairy-tale prince to the folksy Bird Catcher who represents the common-sense philosophy of the amiable, average citizen.

All human life is there, from the sublime to the ridiculous (though even the ridiculous is filled with human warmth). Yet the universal appeal that I had always associated with *The Magic Flute* is apparently not quite as universal as I had surmised. I have encountered people who are musical, who love and appreciate Mozart, and yet have no understanding of this particular work. Robert Donington, in his book *Opera and Its Symbols* (1990), suggests that the key factors that determine an opera's longevity and popularity are its archetypes and archetypal situations. Could it be that for some people the work is just too rich, too complete, too descriptive of humanity, with all its contradictions? Whatever one's view of this masterpiece, it has over the years been able to withstand many attacks, changes, editing, cutting, and added recitatives. As for the interpretations of today's stage directors, a brief inventory of those might well serve the bearer as admission ticket to a sanitarium. Even reputable biographers of Mozart have had their fun. Volkmar Braunbehrens, for example, in his work, *Mozart in Vienna, 1781–91* (1989), decided that Sarastro was nothing but a tyrant since the libretto described him as entering "drawn by six lions."

Notwithstanding the attentions of all these wise men, the continued triumphant progress of *The Magic Flute* seems assured. It appeals to fundamental instincts and fundamental wisdom, and its score represents a synthesis of all that Mozart achieved throughout his composing career. Papageno's ditties are instantly memorable; the choral writing is sublime; the intricate counterpoint is worthy of Johann Sebastian Bach at his best. The recitative dialogue is the model for Wagner's *Ring* narratives, and the Finale of act 2 has a fascinating pyramidal structure. The great writer Hermann Hesse adored Mozart and wrote many beautiful words about music in general. In a 1911 critique of Goethe's *Wilhelm Meister's Lehrjahre*, Hesse includes the following short profile of the era that gave us Mozart and *The Magic Flute*:

> The eighteenth century was the last great cultural epoch of Europe. There was less of pictorial art, architecture in particular, than in earlier times; literature was more significant, and the era reached a breadth and power that embraced all Europe in an international spirit from which we—poor heirs—still receive nourishment. A noble, generous form of humanism and an idealistic belief in the future and grandeur of human culture speaks in all documents of that time, even in the spoofs and satires. Mankind has taken the place of the gods, the dignity of man has become the crowning glory of the world and the foundation of every creed.

Four

Out There in the Dark:
The Crisis of Audiences
and Critics

What Is Musical Illiteracy?

This essay is not a letter to the editor, and its author harbors no illusions about its potential impact. I expect no reforms, and I make no self-righteous assertions or recommendations. I seek merely to describe a problem that has bedeviled several generations of observers and placed the classical music world in considerable jeopardy. If the question posed by my title were put to me in a TV discussion, with the traditional thirty seconds given for a reply, I think I might say that illiteracy in music was identical to illiteracy in language: it means simply that one can neither read nor write. Music simply replaces the *A B C* of the alphabet with the *Do Re Mi* of solfeggio. Since the word *insolfeggiacy* sounds distinctly unappealing, I propose that in this essay we stick with the word *illiteracy*.

Music can be read exactly as one can read a newspaper, a novel, a poem, or the *Tractatus Logico-Philosophicus* of Ludwig Wittgenstein. A cursory glance at the wide variety of publications available at the corner newsstand shows that different papers or magazines are printed with more or less complicated language, with richer or poorer vocabularies, catering to readers of varying degrees of literacy. The differences of difficulty and sophistication are broadly similar to the differences between an Irving Berlin song and the six-part "Ricercare" from Bach's *Musical Offering*. Just as easy access to television has brought a deterioration in reading and writing skills, so the influence of recorded music has had a devastating impact on musical literacy.

People generally seem to regard musicality as an inborn gift that must reveal itself at once. Picture the poor child who—even after a *whole year's* instruction—is still banging around the keyboard or screeching on a clarinet to the patent discomfort of the horrified teacher. The distraught parents are heard to lament that their child apparently has "no ear for music." On the other hand, consider, for example, the works of Ludwig van Beethoven. His life spanned the end of the eighteenth and the beginning of the nineteenth century. His music combines, like that of no other musician, the best elements of each century: the Enlightenment of the eighteenth century and the romanticism of the nineteenth. His works alone inspired the creation of countless symphonic associations. Apart from his nine symphonies, seven concertos, seventeen string quartets, thirty-two piano sonatas, and two-dozen duo and trio sonatas, there are numerous memorable variation works, as well as one of the milestones of the musical theater, *Fidelio*. These works have become the backbone and the livelihood of every orchestra, every chamber music society, and most pianists. Even these bare, statistical facts demonstrate that Beethoven's appeal goes beyond strictly musical values. He is also the only composer whose popular constituency (if that is the right expression) ranges so freely from the sophisticated to the naive.

There is, then, a vast musical repertoire to be studied and enjoyed, and it is intimately linked with man's broader cultural and historical environment. Whereas folk music, or traditional music, is passed on from one generation to the next without its being written down, those works that can loosely be defined by the term *classical* (or *serious*) were written by one person and often subsequently published in multiple printings or engravings. Those works include chamber music, symphonic music, operatic music, sacred music, plus lighter fare such as operettas and hit tunes. Their written form is an essential part of their identity.

In the present environment it seems unlikely that the passive concertgoing public can ever be persuaded to banish their CD players to the closet and dust off their high-school instruments to champion a revival in home music-making. Most members of our contemporary audiences will not understand the C-clef used in Beethoven's time even if they were taught music at school. They will also find it hard to understand new works. Whereas the opera fan may at least have a libretto to study before a premiere, the concertgoer can familiarize himself with older music only. The recording industry is concerned with making profits, not with promoting works of art, so it is highly unlikely that a new orchestral work will be recorded before a performance. The musical sensibilities of a functionally illiterate music lover may be every bit as keen as those of a professional musician, but his illiteracy implies a passivity toward music that must limit his ability to come to terms with a complex composition. Listening to a Webern score without being able to read it must be rather like studying a great architectural masterpiece without having access to the ground plan. One can quite happily contemplate and understand a Swiss chalet without needing to see its blue print, but this is probably not the case with the Palace of the Louvre. The world of music is in this respect analogous to the world of architecture. Most of the music composed over the last 250 years might be neatly divided into two broad groups: popular and serious. Whereas most compositions in the former group might be absorbed and fully appreciated at a first hearing, this is not the case with much music of the latter group.

Taking an "innocent" along to hear Beethoven's *Missa Solemnis* for the first time will not necessarily produce the intense emotional reaction that experienced music lovers take for granted as part of one's first encounter with that masterpiece. There are not many people who enjoy the *Missa* as they enjoy the Fifth Symphony of the same composer. The immediacy of the latter, more popular, work contrasts with the complexity of the former. Both works are universally regarded as memorable, but one should not forget that the word *memorable* can mean both "unforgettable" and "easy to remember." The Fifth is memorable in both senses, but the *Missa*, paradoxically enough, is as unforgettable as it is hard to remember. The relative popularity of a piece of music is largely determined by how easily remembered it is. As for the difference between a thorny classic and a puzzling Schoenberg quintet, that is merely one of good manners. One simply does not question one's admiration for anything bearing the name *Beethoven*, but it is perfectly acceptable to state that one finds no gratification in Schoenberg.

In my view, our music managers and publicists—aided and abetted by music directors—have attempted to present contemporary music in a curious fashion. The demanding new work is invariably jammed incongruously between two familiar old war-horses, so that modern concert programs suggest a rather unpalatable reverse sandwich comprising a slice of tough bread stuck between two slices of top-quality meat. Lest I be charged with rank hypocrisy at this point, I freely confess to having sandwiched Elliott Carter's Piano Concerto between two of the choicest cuts in the repertoire—Dvořák's "New World" Symphony and Wagner's *Tannhäuser* overture. Carter had even assured me of his long-standing hatred for both these pieces, but I argued on that occasion that the premiere of his concerto would be better prepared if combined with two scores that needed hardly any rehearsal. It is patently absurd, however, to claim that this awkward mélange of the popular and the complex represents a coherent strategy. It really is quite difficult, in practice, to juxtapose the old familiar pieces with a work that is alien to the audience's cultural experience. The new, when it eschews any links with the past, can be absorbed only by those who are able to hear the music and read the score (the aural equivalent of the architect's blueprint). Folk music transmitted from one generation to the next does not need a written score, nor do the jazz improvisers. Musicality *per se* has no need of the written musical text, and people's greatest admiration is rightly reserved for those who can sit down and play by ear what they heard for the first time only yesterday. Whereas such gifted individuals can certainly perform this feat with many excerpts from Verdi's operas, I rather doubt that they could do it with the final pages of that composer's opera *Falstaff* (a fugue for ten solo singers, chorus, and orchestra).

It seems that these crucial distinctions between various kinds of music are observed only when box office receipts are the sole criterion for undertaking the program. Pop concerts and arena shows by star tenors are typical examples of such observance. In our regular concert and opera world, however, there is no coherent policy: no commitment to commercialism, for example, and no firm attachment to a particular programming philosophy.

The author Italo Calvino once wrote: "If we assume a reader less cultured than the writer and take a pedagogical, educational, and reassuring attitude toward him, we are simply underlining the disparity." In music, too, we have generally assumed that the listener is less cultured than the composer, and the results have indeed underlined the disparity between the two. This assumption is applied not just to contemporary music but also to the whole field of classical composition. In program notes and in countless lectures and introductory talks we attempt to bridge this perceived culture gap separating the cognoscenti from the hoi polloi, but I believe this is inappropriate. Calvino adds in the same essay, "Palliatives are a step backward, not a step forward. Literature is not school." The world of music is not school, either.

The perceived disparity between public and performer is reflected also in the proliferation of musical contests and the obsession with the stopwatch. Musicians are now expected to be competitors first, not performers. It seems that the manner of presentation is often more important than the quality of performance. This is the case, for example, when a favorite conductor is still being summoned to the podium despite his waning skills. The world of opera is also infamous for stressing the performance rather than the work. When asked why *Falstaff* and *Pelleas und Melisande* are not among the public's favorite works, few in the profession will acknowledge the true reason: that there are no star vehicles or great and easily remembered arias. In the cases of both operas (and in those of several others) it is the work that is the great magnet—but only for those who are more interested in hearing a composition (and watching a play) than in comparing the new protagonist with Ezio Pinza or comparing the new prima donna with Elisabeth Rethberg.

Theodor Adorno's writings deal with all these various points—the incongruity of orchestral programs, their haphazard selection, and the superficial values stressed in promotion and propaganda—and yet I find his diagnosis of the cause unsatisfactory. He denies, for instance, that the disappearance of home chamber music is a prime factor in our malaise, and maintains that media manipulation is at fault. He considers it an established fact, for instance, that the New York critic Olin Downes was sufficiently influential that he could almost single-handedly make a great master of Sibelius (whom Adorno dismisses). Downes did have the music columns of a major newspaper at his disposal, but he could not alone create the popular acceptance of several Sibelius symphonies. Similarly, Downes's rejection of the Second Viennese School caused no substantial damage. Media manipulation is not the main cause of the current malaise; for that we must look elsewhere.

Early in the twentieth century, music and the technology of sound transmission came together to achieve a grand union of two very powerful and influential worlds. There are two schools of thought about this great union. The first, more widely held view is that this union represents a singular blessing upon the musical world. Its miraculous manifestations, they maintain, are manifold. To mention but a few of those manifestations: one can now turn on a radio at seven o'clock in the morning and hear a selection of music ranging from Albéniz to Walton; one can select music according to one's fancy, pluck it from the shelf, and listen to it on whatever playing equipment one chooses to possess; one has an enduring physical imprint of a great musician whose work would otherwise have perished with his or her death; one can experience, in the comfort of one's home, gala events that would otherwise have been quite inaccessible or unaffordable; and one is no longer obliged to listen only to provincial performers (since recorded music grants the listener access to the world's best musicians even if one lives in the most remote location miles from the big city). Just as radio wiped out distance, the advent of recording technology defeated the limitations of time. So the popular view has it.

Then there is the opposite view, which holds that musical composition and living composers have been adversely affected by this grand marriage of technology and music, and that this would still be the case even if the present policies of the recording industry were to change and new scores recorded and distributed at a much greater rate than is the case today. Supporters of this view maintain that the very act of recording music turns a dynamic entity into a static, immutable document. They question the notion that a masterpiece of the performing arts is well served by being made into such a document. In my view, they are right to do so.

The question is well put. Just as great bridges sway with the winds, so do great musical compositions change with the generations. Therein resides their strength, and it is this capacity for change that distinguishes the great from the merely good scores that are indissolubly linked with their particular age. Important performers often re-record the greatest classical pieces after rethinking and rereading the scores. Critics often ponder whether the conductor or pianist has found new insights into the work, whereas they should try to understand how the work has changed. Bach's work is the prime example of music that can change and yet retain or even increase its meaning and appeal over many generations, and nobody objects to the constant re-recording of Beethoven's Third Symphony, because it is installed for all time among the great works of all time and is consequently immune to harm. One wonders, though, if it would have survived so well if the "Prince Rasumovsky Recording Studio" had made an authoritative tape of the work in 1805, with the composer conducting.

Whereas Beethoven and the other great masters are doubtless reasonably safe from harm, living composers must be adversely affected by an environment in which a new work is judged primarily by its competitive worth. An economic judgment has clearly been made by the record companies, which record little contemporary music. On the strictly musical side the jury is still out, and is unlikely to deliver a clear verdict until it is realized that in the great merger of technology and music, there has been only one loser: that loser is certainly not technology.

A Measure of Success

Arnold Schoenberg once said to Alexander Zemlinsky that he would show as little consideration for the public as the public had shown him— none whatsoever. In saying this, Schoenberg evidently assumed that he knew who the public was. It so happens that during the years when Schoenberg and Zemlinsky were holding their famous conversations, the Court Opera in Vienna was refused permission to put on Richard Strauss's *Salome*. The severed head of the prophet was apparently not a fit subject for the stage of the emperor Francis Joseph, who felt that he would displease the Pope if his theater showed a depraved young female kissing the lips of a papier-mâché head.

It seems doubtful that the emperor's stand represented public opinion: the cultural elite of the Austro-Hungarian empire were no more "with it" in this respect than they were "with" the industrial or constitutional progress then being made by other European nations. *Salome* was eventually performed in Vienna (in a privately owned theater) in 1907. This just happens to be the year in which Schoenberg composed his String Quartet No. 2—the work that, according to Adorno, defined the point at which Schoenberg stopped caring about the public.

Mozart once wrote that he would not touch an opera before Rosenberg had seen and approved the libretto. He was referring to Franz Xaver Wolf Graf Orsini-Rosenberg, evidently the forerunner of those who forbade Vienna's Court Opera (and its conductor Gustav Mahler) from putting on *Salome*. So just as in Mozart's day the public could not see *Die Entführung aus dem Serail* without Rosenberg's prior permission, the Viennese public of 1907 could not see *Salome* without permission from higher authority. Both works ultimately became enormous successes and made their composers internationally famous.

Theodor Adorno believes that the public's lack of sympathy for modern music is due to manipulation by the culture industry. Whereas I do not wholly subscribe to Adorno's view, it is quite evident that in the modern American musical world there is a cultural elite in control of musical events just as there was in Mozart's day or in Beethoven's day.

In this respect one might say that the role of Orsini-Rosenberg and the Viennese cultural elite has been played in the twentieth century by presenters like Sol Hurok and managers such as Arthur Judson. One illustration of this point occurred when Judson, who at the time was both manager of the New York orchestra and head of a large talent agency, advised Sir John Barbirolli, the successor to Toscanini as principal conductor of the New York Philharmonic, not to play modern music on his debut performance.

Since Judson used to take commissions from the artists whom he, as chief administrator of the orchestral association, engaged, he wrote to Barbirolli, not to manipulate him, but simply to advise him on his first presentation to American subscribers. He knew that Toscanini was a difficult act to follow and he was doing what any good agent might do to ensure his client-artist was given a warm reception.

Whereas the adherents of Schoenberg apparently despised both the press and the public, Igor Stravinsky understood that without them no music could make much progress. Stravinsky, like Mozart, paid attention to public taste—it was not he who set trends. Stravinsky joined the twelve-tone club late in his life and produced one fine work in that tradition, the ballet *Agon* (1957). His genius, however, is well illustrated by the two symphonies he wrote between 1939 and 1945, which are proof that one could still write symphonies during that period by merely modifying tonality, not abandoning tonality altogether. Besides these and a few scores for chamber ensemble, however, Stravinsky knew exactly where his public was—with George Balanchine and the ballet.

When I had an engagement in the New York area I would sometimes ride with a certain limousine driver who specialized in escorting musicians to and from concerts. His intimate knowledge of suburban music halls and the location of their stage doors was an asset not to be underestimated in a limousine driver. One remarkable feature of our rides home together was that he would invariably ask me whether my engagement had been "sold out." It appeared he had at one time escorted André Kostelanetz to and from his engagements, and that ever since that time the size of the box office takings had been his primary measure of an event's success.

In the world of pop concerts, it is quite logical to equate a full house with success. The public will be drawn to the box office if it is announced that a so-called popular artist, such as Kostelanetz or Arthur Fiedler, will be making an appearance. Unfortunately, however, this simplistic equation (success = sell-out) is frequently used for performances by solo instrumentalists and ensembles. As a result, solo artists (pianists, violinists, cellists, and singers) are exceedingly cautious and conservative in their program selections. My acquaintance with programs and soloists is not unlimited, but I know of only one top performer who goes beyond the standard conservative repertoire: Maurizio Pollini.

One of my earliest memories of life in America is of a 1938 concert given by the Cleveland Orchestra in New York, with Artur Rodzinski conducting and Jascha Heifetz as the soloist playing William Walton's

Concerto. I recall being impressed that the public's unfamiliarity with
the name *Walton* was a stronger factor than its familiarity with that of
Heifetz (notwithstanding that soloist's reputation as a sure-fire draw). A
similar incident occurred in 1974, when I performed Schoenberg's *Gurre-
Lieder* in a major German city on the occasion of the composer's one-
hundredth birthday. Two performances were scheduled, and a few days
prior to the first the local manager regretted not having scheduled a
third, such was the demand for tickets. I was therefore puzzled to see
numerous empty seats at the first concert, but I was assured by the
manager that those seats had been left empty by subscribers to whom
"Schoenberg was Schoenberg was Schoenberg" (never mind whether
it was the Schoenberg of *Transfigured Night* or the Schoenberg of the
Variations).

Any musical performer could tell a dozen similar stories. It is a simple
fact that a program's success depends upon the presence of works by the
great composers of the classic and romantic eras. If those works are also
played by a famous or attractive soloist, then all the better for the box
office. That the composition is more important than the performer is a
healthy sign, but the pressure from those who sell the tickets is often so
great that the same pieces have been brought back too frequently. At
some venues we have reached the point where only three of the seven
concertos by Beethoven constitute a "safe draw." The constant reduction
of repertoire pieces that are considered "draws" is also damaging and brings
to mind an old musicians' joke: How many symphonies did Beethoven
write? Four—the Third, the Fifth, the Seventh, and the Ninth.

This reduction of repertoire in all categories has not in the least
diminished the success of certain top-flight managers and performers who
(like my driver) correctly assume that the ultimate confirmation of their
triumph is the size of the box office receipts. That the modern classical
performer can achieve worldwide success with a very small repertoire is a
bow to the most regressive common denominator in musical taste. Too
much repetition can all too easily reduce even the great milestones of
musical history to common currency.

Perhaps the term *recognition* best expresses the meaning of success,
and therein lies modern music's biggest problem concerning the broader
musical public—the lack of recognized names or links with recognizable

music from the past. In this context it is interesting to note the easy reverence with which the public greets older soloists who are past their prime. On several occasions I have observed, from the podium, the consternation of orchestral players quite nonplussed by the vagaries of the great and venerable soloist. The audience, instead of greeting the performance with an appropriately polite applause, invariably astounds both conductor and orchestra alike by giving the great individual thunderous applause and ovations. One might think on such occasions that the true nature of the great concerto had just been revealed for the first time in a decade.

So how do we explain why a heartless professional hears only the terrible intonation of the world-renowned soloist while the audience responds with such warmth? The reaction of the adoring public has nothing to do with music and rather more to do with Faust's compact with the devil: "When I try to stop time, then I am yours" (very freely transcribed, but the meaning is accurate). The members of the public have come to fantasize that they are again twenty-five (or forty) years younger; they are transported back to the day when the great artist first inspired them to rapture. The reaction of the professional performer, however, is somewhat different. To observe the decline of a fellow performer is simply painful and inspires a fantasy of a different kind. The professional pictures himself deteriorating in similar fashion and hopes to God that somebody will stop him from making an ass of himself when the time comes. Such tales are hardly important in the broader, historical context. The great pianist or violinist must inevitably be replaced, and there the matter ends (although in the case of some great singers, I am sure that we shall never see their like again).

For composers, however, the situation is different—the world of composition has reached an impasse, its progress blocked by the conflicting demands of the great musical masterpieces, a public that thirsts for such works, the living composers desperately trying to make their way, and the presenters who have witnessed the waning enthusiasm of their traditional audience and yet cannot see from where the next audience may come. If a way ahead is to be found, then an effective and independent arbiter must be found. The role of the media is crucial in this respect.

It hurts me to say this, but I believe the very nature of our democratic society is the main reason for the fragmentation in the world of composition and the consequent fragmentation of the musical public. The entire grand opus known as classical music was made possible only with the support of aristocratic patrons. After the collapse of the old monarchies in 1918, the ensuing republican order attempted to continue the traditional system of subsidies. Since democracy never much liked taxation without representation, its attempts quickly foundered. Aristocratic leadership had offered a further powerful incentive toward the flowering of creativity: something against which the artist could kick. From the dramas of Schiller (the archetypal revolutionary) to the farces of Nestroy (whose energy derived from censorship), the best theater has always resulted from the struggle between the artist and authority. The aristocratic tradition, however, was not perfect, by any means. Romantic fool that I am, I continue to believe that if the Weimar Republic had survived, composers would not now be suffering this dreadful confusion about how to write music and about what to write. Such dreams are of no value now.

The closest contemporary relative of the old aristocratic system might be the commission made to a painter. More decisive than the economic and political factors was the personal authority of the aristocratic sponsor to patronize and to pay for whatever he liked, even if his taste was sometimes rather less than "aristocratic." The empress who came to Prague for the coronation of Leopold II was reportedly heard to shout "Che porcherìa tedesca!" (What German trash!) at a performance of *La Clemenza di Tito*. This good lady was apparently unaware of the name Mozart (who was revered in Prague) and cared only for what she liked. There are innumerable stories of similarly asinine remarks by noble persons.

Ever since the early decades of the nineteenth century, when successful works were demanded for repeat performances and then exported and arranged for home music-making, success has become increasingly defined as public recognition. In modern democratic societies, grants and prizes awarded by foundations are the nearest thing that we have to the old aristocratic sponsorship. The difference is that today's foundations do not seem to follow up on what happens to their grants or to the talented beneficiaries of those grants. This clearly shows that grants are no longer intended as a means to procure a work desired by the patron, but rather as a welfare payment to a person considered worthy of the money by a panel of experts. The action is still well meant, and I know that my views must sound churlish to many, but it is a fact that the tradition of individual sponsorship can never be replaced.

When Koussevitzky awarded several commissions for the fiftieth anniversary of the Boston Symphony Orchestra in 1930, it was he who decided which composers should be approached, and he was rewarded with some fine compositions. He was motivated by a sense of *noblesse oblige* (never mind that his *noblesse* came not by the grace of God but by his experiences in Russia and in Paris). In this sense he was behaving as a patron, not as a mere giver of economic support, and the results proved how effective this system can be. It is also noteworthy in this context that Koussevitzky headed from 1924 onward an orchestra that was not unionized until 1942. He was thus free to extend rehearsals if necessary, and the general atmosphere of his orchestra was reminiscent of a bygone age blissfully free of the countless restrictions and regulations familiar in the orchestral world of today.

A Critical Profession

In my effort to understand the current crisis in the music world, I often find myself turning to the essays of Theodor Adorno. Despite having deep reservations about some of his views, I believe he may be the most remarkable of all critics of modern music.

I have, for example, the greatest respect for his general point that modern composers too often just do not know how to compose. He writes in his book *Dissonanzen: Musik in der verwalteten Welt* (1956): "Instruction in composition, particularly in conservatories and music schools, stopped essentially at the level of traditional tonal music, giving the student no serious technical standards for evaluating new music." (I offer my English translation—such as it is—since few of Adorno's writings exist in English.)

If a critic's evaluation of a new piece is to be relevant, significant, and influential, he must demonstrate independence of mind. Unless our professional critics can think independently, then there can be no end to the fragmentation of our musical world or the current confused state of people's musical values. Music criticism must be all-encompassing if it is to have any relevance. If a critic believes that a particular composer has not mastered the craft of composition, then he must have the courage to say so. He will have the authority to do so, however, only if he understands composition and has already obtained and read the score in question.

One salient feature of Adorno's music criticism is that it looks at music in the context of society overall. Perhaps all critics should take this approach instead of sitting comfortably at home in front of the CD player, comparing different versions of Gustav Mahler's symphonies. Adorno's overall view is often blurred by his social philosophy and by his religious adherence to the notion that the only true school of composition is the classic German school. Such criticism is legitimate only if the critic makes it clear that he is expressing a personal view—it is clearly preposterous to offer it as objective fact.

For those involved with public performance, there is clearly a big difference between offering objective criticism and expressing a personal opinion. In this respect I recall Rudolf Bing's relationship with the music of Richard Wagner. His opposition to Wagner was part of a liberalism that he shared with many Viennese musicians of his generation, and he never could resist making cutting remarks about the composer at our meetings. He also produced some of the finest productions of Wagner's works and always ensured that the best casts were engaged to do justice to the roles. In general, however, I believe that Adorno's writing illustrates how music criticism should be done.

Not that it is all the fault of the critics, by any means. It is unfortunate that, in both the United States and Europe, critics who want to write about contemporary compositions often find themselves in conflict with their management. I do not know what the various regulations are, or how those regulations differ from one newspaper to the next or from one city to another, but I do know that publications are often obliged to cover only those musical and theatrical events that have placed advertisements with them. Then, of course, there is the crucial question of editorial policy about music. Even the *New York Times* generally allows its senior music critic only the tiniest space in a Sunday arts supplement many pages thick.

One does not envy the critic who tries to write anything substantial under such conditions, yet the critics must fight this if they wish to play an effective role in helping composers achieve a healthier relationship with the public. In subscription series during winter seasons the influence of the newspaper critic was severely curtailed when it became impossible to publish reviews on the morrow of a concert. Even with four concerts in New York, the earliest reviews appear when it is practically too late for anybody to declare, for example, to a friend: "Hey, we must get tickets for the symphony. It says here in the paper that they have a piece that's really worth hearing."

During the leisurely summer months I often repair to a certain charming coffee house, where the international newspapers may be read for the price of a superb espresso. There I can brush up on the prominent European music festivals in a very pleasurable fashion.

The three festivals to which I generally pay the most attention are those held in Bayreuth, Salzburg, and Lucerne. Whereas at Bayreuth the program never changes, the other two festivals and a host of lesser enterprises are having a devil of a time trying to come to terms with musical modernism without disrupting the familiar programming formulae so beloved of tourists. The festival managers trying to perform this skillful balancing act are subjected to constant heckling by vested commercial interests anxious not to lose their valuable trade. The numerous newspaper reviews of first nights and visiting orchestras' first appearances never seem to mention this fact. Instead, our learned critics prefer to entertain their readers with their usual fine mixture of good writing, generous praise, and well-considered negative comment, concentrating on the respective qualities of two orchestras' woodwind sections or on the sophomoric pranks of stage directors.

I do understand that no human being likes to admit that his job is obsolete, but this is unfortunately the case with the job of the music critic. The *Monday Morning Quarterback* may still have some readers for its sports pages, but for the cultural pages (as they are euphemistically known in the European press) the readership must be infinitesimal. Music criticism has been rendered irrelevant by the forces of promotion and publicity. In the realm of concert music the job is now done by the big record companies, whose superstar artists dominate the big festival programs. When he was head of the Salzburg Festival, the conductor Herbert von Karajan skillfully established an interdependency between the recording companies and his opera performances, but if the recording companies believed that this would be a permanent arrangement, trends at the festival seem to indicate otherwise. This would be a heavy blow for those many music critics content to display their great knowledge of a repertoire that happily matches their record libraries. The press has been at least partially, if not wholly, responsible for the rise of the recording industry to the position of supreme arbiter of musical programming.

Another interesting development in this respect has been the trend for festivals to hold a press conference to announce the program for the following summer's event. This is largely due because many artists now book their engagements absurdly early—sometimes as much as three seasons ahead. It certainly also suggests that the critics and the record companies will have less effect on future programs. In effect the festival management is saying "never mind what you say, we know already what will be given next summer." The press should understand, though, that their reporting is entirely academic and cannot influence the immediate future.

The longer winter seasons present a similar situation. A critic at a New York weekly once lamented to me that nothing he or his colleagues said about the shows at the Metropolitan Opera ever made any difference. It may be true that professional criticism has become irrelevant in the world of opera. One need only consider the tolerance and encouragement accorded by the German music press to those irresponsible stage directors who apparently feel free to do with great operas the first thing that comes into their heads.

Even the more convincing rereadings by inventive directors (I think in particular of Jonathan Miller) tend to disregard the style of the composition when they give the action a modern setting. To do *Rigoletto* in a modern New York Mafia setting is extremely tempting, and yet

Verdi's tunes just do not fit with 1980s New York. The problem with nearly all the so-called new wave stage directors is that they try to force their readings of a given libretto into a musical score that fits only the original version of the libretto.

Opera productions not offering an innovative interpretation of the original have often been condemned out of hand. Indeed, the worst offenders among the stage directors are not only tolerated but "interpreted" by the critics as if they were the most profound scholarly thinkers. The fact is that a public that has become immune to ridiculous tributes will be equally immune to ridiculous negative criticism. It is not unusual for opera reviewers to structure their comments as if they were writing two separate reviews: one about the production and another about the musical interpretation. This approach is quite wrong and shows that the critic does not really understand the nature of opera, whose one essential requirement is that it be a successful combination of stage design and costumes; histrionics and acting; music, singing, and playing. The separate critical consideration of director and conductor is equally deplorable.

I suspect that critics know all this very well, but they also know that if they were objectively to examine most modern productions of operatic masterpieces they would have to conclude that in 99.9 percent of cases the production on stage had no connection whatsoever with the musical score. This is because the stage director generally rehearses the singers for six weeks or so after his own fashion, only for the conductor to take over rehearsals without the slightest idea of the stage director's concept. If only this situation had been appropriately dealt with by the opera reviewers of the last forty years! Perhaps opera directing might then have been left to people who could at least read a score and understand the style of the music.

For several decades composers and opera producers have indulged themselves by writing prefaces to new works that are evidently not quite as self-explanatory as the works of old. The often elaborate and highly philosophical remarks of the composers preempt, of course, the job of the critic. Usually accompanied by music examples, program notes have long been part of the world of instrumental music. They were originally intended to make listeners familiar with the principal themes of a new work and were designed to illuminate a composition's structure for amateur players who might eventually buy the sheet music in an arrangement for four hands that could be played at home.

The program notes of today are generally more reminiscent of a defense plea heard in a court of law than of a sensible introduction to a new score. Similarly, an opera's stage director will nowadays appear on television and radio and write a thoughtful essay in the playbill informing the public what Hofmannsthal "really meant" or how "Da Ponte (Mozart's librettist) was quite wrong." Many critics are thus quite content merely to quote the composers' prefaces in making up their reviews. This is fully understandable, but it does look in general as if the tradition of honorable music criticism has been made largely irrelevant by the might of the public relations industry and by the self-serving biographical comments of interested parties.

The members of the juries also function as critics, and one of my experiences as a jurist brought home to me how irrelevant criticism has become. In 1949 I was among nine jury members asked to find three winners in a piano competition in memory of Sergei Rachmaninov. Even though we could not, in good conscience, find a winner, the chairman assured us that we *had* to give a first prize or the rich ladies who funded the competition would drop the whole thing. We were simply not allowed to award second and third prizes only, whatever our consciences told us. Whenever in later years I asked artists who had sat on juries about their experiences, some two out of three admitted being subjected to similar pressures.

Clearly professional critics are subjected to similar pressures. The real problems of our musical life are those of modernism and its reception and the fragmentation of styles, but critics are clearly uncomfortable discussing these issues and consequently devote their few column inches to reviewing other matters within their competence.

The critic of a major newspaper once wrote nearly every day from one of Europe's grand music festivals without asking whether the (rather conservative) selections at the orchestral concerts made any sense. He confined himself to discussions of orchestral technique and conductors' interpretations. I have no wish to be unnecessarily provocative, but I must say that neither topic is of any importance whatsoever. Who exactly cares about the difference between the woodwind sections of the philharmonic orchestras of London and Berlin? To whom is any similarly fine point of orchestral technique relevant (except those praised or criticized)?

The critics and the musicologists must descend from their ivory towers. They are simply not coming to terms with the relationship between music and the rest of society, and until they begin to do so their work will continue to lack relevance. Over the past fifty years or so the world of classical music has resembled a great river that has overrun its banks to form numerous aimless tributaries. Our task is to channel that river back within its banks. It is vitally important that we have serious critical debate to reverse the devastating fragmentation of our modern musical life.

Five

Of Lunatic Bird Catchers and Other Modern Marvels: Reflections on the World of Opera

The Production of Opera

When Robert Donington died in January 1990, he had just completed his definitive work, *Opera and Its Symbols* (1990). This book explains clearly and simply why certain operas survive for decades while others enjoy only the briefest moment in the sun before being banished to the ignominious darkness of the library shelves.

According to Donington, an opera's survival depends upon its archetypal figures, the relationship between them, and the degree to which the music is memorable. He further concludes that the staging and design of opera settings are inseparable from the style and manner of the score. This latter view has been vehemently opposed over the last forty years. In Europe especially the music critics will not tolerate anything resembling a traditional approach to sets, costumes, or dramatic interpretation. In the United States the jury is still out.

The managers of opera companies seem determined to offer an endless diet of operatic reinterpretation. Even apparently harmless romances like Puccini's *La Bohème* have been served up as operatic nouvelle cuisine—and this, I might add, with the willing cooperation of singers and conductors trained to know better. I hesitate to venture into a territory where expert writers have failed to make their mark, but I do feel compelled to explain to opera lovers just what I understand by the word *staging*.

My experience of operatic staging dates back to the late 1920s when I began to coach singers in operatic roles. I used to play for the singers and their teachers the scenes of operas in which they were to sing (even to the point of giving voice cues or trying to substitute for ensemble partners with my dreadful croak). I would correct enunciation, intonation, dragging, and speeding. I was thus able to learn quite a considerable repertoire at first hand. Later I became a prompter (or maestro suggeritore, as the Italians so splendidly put it) and served as rehearsal pianist while staging was prepared. I played for ballet and translated for German stage directors the words of Italian singers. So it was only after I had served for some eight years as an operatic gofer that I was permitted to mount the conductor's podium.

I had thus been able to observe several stage directors, at the Salzburg Summer Festival during the mid-1930s; in Bologna, Firenze, and Trieste; and at New York's Metropolitan Opera. The one stage director from whom I learned what it means to stage an opera was Wilhelm von Wymetal, who had been at the Met in the 1920s and who would give private instruction in his Vienna apartment. One of my students was a woman named Luise Helletsgruber. A member of the soprano squad at the Vienna Opera, Helletsgruber is also known to record-collectors as a cast member of the early Glyndebourne recordings. When the management of the Vienna opera assigned her the coveted role of Nedda in Ruggiero Leoncavallo's *I Pagliacci*, she felt that she needed private instruction. Having agreed on dates for sessions with Wymetal, she asked me to come along and play while she rehearsed.

For the first forty-five minutes I sat at the keyboard while Wymetal noted down in Luise's score the props that she would need. He warned her that it was an old production and that she should therefore not rely on the theater's props (fan, comb, and so on). These, he said, might not suit her hands and other motor reflexes. We started rehearsing the music, but Wymetal stopped frequently to teach her stage craft. He showed her, for example, how to give the impression that she was addressing a singing partner while maintaining a relaxed pivot to her body, enabling her to sing out toward the audience. I was totally new to the craft of coaching an actor, so I was unaware of just how exceptional a director Wymetal was. Little did I know that I would rarely encounter a director with such an impressive knowledge of the human body and how it should be moved in various situations. When I subsequently worked with Lothar Wallerstein I saw another dimension of histrionic coaching. Wallerstein showed a certain Faninal, in Richard Strauss's *Der Rosenkavalier*, how to walk in such a way that he could show signs, at his very first appearance on stage, of the mild heart attack he would suffer in act 3.

Wallerstein had previously been a student of medicine, Wymetal an actor, and both were very familiar with the music for which they were staging and coaching. Wallerstein always demonstrated in rehearsal a thorough acquaintance with the score's dramatic and histrionic demands. As for Wymetal, he once engaged me to play piano accompaniment at his home. Engaged to put on Verdi's *Don Carlos* in Rome, he asked me to play the score for him so that he could work out, for example, how much music was available to bring on the large crowd and how much time there would be to distribute the crowd appropriately for the auto-da-fé. I had to repeat those passages again and again until he was sure how many people needed how many measures to cover the distance from their point of entry to their place on stage. This whole process required several long sessions. It is no easy matter to learn a score to distribute and move a mass of people.

I am not suggesting that Wallerstein and Wymetal were the only good stage directors, since there are many with whom I have never worked. I confine my views to those directors I observed, but compared with the two mentioned above, the others seemed amateurish and often badly prepared. One particular stage director needed to see an improvisation by the singers before he even knew what was going on. Another director knew the work's libretto and even the music, but was so unsure of himself that the slightest protest or alternative suggestion from a singer could throw him completely and make him very irritated.

My early experiences with the work of stage directors predate the Second World War. Evidently something happened to opera in the postwar era, but I promise you I shall not venture to analyze what that some-thing might have been. The champions of the new operatic school have done more than enough in their various essays to confuse everybody on that point. I will say, however, that the responsibility for so-called New Wave productions lies with the opera managers.

In reviewing Donington's *Opera and Its Symbols* for the *New York Times*, I mentioned a remark made in 1936 by the Viennese publicist Karl Kraus, to the effect that a Prague modernization of an Offenbach operetta was "superfluous." This, I believe, is the key word here. The crucial question for all opera managers contemplating a new production should be, Is this needed? European critics tend to stress the priority given to staging by the European houses, thus implying that while tradi-tional staging will do only for an unsophisticated American audience, European audiences need something newer and more daring. Such a view demonstrates how absurd the argument for reinterpretation really is. It amounts, in my view, to the willful distortion and corruption of language for unsavory purposes.

Whereas deconstruction in literary criticism is harmless enough (since hardly anybody ever reads such stuff), the corruption of operatic language is not harmless. I am reasonably confident that it cannot help John Adams's *The Death of Klinghoffer* become a contemporary *Andrea Chénier* any more than it can kill *Carmen*. I cannot believe that the pub-lic genuinely wishes or needs us constantly to take opera's great librettos and "do something" to them. This does not mean that the sets and cos-tumes of an 1860 production must always be faithfully reproduced. When Otto Klemperer's Kroll Opera House staged Wagner in the late 1920s, they modernized the work without confusing the audience. Another instance of appropriate modernization was the casting of Senta in Wagner's *The Flying Dutchman* as a hysterical girl rather than as a mystic.

On the other hand, numerous great operas are firmly located in a cer-tain time and place. To fool around with *La Traviata* is just plain silly and confuses the public (not, I think, the purpose of theatrical productions). In such instances the task of the director is to give the public as much cultural background as possible. How else can a contemporary audience understand that Alfredo's sister cannot expect to get a decent husband as long as her brother keeps a mistress?

There are many ways in which a theater can supply additional background and the public is infinitely better served by this than by a willful distortion of the libretto's basic premises. A list of all such instances in the world of postwar opera would fill a book so large that no publisher would ever print it. I would say simply this: the ball, so to speak, is in the court of the managers. It is they who must set a policy, if only because there is nobody else left with sufficient authority to do so.

Parsifal and The Magic Flute

In 1969 I was engaged to conduct Richard Wagner's *Parsifal* at the Teatro Colòn in Buenos Aires. The performance was to be given as part of a German-language season that featured several other masterworks, including *Der Rosenkavalier* and *Wozzeck*.

Top-class singers were brought in from all over Europe, and we even had a genuine German stage director. The sets and costumes were of local design and manufacture and, as far as I recall, more or less traditional. By this I mean that they were created in the tradition dominant until 1951, the year when Wieland Wagner began to revolutionize the production of his grandfather's works. Those works included his ten operas, his music dramas, and his *Bühnenweihfestspiel* (Stage Consecration Festival Play), *Parsifal*.

Whenever I conducted opera, I always liked to be present at stage rehearsals because it was often the only way of preventing stage directors from playing havoc with the great works. In the *Parsifal* at Buenos Aires, the final scene was being blocked on stage, and the chorus was being shown when and how to rebel against the king's refusal to open the grail. All was in place for the grand dénouement; the doors of the temple opened and Parsifal duly entered, holding high the sacred lance. I sat and waited, but nothing else happened. No Kundry appeared.

I beckoned to the director, who was standing near by, and asked him in a whisper, "And where is Kundry?" The director, looking visibly perturbed, merely said, "Kundry?" "Yes," I replied, "Kundry. It says in the book that at the moment when Parsifal, the new king, opens the grail, Kundry sinks to the floor, expiring but redeemed." The director very kindly agreed to allow Kundry to come on stage and die redeemed. I later asked him what he thought might have happened to Kundry after we had left her repentant at the holy well, washing the feet of Parsifal. He replied, with the merest hint of hesitation, "In Germany we don't believe in that kind of thing anymore." We did not pursue our conversation.

Of the many operatic "reinterpretations" seen in Europe and America over recent years, not one renders the drama more comprehensible or more meaningful to the spectator—especially to a spectator who has read the libretto beforehand. Having been present at many staging rehearsals since I first worked in opera (1934) I have observed several types of stage directors. Some were familiar with the music and had even been trained as conductors prior to taking up stage management and production, some could not read a note of music, and some barely understood the language in which the opera was to be performed.

The director in charge of the 1969 *Parsifal* had a great deal in common with Götz Friedrich, the director of a *Tannhäuser* that I conducted in Bayreuth three years later. In both cases the motive of redemption that permeates many of Wagner's works was kept from the public. Friedrich's actions are easily explained. Although he was working as a guest director in West Germany, he lived and worked in East Germany and was thus afraid of emphasizing Christian salvation. The Buenos Aires man, on the other hand, was merely following his fancy. His error over Kundry resulted from his superficial perusal of the score. In act 3 Kundry has just four notes to sing, having merely to sing the word *dienen* (to serve) twice. Those words she sings approximately one hour prior to the scene in which she should enter the temple behind Parsifal and Gurnemanz. So it is easy to see how a superficial reading of the score might convince the reader that Kundry had become lost somewhere along the way. The director's conviction that nobody in Germany believed in redemption anymore was all the more reason to ignore poor Kundry, it seemed.

The stage director Robert Wilson has a special gift for the visual composition of light, costumes, and design, and for striking alternations between static and ceremonial movement on stage. His talents have earned him a much-publicized and widely acclaimed career. Yet, even one of Wilson's admirers in the print media had to admit, in reviewing his Paris production of *The Magic Flute*, that the comic scenes did not work quite as well as the serious ones. *Parsifal* and *The Magic Flute* have one major point in common: they are different from their composers' earlier works and cannot be regarded as unified in style. Whereas the latter continues to be the supreme artistic expression of the philosophies of the Enlightenment and of humanism, Wagner's *Parsifal* is a superhuman opus that has aged badly.

Parsifal must be a thorough bore when treated as an opera-oratorio— four-and-a-half hours of ceremonial posing with recitative singing in an incomprehensible language must be a trial even for real Wagner fans. It often seems to me that there is a great deal in *Parsifal* and in other great operatic works that is not being brought out by the stage directors. In Wagner's stage directions for *Parsifal*, the dramatic climax of the entire play is described as follows:

> Kundry, still stretched out, bends over Parsifal's head, gently touches his forehead, and puts her arm intimately around his neck. In this position she sings the words: "Confession shall end guilt and remorse, cognition will make wisdom of foolishness. Know now that love which embraced Gamuret [Parsifal's father], as Herzeleide's [his mother's] ardor bathed him in blessing! She who once gave you body and life, before whom death and foolishness must yield, she brings to you now—as a last maternal blessing—of Love—the first kiss!"

The text from which these lines are translated is printed in the first edition. In my view the phrase "She who once gave you body and life" clearly identifies Kundry as Parsifal's mother. Nonetheless, Carl Waack, for example, in his introduction to the text, never mentions Gamuret and merely tells how Kundry reports his mother's death, awakening in him the longing for her love (which brings him into the arms of Kundry, who presses onto his pure lips the first, hot kiss). Wagner's phrase really is quite a puzzle, however, and suggests a preoccupation with incest that is also apparent in the composer's *Ring* cycle. Wagner's treatment of the family must have been analyzed in countless studies, and yet when it comes to staging these works for the public, it is disregarded.

I would argue that if directors must take a "modern" approach to great works, exploration of points such as this would be more appropriate than the embarrassing nonsense so often presented as profundity. I do mistrust the contemporary habit of hunting for neurotic complexes in the lives of accomplished artists, but the confusion about Wagner's paternity is well documented and it can hardly be denied that the mother figure is noticeably absent from his operas and music dramas. Elisabeth has an uncle, Elsa is orphaned, Lohengrin has a father, Senta has a father, Eva has a father, Wotan has no children by his wife but nine daughters by the earth goddess, Siegfried's mother dies in childbirth, Hagen is the son of a woman who yielded to an ugly dwarf for money, and *Parsifal* gives us a mother who died during her son's absence and a foster mother who wishes to be a mother-cum-lover. One does not need to be a psychologist to find this list rather remarkable.

Let us leave the potentially sublime and return to the truly ridiculous: our two stage directors who chose to conceal from the public that *Tannhäuser* and Kundry gain redemption. My central point is this: an essential element of drama is that the audience should suspend its disbelief as it enters the theater. The stage director should always assume that the audience understands this and always remember that he is not the author of the drama. If he does not believe in a particular element of the drama, he should either offer a sincere reinterpretation of that element or not undertake any interpretation at all. Since drama is fiction, one cannot simply leave out a particular element altogether, simply because the world outside the theater doors has changed.

In the case of *Parsifal* (and of other large-scale music dramas) there is a strong argument for transferring the music to the concert hall. One might give a purely musical rendition of the score or a rendition that includes helpful guidance for the audience, both about the action and about the identity of the players. One can see why it might be tempting to reinterpret the more embarrassing aspects of Wagner's eroticism, but there is no excuse for misunderstanding, misinterpreting, or frankly desecrating Mozart's *Magic Flute*. Notwithstanding the tremendous differences between the two composers, these two works do share some striking similarities. Both plays express their spiritual aspirations through a chorus that represents priesthood: in Mozart the Egyptians are a barely concealed portrayal of Freemasons, in Wagner we have the knights of the grail (the priesthood elected to preserve the chalice in which the blood of Christ was collected). In terms of their dramatic structure, both works have severe weaknesses, but such weaknesses are inherent in any play that calls upon the supernatural to resolve its conflicts. Whereas I might be prepared to accept that *Parsifal* would benefit from directors like Robert Wilson, *The Magic Flute* does not require any tampering from any-body (and that does not mean the opera is easy to produce). On one occasion the directors Brauer and Zankl, who preceded Wilson in Paris by more than a decade, announced their production of *The Magic Flute* as "une version psychanalytique" with Sarastro as "le père castrateur." This is hardly compatible with Sarastro's great aria "In diesen heil'gen Hallen kennt man die Rache nicht" (In our holy halls vengeance is unknown).

Not that directors are alone in their tampering and reinterpreting, as illustrated by the flood of commentary that greeted the Mozart bi-centennial of 1991. In one learned treatise, Sarastro was described as an evil tyrant because "he enters on a chariot drawn by six lions." The same treatise then goes on to quote a letter written by Goethe's mother to her son. From Frankfurt, where she has seen *The Magic Flute*, she tells of the opera's triumphant success. According to her letter, even the Sach-senhäuser (people from nearby Sachsenhausen; broadly speaking, the unsophisticated suburban class) had flocked to the show to see their little children playing the lions, tigers, and other wild animals that gather around Tamino's flute and later pull Sarastro's chariot. A tyrant indeed!

The Magic Flute really begins to cause problems when it is set in any cultural environment outside that of Austria and southern Germany. How painful to watch Papageno not only struggling with the idiom but also speaking with utterly inappropriate accents (including, in this instance, those of High German).

The text is as deeply rooted in Viennese traditions as a *No* play is rooted in those of Japan. Similarly, that *The Magic Flute*, unlike *Parsifal*, cannot be transferred to the concert hall is proof of its miraculous quali-ties. It is, in this sense, superior to all those works that may be just as effective in partial form (such as a ballet score without dance, an opera score without staging, or a Bach oratorio with organ only).

If I were forced to propose a way to make *The Magic Flute* succeed outside its traditional setting, I think I would propose that the spoken text be rewritten in the style of Bertolt Brecht's epic theater and that each theater use as much stage machinery and magic as it could afford. This would indeed be a "modern" approach, but the audience would at least be spared some of the more absurd spectacles offered by modern stage directors.

In Robert Wilson's version of the opera, for example, Papageno's metallic headgear made him resemble nothing so much as a lunatic who had escaped from the asylum with a stolen piece of machinery on his head.

Even the producers of the Salzburg Summer Festival's bicentennial version of the opera could not resist dressing the priests as if they were members of the Hare Krishna cult, and the conductor raced through the brief choral passage that concludes act 1 as if he were being pursued by demons. Since the conductor in question knows German, he must have realized that the text of that passage—a classic distillation of Enlightenment thinking—is among the most crucial passages in the whole work: "When virtue and justice cover the path of the Great with fame, then earth will be like heaven and humans like the gods." We were rushed through it so fast that nobody (not even the performers) could have had any idea what the passage was really about.

Seeing the word *Presto* over the finale, the conductor evidently realized he had every excuse to finish act 1 with a flourish, thus ensuring that the fashionable festival audience would wake up in time to give the cast a decent number of curtain calls. Audiences are often the unwitting victims of the contemporary craze for rereading old texts—be they literary or musical. Early music enthusiasts, for example, have decreed that tempos were faster in the old days. I am always in favor of challenging established tradition, but I am worried by this insistence that there are immutable laws governing tempos. In my view, the only binding law in this respect is that singers should be able to make sense of the words they are singing. In the Salzburg bicentennial performance, the pace of that final chorus in act 1 was such that no singer could possibly give the appropriate emphasis to those deeply significant words.

Even this very brief examination of the two works should show clearly that *Parsifal* is obsolete, while *The Magic Flute* is startlingly relevant to contemporary life. Sarastro's famous aria "In diesen heil'gen Hallen" begins thus: "In our holy halls vengeance is unknown, and if a human being has fallen, Love leads him back to his task." Is it not significant that this particular aria became the opera's hit tune? The central message of *Parsifal* seems to be that, to learn compassion and empathy with suffering, all an innocent needs is for an attractive woman to make a pass at him. There really does not appear to be much else to it.

I conducted *Parsifal* for the first time during the Easter season of 1938. I have since performed it many times and never with anything but the utmost reverence for its marvelous score (which in the 1960s I arranged into a fifty-minute instrumental concert piece). I also find some of the poetry extremely moving and beautiful, but if the best verses are among the greatest moments of the *Gesamtkunstwerk* (total work of art) tradition, the rest of the long score is certainly not. The musical vitality of *Parsifal* would be best served if presentation of the complete work were reserved for the Bayreuth festival. This occasion is still attended by the true believers who insist on seeing every measure and every line as Holy Writ. Let them have their summer pleasure.

Let us end the crass juxtaposition of the original work with fashionable reinterpretation. Why, in the "Good Friday" section of *Parsifal*, set a poetic digression about God and nature on a barren stage offering no discernible trace of nature? Wagner, like Beethoven, was deeply involved with natural beauty, and it is therefore nothing short of cultural treason to place act 2 of *Siegfried* in a setting reminiscent of a mechanical skyscraper. Those readers who have visited Ravello, the southern Italian coastal town where Wagner wrote the scene of Klingsor's garden, will have some idea of how inspirational that setting was. Alas, when I revisited Ravello in 1991 I was dismayed to see how it had been transformed by designers who evidently believed that human beings could out-create nature. Those designers are like many German opera critics, who are so mesmerized by the revisionist values of the stage directors that they never fail to criticize those who courageously adhere to a more representational style of scenic design.

The Magic Flute must be treated with the same reverence as that which is accorded the greatest plays of Shakespeare. It is a detailed and loving portrait of humanity, set as a parable. The dialogue must be so treated or the whole thing will make no sense in the theaters of the world that have no direct link with the spirit that led to the French Revolution. The music should not be handled by those who do not understand the text—modern opera managers apparently think nothing of asking singers to perform music in languages with which they are not in the least familiar. Spoken dialogue should also be handled with extreme care. For decades it has been the custom merely to abridge the spoken dialogue between music numbers, insofar as what remains either makes no sense or is declaimed so clumsily that neither Prince nor Bird Catcher is understandable even to those sitting in the front row.

There is every chance that the dialogue of *The Magic Flute* will recapture its original universal appeal. These days many people tend to dismiss the libretto, but the mere fact that Goethe was tempted to write a sequel to the opera should hint at its true potential. If the dialogue is indeed to recapture its universal appeal, it must be more than revised and edited—it has to be rewritten. This is also true of other great German-dialogue operas. Mozart was extremely critical of Gottlieb Stephanie's use of language in his libretto for the composer's *Die Entführung aus dem Serail*, and both Weber's *Der Freischütz*, and (to a lesser degree) Beethoven's *Fidelio* suffer from the same problem. After Papageno's aria (No. 2) there is a long prose passage that is quite impossible as it stands but which must be retained in some form, because it represents the play's exposition. In the first dialogue, in which Tamino attempts to discover Papageno's identity, the latter answers many questions with the identical words uttered by Parsifal in response to Gurnemanz's queries: *Das weiss ich nicht* (That I do not know). The dialogue cannot be cut because it shows that Papageno is the naive, obverse side of the Prince—not a clown, but the essential simple man whose primary concerns are to make his livelihood, find a woman, and hope for many children.

Rewriting the text of *The Magic Flute* would also require the writer to address the social distinctions that lie at the heart of the play. Whereas the Prince represents the hero who seeks to save and rescue the object of love, Belmonte, Leonore, and Florestan are Tamino's colleagues. The

Three Ladies are there for a musical reason: their trios provide indispensable variety from the set pieces of the five principals. To try to "make something" of the Three Ladies is a waste of the director's and public's time. The presence of the black Monostatos also presents a problem for contemporary productions, namely, How can this figure be incorporated without underscoring the racial prejudices of the plot? When the Moor and Papageno bump into each other the solution generally adopted is to introduce buffoonery, and yet this is neither funny nor accurate. It is a regrettable fact of life that people of one skin color tend to regard those of another as strange, and when the two stammer "that is . . . the dev . . . il cert . . ain . . . ly" they prove that they are no exception to the rule. This particular trap has been with us ever since some of the finest Paminas were sung by black sopranos. Poor Monostatos is thrown into obvious confusion when he has to sing "weil ein Schwarzer hässlich ist" (because a blackamoor is ugly).

Sarastro's male chauvinism is no less embarrassing to modern sensibilities. He sings the following line: "Ein Mann muss eure Herzen leiten, denn ohne ihn pflegt jedes Weib aus seinem Wirkungskreis zu schreiten" (A man must lead your hearts, since woman tends to overstep her range without much guidance). To dodge the issues of racism or sexism by introducing theatrical buffoonery (a technique often employed) is embarrassing, solves nothing, and deepens the confusion. As for the priests, a modern audience generally sees such groups as mysterious and sinister brotherhoods, and yet in Mozart's day the Masons were a liberal assembly. A brief entry about freemasonry in an encyclopedia would surely give even the least-talented director some idea of how to treat Sarastro and the priests (that is, how to manifest their lasting validity as liberals in the modern sense of liberalism, not in the distorted sense understood by political reactionaries).

Whereas the similarities between these two works are several, the differences are few, but more significant. *Parsifal* was begun by a man of sixty-four, *The Magic Flute* by a man twenty-nine years younger; one work is pretentious, the other is not; whereas the pretentious work has aged badly, the unpretentious work is as valid today as it was in 1791 (if not more so). I must say that the aging process in Wagner's work is as audible in the spoken text as it is in the music. The public's continued enthusiasm for productions and recordings of Wagner's works is primarily due to those heroic lady singers who seem to emerge at the happy rate of about one per generation to ensure that a nostalgic public is never deprived of the great outpourings of Isolde, Sieglinde, and Brünnhilde.

The public's enthusiasm has nothing, however, to do with a genuine renewal of interest in his works. In non-German-speaking countries in particular (countries in which the language of the music drama is more of an obstacle than an advantage), the mere existence of a great heroic vocalist is enough to inspire a new production, which will employ all the usual gimmicks in an effort to put a new spin on this venerable *Gesamtkunstwerk*. Giuseppe Verdi, by the way, never claimed that text, decor, costumes, and music should come out of the same egg (as required by the *Gesamtkunstwerk*). His works will last longer than those of Wagner, precisely because the plots of some of his most popular master-pieces have never been taken seriously. They were simply a great excuse for irresistibly passionate music, and nobody cared greatly about the fate of Aïda or Rhadames.

I think it has already become clear which portions of Wagner's works will endure: the great love duets in *Tristan*, *Die Walküre*, and *Lohengrin*, several solo scenes (such as the Immolation, Wotan's Farewell, and Isolde's Love-death), and some grandiose orchestral passages. There were more Mozart works, in more repertoires, at the two-hundredth anniversary of his death, than there were at the one-hundredth anniversary in 1891, more operas, more chamber music, more symphonies (more of everything, in more countries and in more languages). No matter how incensed people may become with the film *Amadeus*, it does illustrate superbly the vitality of Mozart's music—a vitality greater than that of Wagner's music. The first night of *The Magic Flute* took place sixty-six days prior to the composer's death. According to Köchel (the standard thematic catalogue of Mozart's works), it carried the opus number 620. Many eighteenth-century composers wrote hundreds of works, but no composer produced as many vintage works as Mozart. Anyone wishing to compare Mozart with Haydn, for example, should first consider that Haydn lived to the age of seventy-seven, and Mozart died before he reached thirty-six.

Opera buffs may wonder why it is that in every generation there are several conductors who lead superlative performances of *Parsifal* but precious few who can do an equally outstanding job with *The Magic Flute*. The reason is whereas *Parsifal's* score (like those of Mahler's big symphonic works) is loosely conceived and sufficiently broad in scope to allow various interpretations of tempos and emphases, Mozart's score must be interpreted very precisely. Whereas *The Magic Flute* consists of twenty-two concise sections, the *Parsifal* score is made up of several lengthy musical blocks. Mozart's entire opera thus takes less time than act 1 alone of Wagner's work. Bayreuth timekeepers have logged differences of thirty-five minutes between various conductors' renditions of *Parsifal*, but the slightest hurrying or dragging in one of the twenty-two Mozart numbers can change the character and effect of an entire aria or ensemble.

Hermann Hesse, who adored Mozart, wrote in one of his many short pieces on music that *The Magic Flute* was nourished by the humanitarian ideals of the eighteenth century. In my view this great poet and thinker is more perceptive of a work's literary, dramatic, and cultural values than a small band of dilettante German journalists. If this view bespeaks, in some people's minds, a form of old-fashioned conservatism, then so be it—I make no apology.

The careers of theater producers, directors, set designers, and managing impresarios are not in the least dependent upon music criticism. The American music critics are right to worry that opera audiences no longer heed their words. I suspect that my words of wisdom will, like theirs, fall upon deaf ears.

Opera: What Constitutes Longevity[1]

A massive catalogue raisonné, *Annals of Opera*,[2] starting in the year 1594 and ending in 1940, regales us with approximately 4000 entries of first

---

[1] Reprinted by permission of *Daedalus*, Journal of the American Academy of Arts and Sciences, from the issue entitled "The Future of Opera," Fall 1986, Volume 115, No. 4.

[2] Alfred Loewenberg, *Annals of Opera*, 2nd ed. (Geneva: Societas Bibliographica, 1955).

nights, local premieres, translations, and other items of interest. Browsing through the huge tome and its indices, I found one puzzle more intriguing than all the others: why a small number of operas have succeeded and lasted, while many more have been relegated to the shelves. Obvious failures are very easily spotted; they are simply listed, with "world premier" being described in four or five lines. Successes are spread over several columns, indeed, sometimes whole pages of the *Annals*. Such data are eloquent reminders of the fact that instant enthusiasm and lasting validity are rarely synonymous.

For many years, I have watched, coached, conducted, and discussed opera and its problems. I have long been interested in why, for example, *Cavalleria rusticana* (1890) is played everywhere, while the same composer's *L'Amico Fritz* (1891) languishes in the archives. If this were true only of Mascagni's works I should not exert myself. The fact is that there are gaps in our understanding of what constitutes temporary success as contrasted with lasting appeal.

Opera is a composite of many arts and is dependent on a good number of interpreters: painters and architects design the sets that are executed in shops; others deliver the sketches for costumes, in some instances several hundred for the chorus; a lighting expert may do much to help or handicap a production. Such creations are ideally part of a larger concept of a producer (stage director), whose authority and policy decisions have become increasingly important in recent decades. Musical directors, once the undisputed commanders in opera companies, now find themselves in the back seat, sometimes through their dereliction; they do not much care for the new balance of power. Perhaps a close look at those operas that are still with us may provide some clues to the question posed in *Capriccio*: "Prima la musica, dopo le parole, Prima le parole, dopo la musica?"

The survival of the performing arts often depends on the availability of first-rate talent. Eighteenth-century *opera seria* came to an end when the supply of castrato singers dried up, caused in great part by Napoleon's ukase forbidding the operation that prevented the mutation of male voices. No matter how often *Idomeneo* may be edited and revived, there is no chance of hearing the work as it was intended—an important voice in that opera no longer exists. Every generation has witnessed resurrection attempts—Richard Strauss made an elaborate one in the late 1920s—welcomed by all who admired Mozart, who could not get enough of his work to satisfy their appetites. Still, the best efforts are only partially convincing; it is difficult to secure a firm place in the repertoire for this *opera seria*.

Bellini, Donizetti, and Rossini, to name some of the most famous composers, continued to write operas for very great singers, men and women able to negotiate vocal parts demanding acrobatic skills of larynx, lungs, and vocal cords. These works, except for the perennial comedies *Elisir d'amore*, *The Barber of Seville*, and *Don Pasquale* go into limbo for decades until a truly magnetic artist of the caliber of Maria Callas brings about their revival. While it may be impolite to suggest that many of these scores have no intrinsic merit beyond displaying great vocal virtuosity, I do not hesitate to compare such compositions to the music for violin written by Paganini; it is remarkably effective when played by a wizard, remarkably vapid when simply contemplated as music *per se*.

Longevity cannot be forecast for a genre that has uncounted sleepers on library shelves. Who knows which singer of tomorrow will emerge from a vault in Padua or Palermo with a more complex version of *Norma* or a sequel to *Guillaume Tell*? Of titles that have lasted, independent of extraordinary singers on the major stages of the world, one can hardly count more than one hundred.

The best example of an opera that exists independently of the quality of voices is *Carmen*. There is no harder role to cast; yet, not a season passes without Bizet's setting of Merimée's tale being produced. No other opera has been rearranged and revised more, which may be taken as further proof of its indestructibility. Not many other operas belong to this exclusive club. They have found favor on every continent, in every city where opera is part of public entertainment. A large number of other genuine masterpieces, with good librettos and fine scores, are assured devoted admirers, but only in specific places. They represent something else, reminding one of a "vin du pays," which must be drunk where it is grown since it does not "travel well." In this category belong two superb pieces: Debussy's *Pelléas* and Pfitzner's *Palestrina*. There must be many other works that have never traveled, never been widely heard or seen. For many years, Rimsky-Korsakov's *The Invisible City of Kitesh* had a great reputation, yet it never played in the West. Is it possible that this opera, like much of the Slavic repertoire, is fairly inaccessible to audiences that lack a particular cultural background and preparation?

Since most of my argument will be about public reception of opera, and since this is a highly complex subject, my conclusions must be tentative. In recent memory, a concert performance of Debussy's opera was acknowledged by nearly a mass exodus of the audience after the second act, a happening that may be expected to discourage anyone from presenting the work in that city for at least the next decade or two. While such things happen in all the performing arts, they do not fundamentally change the quality of a work's components, which in my view are subject to well-established criteria. The requirements for an opera's long and healthy life before the public are three: (1) memorable set pieces; (2) dramatic situations and *personae* with whom the public can identify; (3) the caliber of the score. It may be difficult for non-musicians to grasp the difference between "memorable pieces" and "caliber of score"; a comparison from gastronomy may illustrate it. One chef produces several outstanding dishes (memorable); another has a very high level of quality whatever one tastes ("caliber of the whole score"). The term "memorable" has two interpretations: easily remembered, and unforgettable. "La donna è mobile" is easily remembered: it remains in the ear; it can be whistled; it is both catchy and unforgettable. The quintet from act 3 of *Meistersinger* cannot be whistled or sung, and much more than one finger is required to reproduce it on a piano. However, once the piece has penetrated a sensitive nervous system it will remain a luminous and unforgettable happening.

It takes a considerable number of memorable pieces, as well as other components, to propel an opera successfully through the requisite two or three hours. It is simpler to state the case in reverse: no opera without memorable moments can enjoy more than limited success, and then with a limited public. Of my examples, both *Rigoletto* and *Meistersinger* meet all three criteria. There is not a weak link in either work, and yet one knows, without needing to see an opinion poll, that a huge difference exists in the number of people who respond to these two works. Many more can and will identify with the drama of Rigoletto: a crippled widower must watch helplessly while his dissolute boss seduces his only child; he hires a hit-man; a warm-hearted prostitute saves the lecherous seducer; and, to add a gothic touch, a curse on Rigoletto by another offended father has been fulfilled. In forty-odd words the essential synopsis is complete.

At least 400 words would be necessary to prepare a newcomer for even a minimal understanding of *Meistersinger*. The piece is complicated on many levels. While the original French story of *Rigoletto* could be changed, with the locale transferred to Mantua, and the king demoted to a duke, one can hardly conceive of relocating Wagner's Nuremberg and calling the work "Le concours de Toulouse." This grotesque fantasy may suggest why Verdi's opera has a different and broader appeal, why it is more easily understood, and why it will outlive *Meistersinger*. Public identification with Rigoletto is not limited by ethnic borders, while Wagner's comedy is rooted firmly in German lore, and is based on premises that have to be known if there is to be more than a superficial appreciation of the work.

FOUR MASTERPIECES

The year 1781 (many years before Napoleon I put an end to castrato singing) was crucial for modern opera. Mozart had just finished *Idomeneo*, and was now embarked on a project he called "eine teutsche Oper," which became *Die Entführung aus dem Serail*. Mozart's stressing of the language—"teutsche Oper"—indicates that at the time it was an extraordinary action to compose a full-length stage play in anything but Italian. Today musicians consider it first of the four greatest opera scores ever written, and its *personae* return in various, but recognizable, disguises throughout the following 150 years of the German repertoire. While academic nomenclature has tagged it *Singspiel* (song-play), defined as a sequence of musical pieces connected by spoken dialogue, this is an inadequate and misleading name. The *Singspiel* of composers Lortzing, Marschner, and Nicolai later became classical operetta, but Mozart's *Entführung* is not light comedy, but a romantic piece like *The Magic Flute*, Beethoven's *Fidelio*, and Weber's *Freischütz*. All four, known to be significant works in German repertoire, owe their vitality and longevity to the German language. One-and-a-half centuries after they were premiered,

The Magic Flute and *Freischütz* remain perennial favorites in theaters of Central Europe where German is spoken and understood. This "orbit" includes Holland, Switzerland, and Scandinavia. *Fidelio*, despite its initial lack of success in 1805, was an instant hit in the 1814 version, as attested by the many arrangements made of several of its pieces. Such transcriptions are the surest, if not the only, reliable sign of genuine success. To print Rocco's aria "for voice and guitar" can mean but one thing: it was popular. Similarly, some eleven pieces from the opera were transcribed and arranged for odd combinations of instruments, all intended for amateurs playing at home what they had heard and enjoyed in the theater.

Weber's *Freischütz*, first performed in 1821 in Berlin, was accepted for production by thirty-three German cities within eighteen months of its premier. In opera houses outside the Germanic language orbit, both *Fidelio* and *Freischütz* were soon complemented with orchestral accompaniments to recitatives, replacing the dialogue, for grand opera in the nineteenth century did not accept spoken dialogue. Berlioz was only one among several less distinguished composers who concocted recitatives for Weber's opus, and, as late as 1939, New York's Metropolitan Opera planned a *Fidelio* revival with recitatives composed by its chief conductor Artur Bodanzky, whose death, however, canceled the production.

In our era of musical purism, which recognizes only what is, or what passes for, authenticity, dialogue has been restored, but without convincing results. *Entführung*, *The Magic Flute*, *Fidelio*, and *Freischütz*, the four masterpieces before Wagner, have all been subjected to grievous mistreatment internationally and even in Germany. After the dreadful *accompagnato* recitatives, stage directors transferred *Fidelio* into a commentary on the Third Reich. Others made *The Magic Flute* into "une interprétation psychanalytique" (as in the case of a Paris production with Sarastro as "le père castrateur"), and *Entführung* in Frankfurt in 1985 became an unrecognizable hodgepodge. Such were the vagaries of some new productions. A 1986 version of *The Magic Flute* from East Berlin approached Mozart and Schikaneder with a Marxist ax: the priests became capitalists, and Papageno-Papagena were portrayed as the downtrodden, exploited proletariat. Such operatic endeavors make one wonder whether these works can exist today on their terms.

Shocked as I am by such misreadings, and astonished as I may be at the venality of opera managers who encourage this vandalism, my fifty-year acquaintance with a non-German operatic world convinces me that dialogue operas are no longer possible on the international circuit; indeed it is doubtful if they ever were. The names Mozart and Beethoven command so much reverence that few commentators, let alone laymen, have the courage to say that dialogue, either in impossible translations and abridgments, or in the original with a dozen foreign accents making hash of the words, has had its day. The theater of the absurd may have been realized when Covent Garden presented a bilingual *Fledermaus*— "hawf English" and "halb Weanerisch"—an eloquent message to the public that neither management nor performers cared very much about who understood what. If international opera houses were patronized only by genuinely interested spectators rather than by unmotivated sub-scribers, dialogue operas could no longer be given. That these operas, during their original runs, and for many years thereafter, did engage audiences, inviting them to identify with their characters, good and bad, is evident from the seminal nature of several *dramatis personae*, starting with *Entführung*.

Selim Bassa, conventionally presented as a cardboard figure, is in fact Sarastro's precursor. Both choose forgiveness over revenge; both nobly resign themselves to unrequited love. Hans Sachs, in *Meistersinger*, faces a similar conflict. Selim and Sarastro represent the best of eighteenth-century humanism; they are incarnations of the *deus ex machina*, a figure that in earlier plays resolved conflict and confusion. Don Fernando in the last scene of *Fidelio* is another true "descendant" of this type, as is the Hermit in *Freischütz*. Finally Lohengrin, transformed by Wagner from a cameo *deus ex machina* to the heroic lead, is the romantic fulfillment of several models: lover, liberator, avenger, justice, and prophet.

The leading ladies, from Constanze on, are passive, noble, and innocent, all awaiting their liberation: Belmonte traveled far to find and free his bride; Tamino penetrated the enclave of a secret order to discover and liberate Pamina; Wagner employed the same motif, having Siegfried liberate Brünnhilde from her enforced sleep. All, too, share a magical instrument: a flute for Tamino; a horn for Weber's Oberon, and for Siegfried, which he plays in his passage through the fire. In *Lohengrin*, the magic horn appears toward the end of the opera, when the protagonist, taking leave of Elsa, presents her with three objects for her resurrected brother: a sword (nothing unusual about that), a horn (to continue the eighteenth-century motif that goes back to Wieland's poem *Oberon*), and a ring. This ring is not a wedding band; rather, it recalls Lessing's play, *Nathan der Weise*, in which a ring symbolizes truth. Finally, the romantic plot prescribes the hero's trial, where he must prove himself: fire and water for Tamino; a shooting contest for Max in *Freischütz*, and fire, again, for Siegfried. In the comedy, *Meistersinger*, the trial is a song competition, with a lovely young girl as the prize. This lover-liberator motif is reversed in *Fidelio*, where the man is in jail and the wife the heroine. The libretto also introduces a novel and very bourgeois character into the gallery of *dramatis personae*: the mercenary father of a marriageable daughter. Rocco is so blindly infatuated with his new helper that he wishes to have him as son-in-law, knowing absolutely nothing of his background. Daland, in *The Flying Dutchman* exhibits the same hasty judgment: a boatload of valuables seems quite sufficient reason for the captain to marry his daughter. In *Meistersinger*, Pogner, the father, is prepared to offer his child to the winner of the musical contest. Of all the operatic fathers, Faninal may be the most ridiculous. His one and only ambition is that the man should have a title; it matters not at all what he looks like, what his age is, or what his manners may be.

The change in the portrayal of heroines from the pure maidens of *Entführung*, *The Magic Flute*, Marzelline in *Fidelio*, Agatha in *Freischütz*, and Elisabeth and Elsa in Wagner's earlier works, to more erotic types, reflects not only a historical change, but also a difference between German and Italian mores. Mozart's Constanze and Pamina are found only in his "teutsche Opern": Susanna in *Figaro* is far from an innocent; Donna Anna is a rape victim; Elvira is an abandoned divorcée. What goes on in *Così fan tutte* between the two couples is anybody's guess, but it is not merely flirtatious. Eros prevails in all three of Mozart's Italian operas, while his two German works are morality plays without overt sexual emphasis.

Most operas with a noble, high-minded couple (Constanze-Belmonte et al.) need as contrast and relief a funny couple (Blonde-Pedrillo, Papagena-Papageno, Marzelline-Jacquino), whose concerns are more earthy, who fight—though not too strenuously—and then make up, who are loyal servants and helpers of aristocrats. Later in the century, they become part of the general plot of most operettas.

Another comic character worth tracing is Osmin, the sixth and last role in *Entführung*. His "descendants" include Monostatos, Beckmesser, and Ochs von Lerchenau. All four attempt to win an unattainable woman. Their failure is in no way tragic; it is cause for general hilarity since they are nasty individuals, meant to antagonize the audience. It is worth noting that the first two of these "fall guys" are non-European, a Turk and a Moor. Later, because of middle-class standards, such characters become members of the same race and class as the rest of the cast.

Today's audiences might have more difficulty identifying with the Sprecher in *The Magic Flute* who informs Tamino: "ein Weib tut wenig, plaudert viel" (a woman does little, chatters much) or, with Sarastro who explains to Pamina why he took her away from her mother: "ein Mann muss Eure Herzen leiten, denn ohne ihn pflegt jedes Weib aus seinem Wirkungskreis zu schreiten" (a man must guide your hearts, since without him woman tends to transgress her own range). Imagine Gloria Steinem as stage director, and what she would do with Sarastro! Yet, to make a real change would be to misunderstand these operatic masterpieces. Sarastro is a humanist of the 1790s, the head of an order, later "reborn" as Josef Knecht in Hermann Hesse's *Magister Ludi*.

If, out of our contemporary type of enlightenment, so different from the eighteenth-century model, we permit the interpreter to become a critic and censor of Sarastro, it will serve neither Mozart's music, rendering it senseless, nor the vitality of the play. Such tampering will not convince the untutored, and it can only offend the educated. To take these works seriously, we must either forget about presenting them as opera, depriving the world of great musical utterances, or find a totally different style like Cocteau's opera-oratorio *Oedipus Rex*, which has a narrator instead of dialogue. As it is, German dialogue opera has not survived—either in undoctored form, or in gratuitous updating, with political text emendations. Seminal influences have come to full bloom in Wagner's works, which have retained their magic hold on an international operatic circuit.

Mercenary elders are common in bourgeois literature; also, in bourgeois opera. The young Wagner created not only Daland, but several other father-figures, including the Landgraf in *Tannhäuser,* as disposed as Pogner in *Meistersinger* to offer his niece as a first prize in a song contest, and King Henry in *Lohengrin,* ready to bless Elsa's bridal bed, soon to be occupied by an incognito husband. While these four—Daland, Pogner, Landgraf, and King Henry—are minor roles, with Wotan we have a figure of much larger proportions, where Wagner's magic is fully developed. Prepared to leave his most beloved child (who only did what he himself secretly wished) asleep at the wayside, for anyone who comes by ("der am Wege sie findet und weckt"), one is reminded of *Fräulein Else* by Schnitzler, a story of a father who bargains away his daughter's virtue to pay his debts. The values of nineteenth-century middle-class Europe are admirably mirrored in such situations.

It is equally intriguing to follow Wagner's development of the lover-liberator motif. In *The Flying Dutchman,* and in the operas that follow, love, sin, and other human indulgences attain metaphysical status. Aside from Elsa, who resembles the passive, innocent model of Constanze, Wagner's women are true heroines. Senta and Elisabeth die to redeem the "eternal" transgressions of the Dutchman and Tannhäuser, respectively. Brünnhilde, by her immolation, redeems not only her father, the god Wotan, but also his kingdom, which in this case is nothing less than the world. All such redemptions, including Isolde's love-death, are grandiose schemes which, surrounded by irresistibly erotic music, bring the public to a state of wish-fulfillment.

Wagner's heroes, with their flaws and sins, appeal much more to people's imaginations than do Mozart's more virtuous lover-liberators. When we use less grandiloquent language than the author, we find many characters redolent of the everyday world. Venus and Kundry, for example, are easily recognized as glorified madams. In a New York *Parsifal* performance in 1942, two young men in uniform were overheard to say at the moment when Flagstad as Kundry, lying on a couch, was pushed on stage: "Guess the girls didn't please him, so they sent the madam." Venus's "customer" is saved from the Pope's condemnation by a miracle, the flowering papal staff, and by Elisabeth's "love-death." Amfortas, who did not resist Kundry, is healed and redeemed by a boy, whose compassion and understanding came to him in a kiss from a woman who embodies the mother-mistress synthesis to perfection.

While I do not know if any psychoanalytical essay on Wagner's figures exists, it seems that even a most cursory acquaintance with Freud's *Kulturtheoretische Schriften* (theoretical essays on cultural subjects) makes clear Wagner's symbolism, as well as the wild reactions, hostile or appreciative, to which he has traditionally been subjected. Tristan betrays his father-figure and benefactor, Marke; Sieglinde commits adultery with her brother. Drugs are used in both instances to shorten theatrically the time between the first infatuation and consummation, and to be safe from the danger of the husband's waking too soon. In *Götterdämmerung* a drug is used to make Siegfried forget both his bride and his oath. Another drug is used in act 3 to restore his memory—all of this to prevent heroes and heroines from appearing completely degenerate. Many "sins" appeal to the darker side of the unconscious: breach of contract is practiced by Wotan; theft is conspicuous in *Rheingold* and *Siegfried*; violent deaths are frequent—through premeditated killings in duels (*Tristan, Walküre*), through spontaneous disgust (Siegfried doing away with Mime), or through a stab in the back (Hagen, who later kills also his half-brother Gunther). Wotan is not only the father of the gods; he has nine illegitimate daughters and a wife who uses her knowledge to blackmail him to gain what she wants, having Sigmund killed. Her defense of marriage and conventional morality is unsympathetically rendered. These situations, with the participants disguised as gods and demi-gods, provide an accurate portrait of the double-standards prevalent in Wagner's world, and, indeed, in our own today.

However disconcerting this may be, Wagner's true magic may lie in his ability to comprehend the taboo dreams and desires of a severely repressed civilization. No other great composer has so many unmusical admirers, who flock to Bayreuth on annual pilgrimages, and fly hither and yon if there is the prospect of a new and promising *Tristan* or *Walküre* production. According to musicologists, there has yet to be written a strictly musical analysis of Wagner, the composer. There is, however, a large bibliography that lists essays on every aspect of his life,

and learned treatises dealing with the music as it relates to the text—
which is quite a different matter from fathoming how he put notes on
the five staffs.

It is in this context that the historic enmity of Brahmsians for
Wagnerites, and vice versa, needs to be understood. It was not the music
as such, but the diversion of the music from the "legitimate" purposes of
the Beethoven tradition to new and unmentionable ones that so enraged
Hanslick and others. For the "absolute" musician, the composer of chamber music, serenades, symphonies, and piano scores, music has no purpose beyond itself. While the famous "feud," like many others in the
world of art (and of politics) was probably overpublicized, it reflected a
profound philosophical disagreement. It is now history, but it still serves
to suggest how the work of two masters can represent the deep duality
within one society that nurtured them both.

RICHARD STRAUSS

Of the fifteen operas composed by Richard Strauss, we can be sure that
three (or perhaps four) are indispensable to any international repertoire.
With the troika, *Salome, Elektra,* and *Rosenkavalier,* the composer made
his outstanding, and probably lasting, contribution. All the remaining
ten works suffer from inferior libretti.

It is generally accepted that the collaboration between Hugo von
Hofmannsthal and Richard Strauss was most fruitful. Extending from
1907, with *Elektra*—actually a finished play when Strauss discovered and
composed for it—until *Arabella,* and Hofmannsthal's death in 1929, the
two produced *Rosenkavalier,* the two versions of *Ariadne, Frau ohne
Schatten,* and *Aegyptische Helena.* Only Romain Rolland doubted that
this was as fortunate a collaboration as everyone claimed. After *Frau ohne
Schatten,* he wrote to Strauss, suggesting that Hofmannsthal's dramaturgy
was more of a hindrance that a help. By that time, Strauss the musician
had already retreated from the road of *Salome* and *Elektra.* Turning to
Viennese comedy and to Molière's era was a counter-move against the
trends shown by Mahler and Schoenberg and indeed by himself in the
two one-act tragedies. Nineteen hundred and nine was the year when he
made his U-turn. It was his respect for Mozart that produced—after

Rosenkavalier—*Ariadne* and then a rewriting of *The Magic Flute*, which was the plan of Hofmannsthal and the composer. Among his other homages to Mozart was his scoring for three women's voices. His own characters, Elektra, Chrysothemis, and Klytemnästra; Marschallin, Octavian, and Sophie; Ariadne, Composer, and Zerbinetta; Kaiserin, Farberin, and Amme, are all modeled on Mozart's own Countess, Susanna, and Cherubino; Anna, Elvira, and Zerlina; Fiordiligi, Dorabella, and Despina. Octavian and the Young Composer are also in the tradition of Cherubino—the very young man, full of passion, half *roué*, half innocent. Sailing under this bland "Return to the Golden Age of Mozart" flag, Strauss employed his ever-present, superb technique of composition to write an admirable work for a combination of *Bourgeois Gentilhomme* and *Ariadne* and, later, a new prologue replacing Molière's comedy. Hofmannsthal and Max Reinhardt visualized the Molière play in Hofmannsthal's German version, with the incidental music, ending with a party *chez* Jourdain at which a whole opera, *Ariadne auf Naxos*, would be performed. This plan was not a success, owing to the inherent incompatibility of theater and opera lovers. The first had no wish to hear ninety minutes of opera after two-and-a-half hours of spoken comedy; the second were uninterested in sitting through two-and-a-half hours of spoken comedy, in order to hear ninety minutes of singing. Hence the later (1916) version with the new Prologue, which also created the Young Composer, as endearing a figure as Cherubino.

Die Aegyptische Helena opens with the premise that the audience is familiar with several versions of the Trojan War. Its libretto is as difficult to summarize as *Il Trovatore*, with music that is not equal to Verdi's. *Arabella*, finally, is an attempt to find a sequel to *Rosenkavalier*, and it has had the fate of most sequels: indifferent reception. The premise that a young man, having obtained the key to a desired lady's bedroom, has a fine time without ever discovering that he is sleeping with someone else may be hilarious in a French farce. In this opera, with the action taking place behind closed curtains, behind the stage set, and during an orchestral prelude that is as weak a piece as the composer wrote, the results are embarrassing. It becomes yet worse when it is compared with its equivalent: act 1 of *Rosenkavalier*, with its "first night" between Octavian and the Marschallin.

Next came *Die schweigsame Frau,* a comedy with millions of notes that went nowhere. Strauss's final four operas, *Friedenstag, Daphne, Liebe der Danae,* and *Capriccio* had only one common denominator: non-theatrical plots. *Capriccio,* a "Konversationsstück" with a book by the conductor Clemens Krauss, was the most successful, simply because it was *sui generis,* making no claim of exceptional dramatic achievement. This work remains a fine essay on the interrelation and interdependence of words and music in opera, a unique old-age credo by a great master who earned the right to close fifteen operas with an elaborate soliloquy.

When Strauss produced *Salome* from a German translation of Oscar Wilde's play, he accomplished the extraordinary feat of emancipating himself from Wagner, while still including special Wagnerian elements. Combining theft, murder, breach of contract, and incest, he added some newly minted perversions of his own, including necrophilia, and he opened up the theme of sacrilege. The action starts with a look at a homosexual page, jealous of Narraboth's infatuation with Salome. Aside from her advances to the prophet, she is ogled and propositioned by her stepfather in the presence of her mother, who, haranguing her husband, reveals that he is the son of a camel driver and thief. An anecdote has a London subscriber turning to her neighbor at the point when Herodias and Herod bellow insults at each other, commenting: "How unlike the home-life of our own dear Queen!" With this lurid titillation came music that lasted from start to finish less time than the longest act of Wagner. Strauss had applied the lesson that orchestral compositions should not be in four movements but in one, which made him the *non plus ultra* of the symphonic poem, before he embarked with the same idea of condensation on opera: it need not have three acts; one was enough. After *Elektra,* which includes matricide among other post-Wagnerian themes, and which also confirmed the composer's genius, he applied some kind of brake, as suggested earlier, and moved away from such subjects.

THE TWENTIETH CENTURY

No other composer of German opera was able to shake the shadow of Wagner; three of them—Schreker, Korngold, and Pfitzner—wrote between them at least another fifteen operas, of which none comes near

Strauss's vital works. Schreker and Korngold had also found the need to incorporate unusual erotic titillation, but, easy to say in hindsight, it was all too obviously calculated, rather like some of the more questionable periodicals that hover between literature and pornography. Music for such texts cannot be sustained for long without becoming cloying.

Pfitzner went in the opposite direction, avoiding eros in most of his compositions. His *Palestrina,* subtitled "a musical legend," may be thought to represent the prototypical "vin du pays" opera. It dates from 1917, was conducted on its first night in Munich by Bruno Walter, and has since been included in the repertoire of all the larger German houses, but only for a handful of performances each year. In my student days, in Vienna's State Opera, it was given twice each season, before a half-full house, with priests and music students replacing subscribers. While in Vienna I never missed a production of *Palestrina,* and I had one of the great thrills of my long musical career when I conducted the work in the same house, where, forty-one years earlier, I had stood for the entire four-and-a-half hour performance seventy-five feet behind the conductor's podium.

The strength of the work lies in the contrast between the inner life of the artist, symbolized by Giovanni Pierluigi's struggle to compose, and the cold response prevailing at the Council of Trent, where the composition, commissioned to save the true church music from decline into banality, receives a one-sentence mention, when Borromeo says "Die Messe wird geschrieben."

The high point is reached late in act 1, when Pierluigi, left alone after a grievous misunderstanding with Borromeo, is visited by nine dead masters of music—from Josquin des Près on—who, in a sublime scene, inspire him to write the mass. For me and for a tiny group of sympathizers, this half of the act with the nine masters, followed by the onstage composition of the mass, constitutes a truly "memorable" moment in opera. The balance, consisting of at least another two hours of music, has no more than a few fleeting passages of extraordinary quality, and I know that my devotion is unlikely to be translated and played in international revivals; the work is strictly for parochial consumption.

Surveying the German repertoire, it appears that Wagner led it into a cul-de-sac, from which it was rescued by the social revolution, following the First World War. Alban Berg's *Wozzeck* and Kurt Weill's *The*

Threepenny Opera were not only filled with genius and contemporary significance, they pointed the way to a vital musical theater, without ties to the previous century. The year 1933 and the incoming Nazi tyranny ended not only the Weimar Republic, it stymied the best creative talents, or forced them into an exile where they could not function without abandoning their principal interests; Weill is one prime example. Germany was not the only country hostile to these new ideas and sounds. Other countries also became artistically conservative, through a strong draft of crass mercantilism that had room for neither the experiments, nor for the social critique found in these new works. The Third Reich, during its twelve years, killed German opera, just as Napoleon had killed *opera seria*, but while one acted from humanitarian motives, the other effectively crushed freedom of expression.

It can be no coincidence that Schoenberg's *Moses and Aaron* and Alban Berg's *Lulu* remained fragments. They could be final, yet incomplete, "torsos" of an era spanning 154 years, from *Entführung* to the death of Berg. If I do not take into account the labors of Cerha, who finished act 3 of *Lulu*, this is neither inadvertent nor meant to be censorious. The significant fact is that the composer did not, or could not, finish his work.

THE LATINS

The international opera circuit today resembles an informal cartel, presenting more or less the same leading singers, conductors, designers, and directors and, with some considerations of local pressures, the same basic repertoire. No more than twenty German works return regularly, of which ten are by Wagner. A count of French works, with *Carmen* and *Faust* as flagships, would hardly reach ten titles. There is no French composer equal to either of the giants, Verdi and Wagner. The problem is compounded by the notorious difficulty of singing in French, which, unlike the other major opera languages, German and Italian, has never been mastered by foreigners. Since French composers chose some of the greatest literary masterpieces for their libretti, the poor quality of that repertoire cannot be caused by inferior plays; indeed, it may be caused by the opposite: composers were too ambitious, and chose subjects above their creative capabilities. Ambroise Thomas went "right to the top of

Olympus," using *Hamlet*, and Goethe's novel *Wilhelm Meister* for *Mignon*. Massenet also used Goethe's *Werther* and composed a *Don Quixote*. Goethe's *Faust* seems to have been more accommodating; Berlioz did it nobly, though with a caveat, calling the piece an opera-oratorio; its success lies in this latter guise. Gounod, whose *Faust* has remained an international hit, also composed *Romeo*, which, like Bellini's, cannot be accepted by Shakespeare readers, since the poetry of the author's verses becomes laughable when Juliet starts in on roulades and cadenzas. Such *coloratura* is easily associated with frivolity, which makes a Manon acceptable, and a Juliet unacceptable. *Samson and Delilah* will be with us as long and as often as there is a popular contralto who fancies herself a Mata Hari. Aside from the difficulties of singing French, the basic problem of the repertoire seems to be the ambivalence of composers like Gounod, Massenet, and Thomas, who hover constantly over an imaginary fence that divides opera from operetta. Jacques Offenbach gave us a masterpiece in *The Tales of Hoffmann*, but for the rest of his life stayed with the lighter genre where he was not only more at home, but where he achieved an unparalleled, long success, extending far beyond the borders of France.

Verdi, to date, is the only composer capable of matching Shakespeare's genius when using his plays. Even Wagner only once adopted a Shakespeare piece, *Measure for Measure*, for *Liebesverbot*. With unfailing instinct he left the bard alone after that. Altogether, Verdi's selections are first-rate plays, but it took him time to grow until he became the peer, not only of Shakespeare but of Schiller as well. *Die Jungfrau von Orleans* was used for *Giovanna d'Arco* (rarely if ever revived today); *Die Räuber* for *I masnadieri* (again, rarely played now); *Kabale und Liebe* (*Luisa Miller*) was brought back in several major houses, including the Metropolitan in New York. Finally, with Verdi's 1867 *Don Carlos* we find the supreme master.

The Shakespeare-Verdi connection needs little comment. In 1847, Verdi learned from the Florentine impresario who had commissioned him that the roster consisted of several well-known singers, yet lacked a first tenor. Familiar with the virtues and deficiencies of available talent, he decided that the libretto could not be based on a love story, so he and the librettist arrived at the decision to try *Macbeth*. He was only thirty-four then, and, after tackling Shakespeare once, he waited decades before attempting *Otello* and *Falstaff*. For those later works he had a great collaborator in Arrigo Boito; it may be heresy to suggest that he, a composer, made better libretti than many professional writers. From even this small selection of great books adapted as opera texts, there is only one conclusion to be drawn: great plays and great novels do not great composers make.

Since major opera houses today perform regularly at least twice as many Italian operas as German and French operas combined, and since certain of the musical scores are pot-boilers of the most banal type (by popular composers Ponchielli, Leoncavallo, Mascagni, and Giordano), some criterion other than excellence must explain why they survive, and why they retain the loyalty of a large public. Perhaps Puccini's great triumphs, and the constant showing of some of his works may provide a clue to the nature of irresistible operatic plots. As language *per se* loses meaning for the public, through larger auditoriums and the growing orchestral role, distorting or concealing the words, the visual understanding of the situations onstage becomes all the more important. Exotic settings, as in *Madama Butterfly* and in *Turandot* (perhaps even the Far West in *La Fanciulla del West*), give at once a visual message, answering at least one question: Where are we? It is a moot point whether *Aïda's dramatis personae* were invented to celebrate the Suez Canal, or whether Verdi felt that the visual contrast of Copts and black Ethiopians would stress visual over linguistic communication. Yet, visual confusion, to illustrate the other side of the issue, has prevented some of the most glorious Verdi scores from achieving their deserved status with the public. Without having read the libretto carefully, one finds it impossible to follow the relationship between the young Boccanegra and Fiesco. It is even more difficult to suspend disbelief when Alvaro "disarming himself, throws away his pistol which accidentally kills the Marchese."

Opera fans of my generation, and of an earlier time, will recall that for many years fewer Verdi operas were performed than is now the case. It took several determined artists, among them the author Franz Werfel, to open the stages of internationally oriented houses to more than six to eight Verdi pieces. The inconclusive evidence of longevity is illustrated by a comparison of Verdi's operas regularly performed sixty years ago, with those produced today. At that time, there was no regular showing of *Macbeth*, *Ernani*, *Vespri Siciliani*, or *Luisa Miller* and, in Vienna, no *Forza*, no *Simon Boccanegra* or *Don Carlos*, which had to await the imprimatur of Franz Werfel's translations and adaptations to be accepted for performance. Incredible as it may seem in 1986, it required enterprising managers to extend the Verdi repertoire beyond the four works that have been and remain today as popular and well known as any music can ever be: *La Traviata*, *Rigoletto*, *Il Trovatore*, and *Aïda*.

INTERNATIONAL OPERA

The process of enlarging the repertoire started in the 1930s, when air transport began gradually to change the rules and problems of casting opera. When a Bulgarian tenor was discovered by an enterprising agent from Germany, where most repertoire houses are located, and where the largest number of singers are needed, he had to learn his roles in German, or in any one of the twenty languages that were the rule in European opera lore. In the *Annals* one can read precisely when *Tosca* was translated into Lithuanian, Hebrew, and eighteen other languages between 1902 and 1925. If the tenor was good, he would discover that his German Manrico was useless for La Scala, the Palais Garnier, or the Metropolitan. With ease of transport, however, performances in the original language became a matter of course. A few festivals began to do their casting from several countries, and they performed those works that previously had been done in the vernacular in Italian. Salzburg was among the first to perform Mozart with an international cast of singers. The system soon spread to regular winter seasons. Its combination of practicality, convenience, and artistic rectitude guaranteed its success. Whether the eloquent pleas for original languages were genuine or not is scarcely germane; vernacular for opera is now the rule only in third-rate provincial companies.

Italian opera, and not only by the masters Verdi and Puccini, has done best during this period of internationalization. The language is by far the most appropriate for *cantabile* (singable) works, and it is easier to pronounce than any of the others. Today, the "elegant" and "snobbish" solution is to sing everything in the original. This reaches a point of absurdity when Russian and Czech works are taught by rote to chorus members and solo singers who have no idea of their meaning. If one does not know a language profoundly and intimately, one cannot color the voice to express the words. Today, the entire question is merely another expression of social stratification: where one finds two companies, the expensive one plays in the original, the less expensive one in translation. Lead singers with major reputations perform in the original; others, in the vernacular. One of the upper echelon's punishments for this insistence on authentic language is the increasing number of high-priced singers, with incomprehensible histrionic vagaries. In the great houses there seems to be no problem of total suspension of disbelief, and priority is placed entirely on vocal prowess. When Tosca will not even pretend to jump, and walks off into the wings, who needs a libretto or a stage director? And when La Scala produces *Eugene Onegin* in the original language with an Italian Tatiana, an American Lensky, and an English Onegin, all under a Japanese conductor, none of them familiar with Russian, it becomes manifestly clear that nobody really cares what the whole piece is about. What then are the role and importance of the third criterion: the quality of the complete score?

THE MUSICAL SCORE

Musicians have always been unhappy with the knowledge that their evaluations of operas as compositions may not be shared by the general public. If we poll a group of professional musicians with the question, "Which Verdi opera is the best composition?" a large majority will vote for *Falstaff*, and a sizable minority for *Otello*. If a similar question is put to regular subscribers of a great opera house, the majority will probably vote for *Aïda*.

For music lovers who have not studied musical composition, it may be difficult to accept that there are judgments that go beyond subjective likes and dislikes. Theoreticians and many musicologists have failed to advance a general awareness that music is composed according to laws, and that it is possible to call a piece better or worse.

Mozart, in a letter to his father written at the time of the composition of *Entführung*, explains how he was aware of his methods, and what their ultimate effects were intended to be. The letter, more enlightening than a hundred pages of criticism, illustrates what the music is intended to express. Mozart writes:

Mon Très Cher Père!   Vienne, ce 26 de Septembre, 1781

Forgive me for having made you pay an extra heavy postage fee the other day. But I happened to have nothing important to tell you and thought that it would afford you pleasure if I gave you some idea of my opera. As the original text began with a monologue, I asked Herr Stephanie to make a little arietta out of it—and then to put in a duet instead of making the two chatter together after Osmin's short song. As we have given the part of Osmin to Herr Fischer, who certainly has an excellent bass voice (in spite of the fact that the Archbishop told me that he sang too low for a bass and that I assured him that he would sing higher next time), we must take advantage of it, particularly as he has the whole Viennese public on his side. But in the original libretto Osmin has only this short song and nothing else to sing except in the trio and the finale; so he has been given an aria in act 1, and he is to have another in act 2. I have explained to Stephanie the words I require for this aria—indeed I had finished composing most of the music for it before Stephanie knew anything whatever about it. I am enclosing only the beginning and the end, which is bound to have a good effect. Osmin's rage is rendered comical by the accompaniment of the Turkish music. In working out the aria I have given full scope now and then to Fischer's beautiful deep notes (in spite of our Salzburg Midas). The passage "Drum beim Barte des Propheten" is indeed in the same tempo, but with quick notes; but as Osmin's rage gradually increases, there comes (just when the aria seems to be at an end) the allegro assai, which is in a totally different measure and in a different key; this is bound to be very effective. For just as a man in such a towering rage oversteps all the bounds of order, moderation and propriety and completely forgets himself, so must the music too forget itself.

But as passions, whether violent or not, must never be expressed in such a way as to excite disgust, and as music, even in the most terrible situations, must never offend the ear, but must please the hearer, or in other words must never cease to be *music*, I have gone from F (the key in which the aria is written), not into a remote key, but into a related one, not, however, into its nearest relative D minor, but into the more remote A minor. Let me now turn to Belmonte's aria in A major, "O wie ängstlich, o wie feurig." Would you like to know how I have expressed it—and even indicated his throbbing heart? By the two violins playing octaves. This is the favorite aria of all those who have heard it, and it is mine also. I wrote it expressly to suit Adamberger's voice. You feel the trembling—the faltering—you see how his throbbing breast begins to swell; this I have expressed by a crescendo. You hear the whispering and the sighing—which I have indicated by the first violins with mutes and a flute playing in unison.

The Janissary chorus is, as such, all that can be desired, that is, short, lively, and written to please the Viennese. I have sacrificed Constanze's aria a little to the flexible throat of Mlle. Cavalieri, "Trennung war mein banges Los und nun schwimmt mein Aug' in Tränen." I have tried to express her feelings, as far as an Italian bravura aria will allow it. I have changed the "Hui" to "schnell," so it now runs thus—"Doch wie schnell schwand meine Freude." I really don't know what our German poets are thinking of. Even if they do not understand the theater, or at all events operas, yet they should not make their characters talk as if they were addressing a herd of swine. Hui, sow!

Now for the trio at the close of act 1. Pedrillo has passed off his master as an architect—to give him an opportunity of meeting his Constanze in the garden. Bassa Selim has taken him into his service. Osmin, the steward, knows nothing of this, and being a rude churl and a sworn foe to all strangers, is impertinent and refuses to let them into the garden. It opens quite abruptly—and because the words lend themselves to it, I have made it a fairly respectable piece of real three-part writing.

Then the major key begins at once pianissimo—it must go very quickly—and wind up with a great deal of noise, which is always appropriate at the end of an act. The more noise the better, and the shorter the better, so that the audience may not have time to cool down with their applause.

I have sent you only fourteen measures of the overture, which is very short with alternate fortes and pianos, the Turkish music always coming in at the fortes. The overture modulates through different keys; and I doubt whether anyone, even if his previous night has been a sleepless one, could go to sleep over it. Now comes the rub! The first act was finished more than three weeks ago, as was also one aria in act 2 and the drunken duet (*per i signori viennesi*) which consists entirely of my *Turkish tattoo*. But I cannot compose any more, because the whole story is being altered—and, to tell the truth, at my own request. At the beginning of act 3 there is a charming quintet or rather finale, but I should prefer to have it at the end of act 2. In order to make this practicable, great changes must be made, in fact an entirely new plot must be introduced—and Stephanie is up to the eyes in other work. So we must have a little patience.[3]

Nobody can decide why one listener finds the aria of Leonora in *Il Trovatore* known as "Miserere" superior or more memorable than "Pace, pace mio Dio," which is also sung by Leonora in *La forza del destino*. No attempt along these lines is possible. One can, however, explain why one piece is a better composition than another. An aria consisting of a melodic line given to the voice, accompanied by appropriate harmonies in orchestral passages consisting of arpeggios (*Pace, pace*), or of a constant exciting rhythmic pattern (*Di quella pira*), or by instruments following the voice in unison, is inferior as a composition to one that has obbligato solo passages in one or more instruments. Mozart has "Martern aller Arten" accompanied by a quartet of four solo instruments and the

3 "Mozart to his Father," *The Letters of Mozart*, vol. 1, 2nd ed., trans. Emily Anderson (London: Macmillan, 1938). Reproduced by permission of Macmillan, London and Basingstoke.

full orchestra; in *Figaro* several pieces feature wind soli; a clarinet solo competes with Cherubino's voice; oboe and bassoon with the Countess and Susanna in the letter duet; three woodwinds are interwoven in Susanna's "Deh vieni, non tardar." Zerlina in *Don Giovanni* is accompanied by a much feared and respected cello solo, and in *The Magic Flute* the magical instrument is "played" by Tamino while he pauses in his singing. A list of similar pieces, distinguished by an intimate competition of voice and instrument(s) could also be mentioned. Such compositions are, all things being equal, superior to the voice with vamp only. Verdi used the obbligato instrument to telling effect in "Corteggiani, vil razza," a bravura cello solo, and again in "Dormirò sol" (*Don Carlos*). In ensemble composition, the level of artful voice setting depends on the diversity, and variety, given to the ensemble members. The sextet in *Lucia* is less involved and less sophisticated than the quintet in *Meistersinger*. As composition the latter is superior to the former, though Donizetti has found an unforgettable tune that can be whistled or sung without any accompaniment, an impossibility with the quintet music of Wagner, who works instruments in with voices in such a way that any attempt to do it *a cappella* is unsuccessful.

For the first decades of nineteenth-century opera, the continuity alternates between recitative and set pieces. Later, the recitative with keyboard accompaniment disappeared, and more care was taken to do something dramatically significant with the passages between set-pieces. Here lies the great quality difference between the masters and the journeymen.

If one wished to study this particular development at its most stunning, one need only follow the chronological progression of Verdi's compositions. With *Falstaff,* his final piece, he reached a seamless continuity rare in any composer's operas. There is no distinction between set pieces and recitative. While one can make the same claim of smooth continuity lasting two-and-a-half hours for *Rheingold,* it consists only of recitative, with hardly any *melos* rising above declamation. In contrast, *Falstaff* is an amalgamation of the two basic elements that have defined opera for nearly three hundred years.

Parsifal is perhaps Wagner's most seamless work. Nothing can be excerpted; even the Prelude needs some concocted ending for concert

use, and the famous "Good Friday spell" is an arrangement and condensation of the scene, minus the voices of the two singers. The long score
is a continuous composition, with that uncanny mixture of declamatory
and arioso treatment of the voice parts. Notwithstanding the wide gap
between *Falstaff*, a Shakespearean comedy, and the *Bühnenweihfestspiel*
(Wagner's title, meaning a sacramental stage festival play), both composers paid for the seamless continuity with the loss of genuine inven-
tions for solo or ensemble numbers. A parallel can be found in nature:
a *Trovatore* or a *Tristan* resemble alternating peaks and valleys, while the
seamless masterpieces mentioned proceed like a mesa on a high, exquisite plateau, with hardly an apex anywhere. Debussy's *Pelléas et Mélisande*
belongs to this small and exclusive club, only more radically so, through
its avoidance of any set pieces and ensembles.

The final fugue in *Falstaff*, Verdi's "calling-card" showing that he
could also emulate Bach when he wanted, is, like the final septet of *Don
Giovanni*, a coda without dramatic significance. A dramatic ensemble,
probably never equaled, is the finale of act 2 in Mozart's *Figaro*: here
every portion of the fifteen-minute piece is marked by an increment in
the vocals, from duet to septet, via trio and quartet, and all the while the
action is advanced. This portion stands in splendid isolation, since most
other great ensemble pieces take place when the action is halted. A small
selection of the best ensemble compositions in opera would include
everything by Mozart, the Canon in *Fidelio*, the prestissimo in *l'Italiana
in Algeri*, the quartet in *Rigoletto*, the trio in *Rosenkavalier*, the *Meistersinger* quintet, the scene of the nine masters in act 1 of *Palestrina*, several
large ensembles in Verdi's works, and especially the triumphal scene from
Aïda, where three sharply profiled themes (the chant of the priests, the
triumphal march, and the soaring cantilena of the high solo voices) are
joined in a masterly counterpoint, quite similar to the moment in the
prelude to the *Meistersinger* where three themes appear together in a
splendid climax. It is often mentioned with some acerbity that musicians
of German background extol polyphonic composition beyond reason.
True or false, the examples from Verdi's operas show that an Italian master
of genius found polyphony an appropriate climax on several occasions.

Avoiding technical language, opera composition consists of inventing highlights of a memorable character, with "stuffing" in between.

More and better highlights will be popular in wider circles, and assure a longer life to an opera as a whole. The quality of the stuffing is more dependent on the libretto than on the musical inventiveness of the composer. The best example of that thesis can be found in Richard Strauss. His supreme facility with notes enabled him to make appropriate sounds with very little substance. In his three major works, stuffing escapes undue notice thanks to the brevity of the one-act plays *Salome* and *Elektra*, and in *Rosenkavalier* by the continuous charm and humor of the stage action. Indeed, Strauss probably has the largest amount of stuffing in his stage works, compared to the other prominent composers of the era. Wagner, too, depends on filler music, particularly in expository scenes of the *Ring*: Wotan's long narration in act 2, *Walküre*, the two Alberich scenes in *Siegfried* and *Götterdämmerung*, and the Gibichungen scene prior to Siegfried's arrival. Quite different in compositorial value and art are the expository scenes in act 1 of *Siegfried* (Wanderer-Mime), and the Norns in the Prologue of *Götterdämmerung*.

SOME CONCLUDING REMARKS

If the panorama of nineteenth-century opera shows a puzzling contrast between the German and Latin sides, it is probably due to two developments: an unparalleled wealth of instrumental music in sonata and symphony, emphasizing chamber music ever more and, connected with it, the fast growth of the piano as an indispensable part of a bourgeois household. This put a premium on the production of vocal chamber music, otherwise known as the lied. German composers wrote more lieder and fewer operas. The four eminent masters of the lied, Schubert, Schumann, Brahms, and Wolf, could not create between them one opera that lived; Brahms never even tried. Poets of the romantic era produced irresistible verses, and the musical emphasis on home activity contributed to an avalanche of great songs from those four composers and from lesser masters.

Chamber music, and even orchestral symphonies, did not seem to have taken up much time of Italian and French composers. Only toward the end of the century, when the great poets Baudelaire, Verlaine, Mallarmé, et al. made their impact, did *chansons* by Duparc, Debussy,

Ravel, and Poulenc appear. Here too, the song composers did not excel particularly in opera. A lied (or chanson), accompanied by one keyboard instrument, is vocal chamber music when compared to the demands made on opera singing. Just as the great lieder creators did not find opera congenial, so does the reverse hold true: hardly any songs were composed by the Italian masters of the *teatro lirico*.

Writing music for the voice is then the central issue. Since all vocal music must act symbiotically with the words, vocal style is influenced, if not to say inspired, by the type of text before the composer. As the German romantic composers drew from the poets Goethe, Mörike, Eichendorff, and others, as their song cycles became available in music stores for the pleasure of *Hausmusik*, Mozart's *teutsche Oper* (or *Singspiel*) entered the amusement sector of the music establishment, and became operetta. Here we come full circle in demonstrating why only three or four specimens of that genre survived by dint of the names Mozart, Beethoven, and, to a lesser degree, Weber.

This split, placing the "serious" composers of the German orbit into the camp of instrumental and vocal chamber music, never occurred on the Italian side of the Alps. Perhaps the curious preference of Latin composers for German drama and Goethe novels was due to the fact that in Germany the classics, such as Schiller and Shakespeare, were virtually part of everyday drama repertoire, hence composers neither needed, nor dared, to rely on plays that had a vitality of their own. The verse plays were presented in a style that was heightened recitation, not too far from pitched singing. I remember the actors who played "die jungen Helden"—the young heroes—Max Piccolomini, Mortimer, and Marquis Posa with stentorian exertions, projecting the noblest sentiments of their roles. Only ideal Italian tenors could be selected to make a similar impact on an audience. Italian opera never experienced any "defections" from important composers. There is no symphonic repertoire, nor chamber music out of Italy, and anyone looking for Italian contributions must go back to the baroque era when Vivaldi and others flooded the music world with an encyclopedic variety of pleasant musical entertainment. Both *opera seria* and *opera buffa* continued, undisturbed by the schism, into the nineteenth century and, as we see today, have lasted better than the more problematic German repertoire.

The lack of a strong representation of Slavic operas on the international stage stems from the same parochialism that derailed the German *Singspiel*. Three Smetana operas were popular for a time, particularly in Vienna, where Mahler favored Smetana's *Bartered Bride*. But by 1950, the only occasional representatives of the Slavic orbit were Moussorgsky's *Boris Godunov*, and its revisions, and the Tchaikovsky operas, because of the composer's recognizable magic touch.

International survival of any operative work, regardless of its standard and rating by experts, depends most on the quality of its memorable moments. The total composition is of concern only to the professionals and others who are musically initiated. The importance of the libretto, however, has declined over generations of spectators who no longer find it compelling to participate emotionally in Rigoletto's grief or in Cio-Cio-San's tragedy.

Modern stage directors indulge in philosophical, cultural, sociological, and political prefaces, statements, and interviews to explain what Mozart, Wagner, or Puccini "meant." All these *obiter dicta*—*if* taken seriously—aim to reinvolve a public that has lost the identification and compassion indispensable to opera if it is to be the total experience it was intended to be. There are many sublime scores, and many attractive scores, which, given the right treatment, would bring the public back into the environment out of which each of these works emerged.

Conducting the New York Philharmonic (27 April 1989).

Receiving a helping hand with the score for David del Tredici's *Final Alice*.

The hands of the maestro.   © Luigi Pellettieri.

Erich Leinsdorf.   © Lisl Steiner.

In Leningrad, talking with Russian students (1976).

The New York Philharmonic rehearses in Leningrad.

Erich Leinsdorf rehearses Mozart's Concerto for three pianos, with Rudolf Fikursny and Carlos Moseley.

Leinsdorf, Rudolf Fikursny, and Carlos Moseley leaving the stage after playing Mozart's Concerto for three pianos.

In rehearsal.

Photograph: Anthony Crickmay.
From the collections of the Theatre Museum, V&A.

In rehearsal.

Rehearsing for *Ariadne auf Naxos* at Carnegie Hall, with Sandor Konya, Claire Watson, Beverly Sills, and John Reardon (18 January 1968).

At Tanglewood, beckoning the soloists to take their bows.

Erich Leinsdorf conducting.
A Ramon Scavelli photograph.

Erich Leinsdorf.   Robert M. Lightfoot III.

Six

Aspects of the Symphony

The Symphony as Social Phenomenon

I believe that American music institutions have remained virtually static since around 1936. Having apparently lost their taste for the open seas of innovation and discovery, they have been content to remain safely anchored at their comfortable moorings.

By 1936 the major orchestras of the United States had become the equals, in terms of ability and stature, of any comparable music ensemble in the world. American opera, from New York to San Francisco, had benefited from the discovery of several great singers; a substantial influx of cultured refugees from Europe had augmented American concert audiences; and many accomplished composers (such as Arnold Schoenberg), writers, and performers had chosen to live in the atmosphere of personal freedom offered by the United States. Few, however, seemed aware that a summit had been reached, and that consequently the only way back was downward. Even the ensuing years of war sometimes seemed like a boom time for the entire entertainment industry.

Few people seemed to be worrying too much about the future, notwithstanding the notorious and rather tragicomic exchange between Arnold Schoenberg and the author Thomas Mann. In his 1947 novel *Doktor Faustus*, Mann credited his fictional hero, Adrian Leverkühn, with the invention of the twelve-tone method of composition. Schoenberg accused Mann of having endangered his (Schoenberg's) posthumous reputation by not crediting him with the invention of the system. Mann replied, in his best ironic style, that the next edition of his book would be dedicated "To A. S., the real one" (*Dem Eigentlichen*).

It seems that even after 1945, when life gradually began to return to what is often rather euphemistically termed a "normal" state, very few senior representatives of the U.S. concert scene noticed that a "funny thing was happening" at the box office (and indeed at the record store). It was happening, nonetheless. Young people had begun to hunt for Vivaldi, not Tchaikovsky, for Landowska, not Rubinstein, for consorts, not philharmonics, and for a viola da gamba, not a cello. In short, they wanted pre-1800 music.

If this phenomenon was indeed observed by the councils of the symphony boards, nobody did much about it. No one, apparently, did anything to render the offerings of the symphonic societies more attractive to the younger generation, which made the greatest financial contribution to the classical music season and which had all but turned its back on the music of the nineteenth century. In fact, if any clear policy can be identified at all, it went rather in the opposite direction. Conductors fell over each other to put on the blockbusters of Bruckner, Mahler, and Shostakovich, the mammoth productions of Berlioz, Schoenberg's post-Wagnerian *Gurre-Lieder*, and the marathon mysteries of Messiaen. It was as if the survival of the symphony could be assured only by hypertrophied displays of romanticism. It is worth remembering in this respect that those post-1900 works that were still included in the basic classical repertoire were—in style, manner, and harmony—either identical to or highly derivative of late nineteenth-century scores.

That the leaders of the music establishment should have become distracted from the long-term picture is in some respects unsurprising. During the immediate postwar years there were certainly many short-term concerns that were more pressing. Fundraising, for example, had to be totally reorganized. Its focus had to be shifted away from the donations of financially hard-pressed individual sponsors and toward the contributions of corporations and wealthy private individuals. That reorganization required new staff, and budgets rose in consequence. Then the year-round musicians' contract was introduced. This contract was (and still is) a very costly institution, and one that failed to reflect the real level of demand during longer seasons.

These developments must at least have been on the agenda of board meetings and managers' conventions. The American Symphony Orchestra League certainly responded as it should—providing a wealth of services, publicity, and statistics. All the while something else was happening. Apparently unnoticed by board members and managers alike, a veritable avalanche of "new" compositions was on its way. The early music movement and its exponents were swiftly taken up by ad hoc groups, which shrewdly secured their public appeal through innumerable recordings. Yet, something was amiss.

The world's music libraries are crammed with the works of seventeenth- and eighteenth-century composers whose names should not even be mentioned in the same breath as Bach, Handel, or even Vivaldi. The works of these composers are wholly unoriginal, and yet we were suddenly assailed by hundreds of concertos, cassations, serenades, *Tafelmusiken*, sarabandes, courantes, gigues, and other solo pieces for wind instruments. These pieces, which possess virtually no genuine substance or musical invention, are yet unfailingly charming to the ear when played by a new generation of skilled brass and woodwind virtuosos.

In my (evidently heretical) opinion, this phenomenon is neither memorable nor courageous. The music played is mostly predictable, undistinguished, and routine—background music that passes the time pleasantly enough when you have other things to do. This music generally turns up in symphony programs only when it is time to feature the orchestra's piccolo player. At such times the audience is generally regaled with a Vivaldi concerto or (when the conductor gets seriously radical) a concerto for mandolin or four harpsichords. The "modernist" repertoire has met a similar fate. It is generally left to specialized enterprises such as "composers' alliances" or "new-music societies" and makes only an occasional appearance in the first half of subscription programs (always countered in the second half, of course, by a famous popular soloist play-ing a famous popular concerto).

It is an indisputable fact that scores composed during the period 1760–1910 (broadly speaking, from Haydn to Mahler) were created, per-formed, and/or published to meet public demand. Instrumental music composed during this period came primarily from north of the Alps, vocal music for the lyric stage primarily from the southern side. It is also a fact that genuine demand for new symphonies and new operas abated as Europe was plunged into the Great War of 1914–18.

The United States imported primarily symphonic music and formed symphony orchestras that could be maintained without government funding. Opera, a much more expensive affair, was limited to New York's Metropolitan Opera. San Francisco and Chicago enjoyed the odd moment of glory, but were largely dependent upon the generosity of a few very wealthy people. In America, both opera and symphony were founded largely upon music whose validity had already been seriously questioned by around 1907. That was the year in which Schoenberg wrote his String Quartet No. 2, the composition that marked the defini-tive transition from extended chromatic tonality to atonality.

Alban Berg, in his lecture introducing *Wozzeck* to German provin-cial opera subscribers, wrote that in his view atonality was only valid for small pieces, and that the longer musical forms—opera, oratorio, and the symphony—needed the central pillar of tonality (or, as he then proposed for *Wozzeck*, at least the replacement of that center pillar by something else). If the composition of symphonies became impossible without tonality, what happened to tonality after 1900? It is quite likely that every composer, musician, musicologist, and critic will have a different explanation for this. I should like to submit two (not necessarily original) explanations of my own.

The first explanation is musical. The ecstasies and excesses of passion (erotic or religious) were best expressed in music that was multi-directional. Such music was not used, however, until around the time of Wagner's *Tristan und Isolde* (1859) and required the diminished seventh chord—a piling up of three minor thirds whose flexibility is such that a simple half-tone shift in one of the four tones can establish several tonalities. The resultant chromatic harmony is like the *étoile* of Paris and

Washington town planning: a roundabout that permits travel in several directions. The classic diatonic harmony, in contrast, is like a straight road along which the composition travels and then returns (exposition of two themes—reprise of exposition (varied)—concluding coda).

Bach rarely used the diminished seventh, and then only to express something complex and negative. In his Cantata No. 102 ("Herr, deine Augen sehen nach dem Glauben"), the first time the text speaks of "betrübte Schatten" (sorrowful shadows) the syllable *trüb* is sung over a diminished seventh. The opening of the last piano sonata by Beethoven (No. 32 in C minor, Op. 111) is another of the many illustrations of how powerful this harmony can be, if used sparingly; however, Liszt, for example, later used the device so freely that it became unbearably banal. The form and underlying spirit of the symphony is just not well served by this gateway to chromatic variety, which is best suited for dramatic music (for opera, orchestra, or chamber ensemble).

It is no secret that, between *Tristan und Isolde* (1859) and the period of Mahler and the Schoenberg school, the development of music was characterized by a trend toward the expression of the ecstatic and the extreme. Consider Brahms and Wagner. Those who feel that music's greatest moments are from the classical symphonic tradition are essentially Brahmsians. Here is bourgeois music in the tradition of Beethoven's positive, optimistic, heroic, and often humorous rhetoric. Wagnerites, on the other hand, are transfixed by music's appeal to man's hidden, antisocial, even criminal drives. Here are all the questionable vices and aberrations, the transgressions of the legal code and the moral consensus. The chromatic tradition gives us adultery, incest, and matricide (*Elektra*); necrophilia (*Salome*); and other, similar delights. César Franck's chromatically inclined *Symphony*, by the way, is pitched somewhere in between the two great traditions, achieving a kitsch that I find rather attractive.

My second explanation is political, and concerns the collapse of Europe's aristocratic hegemony in the wake of the First World War. The entire upper echelon of symphonic and concerto composers lived in cities and countries ruled by the Habsburgs, Hohenzollerns, Wittelsbachs, Romanovs, and the lesser principalities of Central Europe. In Italy the music world was structured somewhat differently, being centered upon opera, but it, too, collapsed in 1918. The consequence of this was that music composition became fragmented, splintering off in several distinct directions. The trend toward fragmentation was favored by the creation of the Weimar Republic and the states created by the western Allies. The 1920s pitted Schoenberg against Stravinsky just as Wagner had been pitted against Brahms. Those young people who have in recent years escaped into the appreciation of baroque and pre-classic music find Stravinsky more appealing. Like the collapse of the old political order, the collapse of tonality and the symphony were so dramatic in their effects that even today those effects have still not yet been fully absorbed. What has driven young people away from the music of that glorious century that began with Beethoven and ended 113 years later with Stravinsky's *Rite of Spring*?

There is an important link between the music of the eighteenth century and those of Stravinsky's works that were composed after his three great ballet scores. With Stravinsky's later works, music was no longer "connected" in the sense that it had been since the French Revolution. By "connected," I mean that which is written to be understood, enjoyed, and appreciated only by a limited constituency of highly educated people who can associate a great composer's work with the rhetoric, the poetry, the pictures, the architecture, and all the other cultural factors influencing a score.

Except for a few exceptionally vital works, the symphonic form has been largely dormant since Mahler. I have performed, with conviction and pleasure, symphonies by Prokofiev and Shostakovich. Whereas the works of those composers are essentially imitative of what has gone before, those of Stravinsky are new and contemporary. I have also performed (in this case with more pleasure than conviction) the symphonies of Bohuslav Martinu. I do not consider Martinu to be imitative in the sense of the Russians Prokofiev and Shostakovich; the British composers Arnold Bax, Arthur Bliss, William Walton, Sir Michael Tippett, Sir Edward Elgar, and Ralph Vaughan-Williams; or the Scandinavian Carl Nielsen. Like Igor Stravinsky, Martinu sought to write "unconnected" symphonic works, but Martinu did not have Stravinsky's "ear," and so his orchestral scores lacked any real variety. In this respect he was like Bruckner (with the obvious difference that Bruckner's appeal, though still limited, owes much to his moving affinity with Catholic mysticism).

I should make it clear at this point that I wholeheartedly reject the notion that the German school of composition is the only true school. That is a view propounded in Berlin and Vienna and I will not be associated with it. I know some readers will still insist upon interpreting my previous paragraphs as the snobbish conceit of the Central European, but I promise you that I do not, in any sense, look down upon those composers just mentioned. As a musician who has performed and still performs concerts with symphony orchestras, I have presented a very large and varied repertoire during my career. Like other curious and impatient persons, I have not entirely given up hope that neglected masterpieces will be rediscovered. Indeed, my optimism has frequently been rewarded by the discovery of many attractive, fascinating, and challenging masterpieces, but these works have never been in the form of a symphony.

The symphonic form is clearly defined. Benjamin Britten composed many fine works and Elgar's *Variations* are a masterpiece, but these works do not have the impact of the complete symphonic form. Variations that are independent of larger works are not effective with the public, even if the composer is a great public favorite—consider, for example, the following three masterpieces by celebrated composers: the *Haydn Variations* of Brahms, the *Variations on an Original Theme* by Dvorák, or *Don Quixote* by Richard Strauss.

The symphony is a social phenomenon. In evaluating a symphonic work, one cannot limit oneself to considerations of technique, style, and form. Such an evaluation will rarely reveal, for example, the true reason why one work fails to stand the test of time while a second is welcomed into the basic repertoire. The critic must go beyond a purely academic approach, and the answer he will generally find is that the first work is frankly irrelevant to the public for whom it is played. Here is the essential paradox of the symphonic composition as a social phenomenon: whereas in feudal society composition was free, in modern democratic societies music has been loaded with innumerable premises.

An example of such a premise is the unwritten (but ever-present) demand for "uplifting" or "life-enhancing" music. The bicentennial celebrations of Mozart's death have sent the musicologists scurrying around to explain the Mozart phenomenon, and it seems that every composition must be endlessly diagnosed according to the perceived psychological traits of the composer. Nevertheless, a thorough reevaluation of the dramatic social changes wrought by the French Revolution would be infinitely more enlightening in this respect. There is a small and elite club of intellectual giants who lived during the period of the French Revolution and sought to reconcile the theories of the Enlightenment with those of romanticism. Its members include Immanuel Kant, Thomas Jefferson, James Madison, Johann Wolfgang Goethe, Friedrich Schiller, Joseph Haydn, Wolfgang Amadeus Mozart, and Ludwig van Beethoven.

Between 1914 and 1918 the map of Europe was radically redrawn. The worlds of the opera, of the symphony concert, of symphonic institutions themselves, and of many other musical manifestations were similarly shaken to their roots. The ensuing interregnum of the Weimar Republic was all too brief, and its horrors clearly were neither enlightened nor romantic. Those members of the old musical public who survived the war clung desperately to familiar works, while modern composers resembled a hiking party lost in the forest, with each member of the party heading off in a different direction to hunt for the trail. Confronted with the hesitancy of contemporary composers, alienated by the older tradition to which their parents and grandparents clung so desperately, young people sought refuge in the music of the Enlightenment. They also fled to those modern composers who had correctly diagnosed the passing of Grand Opera and the one-hundred-piece orchestra.

I trust it is not too shocking to certain cultural sensibilities if I compare some of the errors made by American music management to those of the big Detroit automobile manufacturers, who did not understand the trend toward the small, toward reduced consumption, and toward serving a broader range of customers. With the example of Detroit clearly in mind, it is easy enough to guess at the missed opportunities in music. There are many cities in the United States with symphony orchestras of seventy, eighty, or ninety members (the big six or seven engage over one hundred). If only the music management of thirty years or so ago had reduced the size of their orchestras to around fifty players, then we may have avoided the modern crises. Such a move would have been eminently feasible if each city also established a first-rate conservatory that turned out graduate students who could fill in the missing instrumentation if a selection really demanded sixty or seventy players.

The symphonic repertoire can be served perfectly by ensembles well below the hundred-member mark. Not only baroque and pre-1800 music are both well served by wind and brass sections of eight to fourteen members; most orchestras have twenty-four wind and brass players under permanent contract. As for strings, their numbers in concert are optional. The Berlin Philharmonic, which has a larger personnel roster than the major U.S. orchestras, plays most of its regular concerts with fifty strings, compared with around sixty-five in the United States. If this large membership is maintained to cope with an unrelenting program schedule, it is fully justified; however, to keep twenty to thirty players on annual salaries, with only an intermittent need for their services, is musically and financially absurd. There is a vast repertoire of great works by the major composers that requires only a smallish orchestra.

Had there been timely recognition of the trend toward eighteenth-century music and certain modern compositions for chamber orchestra, the current critical situation might well have been avoided. The great orchestras of the United States (and at least ten of these have the potential to be great in a repertoire spanning three centuries) have received little guidance from either their public relations experts or their music directors. Take the Rochester Philharmonic, which at one point functioned successfully by following exactly the recipe outlined above. Columbia Records came to us for a series of classical works after their flagship, the Philadelphia Orchestra, asked to be paid as if the music were scored for 106 musicians. In Rochester the local musicians' union cleverly argued that only the permanent fifty players needed to be paid. Columbia saved money and we also did very well financially. Things changed, of course, in Rochester, and for the usual reason: a lack of understanding from the lay board of directors. Everything fell apart with the death, in 1953, of the one manager who could handle everything.

So it is, in 1990, with the broader picture. How can we cure the current malaise? By addressing the financial crisis, partly through flexible rostering that includes first-rate student players, and partly by winning back the younger audience through a broader cultivation of pre-1800 music, which would reclaim early music (and the financial rewards of playing it) from the consorts and the academies.

When a Symphony Is Not a Symphony

Beethoven's Third and Ninth Symphonies are both blessed by final movements of an unparalleled magnificence. They are so masterful, in fact, that some composers have been noticeably reluctant to attempt their fourth movements—perhaps for fear lest they suffer by comparison. Was it more than just coincidental that Bruckner ended his career without ever having written a traditional fourth movement, or that Mahler, like Bruckner, chose to end his third and ninth symphonies with an adagio?

During the late nineteenth and early twentieth centuries it was a commonly held belief among German musicians that either Beethoven or the Fates had put a hex on anyone planning to write anything beyond a ninth symphony. It is said that Gustav Mahler, in calling his *Das Lied von der Erde* a "symphony for tenor and alto," was merely trying to fool the Fates. Described in correct music terminology, the work is "six songs with orchestra." Even if it is the finest and most balanced of all Mahler's compositions, and even if Mahler wrote the word *symphony* on the score's first page, it is nonetheless not a true symphony—despite musicologists' assertions to the contrary. There is no hex on the number nine.

Consider the following: there are adagios as final movements in Tchaikovsky's Sixth, Bruckner's Ninth, and Mahler's Ninth. Tchaikovsky completed his Sixth Symphony in 1893, shortly before his suicide, while Bruckner wrote his Ninth Symphony between 1891 and 1896 (he died in October 1896). Mahler composed the final movement (Adagio) of his Third Symphony very quickly in 1897 and his Ninth Symphony in the early years of 1900 (Mahler died in 1911, without ever having heard his Ninth Symphony). There appears to be a definite link between the death of Tchaikovsky and the composition of the Adagio of his Sixth Symphony, although with Bruckner and Mahler the connection is less clear.

According to the *New Grove Dictionary of Music and Musicians*, Bruckner was "the first symphonic composer to take up the metaphysical challenge of Beethoven's Ninth Symphony." This is meaningful only to those who endorse the Germans' insistence on giving a metaphysical dimension to anything beyond the complexity of a Strauss waltz.

Bruckner did not like to vary the meter in the outer movements of a four-movement work. In eight of his nine symphonies the first and fourth movements are in duple time (which divides the pulse by two or by four). Beethoven also wrote outer movements in duple time, but the only symphony in which both first and fourth movements are in the same meter is his Second Symphony (generally considered to be the least accomplished of his nine). I am a devoted admirer and enthusiastic performer of Bruckner's music, but I nonetheless believe that whereas each of Beethoven's nine symphonies had a different message, those of Bruckner all contain essentially the same message. Bruckner was a disciple of Wagner, whose bewitching harmonies he tried to incorporate in symphonic form. This statement is not intended to detract from Bruckner's creative contribution to late nineteenth-century music; *The New Grove Dictionary*'s assertion that Bruckner was the first symphonic composer to challenge Beethoven's Ninth is correct to a certain extent, since Bruckner was among many nineteenth-century composers who were smitten by the opening of Beethoven's "Choral" Symphony. That opening appears in Wagner's *Faust* overture, in Schoenberg's sextet *Transfigured Night*, in Robert Schumann's *Faust* overture and, of course, in Bruckner's Third and Ninth. The Scherzo of the Beethoven work was also much copied, becoming a model for several scherzos that were not quite as amusing as their Italian title might imply. The slow movements of Beethoven's Third and Ninth also constituted an entirely original departure from the classic second movements of Mozart and Haydn (and indeed of Beethoven's other symphonies). In that way, the two symphonies also gave new meaning to the word *adagio*, which Haydn and Mozart had used mostly for the introductory sections preceding the body of an overture or a sonata movement. Many conductors unfortunately believe that they serve Haydn and Mozart better by playing their adagios as if they belonged to the Beethoven canon.

Bruckner's best slow movements are modeled after the Adagio of Beethoven's Ninth. After struggling on eight separate occasions with a final movement (for which he had always lacked Beethoven's inventiveness), Bruckner must have felt that with his Eighth he had done his best fourth movement, because he left the ninth with only three. Perhaps he was simply no longer physically and mentally strong enough to add yet another enormous tonal block. Bruckner came to the symphony by a different route from that taken by the classic trio of Haydn, Mozart, and Beethoven, whose symphonies were matched by a larger number of sonatas and duos, trios, quartets, quintets (all of which are structured like a symphony).

It seems that one must either change the definition of the term *symphony* in describing the works of Bruckner, Mahler, and some twentieth-century composers such as Shostakovich, or simply allow that their works are not traditional symphonies at all. In choosing either course, one will find that Mahler composed just one symphony (his First). Whereas its thematic material is not symphonic, he did succeed in constructing a classic symphonic structure in four movements. The best themes for symphonic composition are partially developed motifs that have the potential to be developed into climaxes. The best tunes do not make the best themes. This is because a good tune is by definition fully developed and thus does not require further development. In Mahler's First, two major melodies are taken from his "Wayfarer" songs, and the canon in the third movement is that old favorite, "Frère Jacques."

The progression from the opening "mood" music—marked in the score "Wie ein Naturlaut" (like sounds heard in nature)—to the grand peroration of the final pages is among the finest compositional devices ever written in the style of cyclical symphonic writing. The word *cyclical*, by the way, describes the use of themes or motives in more than one movement of the same piece. This had rarely been done by the great classical composers, and by quoting in the fourth movement of his Ninth the themes of its first three movements, Beethoven was again blazing a trail for future composers to follow. The best known of the cyclical symphonies are Tchaikovsky's Fifth, Dvořák's "New World" symphony, and Schumann's D minor Symphony. The masterful way in which the opening of Mahler's First is transformed in the work's closing movement foreshadows the difficulties Mahler would later encounter in concluding his scores.

The art of variation (the single greatest art of composition) is here achieved only by more intense orchestral coloring, which again shows that symphonic invention and development were not natural to Mahler, whose greatness lies elsewhere. Mahler was the first composer to bring the angst of the individual into the world of instrumental music. Since he arrived at the symphonic form via the lied—a music form in which he is one of the great masters—it is not surprising that his greatest writing is found in his middle movements. These include the two night-music sections in the Seventh, the Scherzos of the Sixth, Seventh, and Fifth, the middle movement of the Third, and indeed all those which, like those of the First, use the tunes of existing songs.

It can never be sufficiently stressed that one should not link Mahler too closely with Bruckner. If they do share anything significant (besides the length of their works), it is that both have enormous problems with their final movements. Mahler, being the cannier of the two composers, avoided the issue by using voices in his Second, Third, Fourth, and Eighth (which is more oratorio than symphony), and in his *Das Lied von der Erde*. These works with voices were popular in Europe much earlier than the three great instrumental works, the Fifth, Sixth, and Seventh. In fact, the first performance of the Sixth by the Vienna Philharmonic took place no less than twenty-seven years after the 1906 premiere in Essen, Germany.

Mahler, then, was not even attempting to continue the traditions of symphonic writing, whereas Bruckner certainly was. Mahler became an icon for the Second Viennese School. His angst-filled works were the direct inspiration for Schoenberg's *Erwartung* and for the greatest master-piece of twentieth-century music-theater, Alban Berg's *Wozzeck*. Mahler's Sixth has the power to leave the most optimistic listener weak and depressed, while the Fifth is weakened by the composer's attempt to introduce false and unconvincing optimism into four otherwise quite neurotic movements. I should add that I love to play all these works.

Until the third and fourth symphonies of Brahms and the last by Tchaikovsky, the classic and romantic composers had never concluded their symphonic works on a negative, pessimistic, or tragic note. The tragic or pessimistic endings common in music of the late romantic era reflected the uncertainties of the general political sphere. The historical position of the great European monarchies (particularly of the Habsburg empire) was becoming increasingly precarious. Brahms, Bruckner, and Mahler spent a good portion of their creative lives in Vienna, where signs of the coming catastrophe of the Great War were everywhere to be seen.

The days of the classic symphony—a four-part music structure with contrasting themes and an affirmative conclusion—were clearly numbered.

I see Brahms as the direct link between Beethoven and the Second Viennese School. Brahms gave to the composers of that school the confidence that there was still some life left in the old forms. One might see Mahler's music as the transition from the spirit of the eighteenth century to radical expressionism. I believe that Mahler's Ninth Symphony is the work that represents this new spirit, in that it does not offer the compromises still apparent in his Fifth, Sixth, and Seventh.

Beethoven was a disciple of Haydn and, of course, knew Mozart's music intimately (often emulating patterns and schemes as they appear in Mozart's music). Nonetheless, his music goes beyond the perfect order of Haydn's and Mozart's world, becoming a kind of medium for the expression of the divine. Its power remains undiminished today, sending the listener away filled with confidence in the "future and grandeur of human culture" described so aptly by Hermann Hesse in his 1911 critique of Goethe's *Wilhelm Meisters Lehrjahre*.

Beethoven's symphonies represent the pinnacle of musical creativity. Wagner maintained that since the Ninth Symphony was so perfect there was simply nothing more to be said by music alone. Consequently, he said, music would have to proceed by linking up with other art forms. With all due respect and admiration for the efforts of Schumann, Mendelssohn, Dvorák, and later British composers like Edward Elgar, none of their beautiful works disproves Wagner's contention.

Seven

Reflections on the Revolution: The Power (and the Perils) of Recorded Music

Recording and the Contemporary Composer

Those who argue for the superiority of live performance over recordings maintain that only a live audience can guarantee the sense of mutuality that alone can make a musical experience unique. When one attempts to repeat that sense of mutuality, they say, the music is no longer unique.

I recall a lieder recital in which Lotte Lehmann was accompanied on the piano by Bruno Walter (with me turning the pages). After performing a selection of Schubert lieder, we went backstage. Lehmann was recalled and showered with so many bravos and so much applause that she finally asked Walter whether we should repeat the last number. "Never repeat," answered Walter, before going on to explain that one could never perform the same piece twice in exactly the same way, and that there would always be those in the audience who would ask why the second rendition had not been as good as the first or vice versa. "No matter which it is, you cannot win if you repeat," he added.

A recording is another matter entirely. A recording will sound the same no matter how many times one plays it, and if it does not always have the same effect upon the listener, the recording equipment is not to blame. The element of uncertainty that precedes a live concert is due to its being a *performance*, without retakes, without corrections, but with another unpredictable element: the presence of the audience, whose collective mood and personality can and do affect the performer in many different ways. Few performers would deny that the presence of an audience has a tremendous influence upon those on stage. Indeed, that influence is arguably as great as the influence exerted on the audience by the performer.

Just as an audience that coughs its way through a soft passage can quickly demoralize the most professional performer, so can an enthusiastic audience inspire those on stage to perform with renewed vigor. Certainly my experience of repeat programs taught me that no two performances are ever alike.

Prominent musicians are accustomed these days to being bombarded with recordings made by composers seeking a performer for their works. Indeed, so widespread has this practice become that when a musician friend of mine once told such a composer he would prefer to look at the score rather than listen to a recording, the astonished composer was obliged to beg for more time, saying he did not have enough copies of his score at hand.

These recordings are generally made under the most awkward conditions, and the composer rarely has the means to secure the necessary professional help; however, those composers whose scores are, shall we say, not very readable have little choice but to pin their hopes upon such recordings. The major international recording companies are generally reluctant to produce contemporary music emanating from composers of radical—or even moderately traditional—schools, because such music rarely meets their sales projections.

True, recording companies are sometimes faced with the nasty problem of a valuable contract artist who wants to do something a little unusual. In such cases it is the task of the Artists and Repertory chief to impress upon those doing the sales projections (who will be virulently opposed to the piece in question) that even if the piece does not sell, there is something to be gained from recording it, because it will keep the valuable artist safely in the fold. Some unlikely recordings have been made in this way, but nobody ever expects such recordings to become the norm just as nobody expects the recording industry to demonstrate altruism concerning the offbeat composer. The dedicated avant-gardist may protest about this state of affairs, which has certainly had a negative effect upon contemporary composition, but the unfortunate truth is that the recording industry has always been a profit-oriented business just like any other.

The advent of recorded music has brought considerable advantages. After making their initial investment of television, radio, or playing equipment, listeners now have private access to a bewildering array of recordings. The fact remains, however, that recordings are quite different in nature from a live performance in the presence of the musicians and of hundreds or even thousands of other people. I am aware that this distinction may seem somewhat academic to those readers who (like myself) enjoy listening to music in the comfort of their homes. One has no driving to do, no expensive concert or theater tickets to buy, no babysitter to organize. Yet, the modern recording industry has had a dramatic impact upon composers and the status of contemporary music.

Who is ultimately responsible for this situation? It is certainly true that big symphony orchestras generally play older music on their world tours, that they generally play music that they themselves have recorded, and that their recordings are generally available in the lobby for concertgoers to purchase on their way out of the hall. Nevertheless, the recording industry alone is not responsible, for there are several other factors involved. The sense of confusion frequently expressed by modern composers reflects a greater confusion among the three dominant forces of the U.S. music industry: the boards of music organizations, which are usually composed of well-meaning laypeople competent only in the financing of non-profit organizations; the composers' organizations, which have enlisted the support of governmental and private organizations to win finance and public performance of their works; and the recording companies, which control the programming of their contracted artists. In my view, not one of the three has shown any real concern for the overall plight of "serious" music in the United States.

The boards point proudly to their programs of educational concerts, and yet I believe those programs to be wholly ineffective. Few would deny that the pervasive influence of the media in our society has short-ened people's attention spans considerably, and that the music education programs have similarly affected young concertgoers. How can young people be expected to appreciate a great classical symphony by Haydn if educational programs cut the symphony down to five minutes from twenty-five? I have for this reason had very little to do with such programs. In fact, in the one and only educational concert I ever did, I refused to do excerpted portions or single movements. Being a pragmatist I selected only short, but complete pieces.

These programs will not succeed in winning back the younger audience. The critical problem of how to achieve this goal is the subject of frequent debate within the industry, but one of the two major conclusions usually reached is simply wrong. I agree with the first conclusion, that pricing policies should be changed to attract younger people, but competition from recorded music (usually identified as the second culprit) cannot be blamed in this respect. Not one of the advances in music technology has adversely affected concert attendances. Quite the contrary, those advances have encouraged people to see those performers familiar to them from recordings, television, or radio. The trouble is, though, that the music in question is generally limited to the old war-horses of composition.

As for the composers' lobbies, let us consider the two most successful champions of popular classics, John Williams and André Kostelanetz. The magnetism of the name Kostelanetz stems from his long-running series of radio concerts. Broadcast in a pre-TV age, those concerts introduced his name and the music that he played to people who would never become familiar with the names of those distinguished conductors who performed regular subscription concerts in the very same hall Kostelanetz used for his radio recordings. The free concerts given by John Williams at Boston's Esplanade, combined with his regular annual nine weeks with the Boston Pops, were a surefire way to make him better known than the incumbent maestro playing to a very geriatric Friday matinée crowd. Mr. Williams may not be recognized by the guests at table No. 13 in Boston's Symphony Hall, but his concerts and his screen credits make his name known worldwide.

Commissioned compositions that I either performed or heard early in their career were given few repeats beyond their first outing. This has been the source of much open lamentation from composers and their benefactors, but it seems there is just no desire among the public to hear something new simply because it is new. There should be such a desire, and I believe that there would be, if only more young people would listen to music and study music, if only more educated people would read more about music, and if only music were appreciated in a broader cultural and historical context than is the case today.

Concerning this last point, is it not significant that only one player in a major American symphony orchestra knew what the word *Mathis* referred to in the title of Paul Hindemith's opera *Mathis der Maler*? I wonder how many amateur linguists are aware that certain themes of Béla Bartók cannot be codified into traditional musical notation because they are an approximation of Hungarian language accentuation. I wonder how many people have ever pondered the third of Richard Strauss's *Four Last Songs* for voice and orchestra with reference to the Hermann Hesse poem upon which it is based? Perhaps a college poetry course might discuss Hesse's poem in the light of the music. Perhaps Bartók's *The Miraculous Mandarin* might be accompanied by photographs of the original ballet choreography. Perhaps an exhibition of Matthias Grünewald's pictures might be accompanied by Hindemith's opera music. There is hardly a single well-known composer whose works might not be revealed to the nonmusician for their relationship with the other arts.

This is true not only of titled scores. The number of works designated by the word *variations* is legion—and yet the word is not evocative of anything in particular. Perhaps a little imagination might reveal that these works are like several shots of the same person taken from different angles, in different moods, in different circumstances, or engaged in different activities. A creative writing instructor might run a few recordings of famous variation works, such as Edward Elgar's *Enigma Variations*, before asking the class to listen to and describe Johannes Brahms's *Variations on the St. Anthony Chorale*. Whereas the latter work explores eight moods of the same person, Elgar's piece describes eight people. The composers therefore treat the basic thematic subject quite differently.

I should add, however, that the compositional style dictated by commissars of the former Soviet Union demonstrated quite clearly that there are limits to this cross-fertilization process. Self-conscious attempts to link art to political culture have not always been particularly successful. Similar attempts have been made in the United States, but are rather less visible because the U.S. government is less concerned with the control of its artists and their style. One of my favorite recollections of such an occasion was an attempt by New York's Metropolitan Opera to assist in the birth of an American opera during the 1940s. The manager of the Met, Edward Johnson, had been a tenor and in 1931 had sung the role of the protagonist in Deems Taylor's *Peter Ibbetson*. He wished perhaps to be remembered as one of the few musicians ever to spawn a viable native opera. The young William Schuman was involved, spending a season as a guest observer of the Met's operations. There was also a poet, Christopher La Farge, who was assigned to provide a libretto for Bill Schuman's music. I lost count of how many times Schuman lamented "all I ever asked of Christopher was that he stay away from Indians as a subject" (or words to that effect). When the poet delivered his libretto, its title proved to be *Mesa*, it was based in New Mexico, and American Indians were there in abundance.

On the other hand I remember conducting Louis Gruenberg's *The Emperor Jones* in 1946. I do not find the composition remarkable, but Eugene O'Neill's plot and text were excellent, and with Lawrence Tibbett singing the lead it was certainly a very worthwhile effort. Just as composers never write their greatest works early in their careers, so must any nation be content to wait a few years before its magnum opus is created.

Just as the advent of copyright caused the metamorphosis of a service into a property, so the advent of recording transformed music from a means of communication to a one-sided statement. The invention of the phonograph, the radio, the television, and the video recorder brought a revolution to home life almost comparable to those wrought by the electric light and running water. Yet people washed before there was running water, they had candle light before they had electricity, and—judging by Shakespearean theater—the lack of a computerized lighting panel did not adversely affect the talents of dramatists or other writers. People also had music in their homes prior to the invention of the radio.

There is no doubt that radio, television, and so on are all great social services, which provided genuine cultural advantages. That every invention can be misused and abused is merely a reflection of the perverse instincts of humanity, and should not be held against the inventors or the distributors of these great advances. The advent of recording has effectively enabled the music industry to distribute documents of masterpieces that in their written form could be deciphered by only a few well-instructed professionals. The resident of an Italian mountain village who rarely has the opportunity to travel to Milan can now listen to opera in the best possible reproductions at a cost that is comparable to that of a visit to La Scala. He also enjoys the obvious conveniences of listening to music at home.

Music lovers probably also find that the recorded version of a symphony sounds much better than the version rendered by the local symphony. There are certainly significant differences between the standard of a recorded opera, featuring leading singers of the international circuit, and those of the civic opera in Annecy, Brno, or in any similar small provincial town. The residents of such towns can now watch a Salzburg production of a Mozart opera on their television screens. The production will doubtless feature the most expensive musical talent, playing before an audience that has paid the highest prices.

Of course, American readers may ruefully contrast this agreeable picture with their rather less agreeable domestic situation. Radio stations that play good music are rapidly being sold out to the rock music industry, the televised glamour of a Metropolitan Opera telecast is a relatively rare phenomenon, the regular radio broadcasts of some prominent orchestras have ceased for lack of an underwriter, and the great American orchestras do not record nearly as frequently and effectively as their European counterparts.

The leadership of the American music establishment must shoulder the responsibility for this unfavorable situation. The musicians' unions set prices that made America noncompetitive, and the boards of directors erred in not putting up an effective fight. Because conductors, singers, and virtuosos give priority to engagements located near to the site of their next recording, American venues have become second-choice venues for most major artists.

During my various recording activities I encountered many Artists and Repertory people. Of those whom I observed, at least three were out-standingly talented. Their preparation for a project was so thorough that they seemed to have a more intimate relationship with the composition at hand than some of the musicians.

I do not refer here to the producers, who sit score-in-hand like Beckmesser marking errors and asking for retakes. The people I am refer-ring to are those who scurry to and fro, changing microphones or the placement of voices or instruments, suggesting to the performers a differ-ent approach here or stressing a nuance there. These people are not just "with it," they are "it." It is arguable that they should be given credit, not merely as Artists and Repertory officials, but as members of the perform-ing team (as happens in the world of rock music). Whereas these gifted recording experts should be given credit for countless superb recordings, they should also shoulder responsibility for their part in the failure of cer-tain recording artists who attempt to make a career as live performers.

In the late 1940s, just after the Second World War, a certain European pianist was announced for his American debut in a recital at New York's Town Hall. The artist's arrival having been duly heralded by a series of recordings, his name was sufficiently well known to ensure a sold-out debut concert. Then came the letdown. Poor media reviews were combined with a negative reception in the cloistered but all-powerful world of the conservatories. His recordings, it was decided, had been crafted by a clever sound editor and live performance did not live up to the expectations they had generated. Even if the hoped-for career as recitalist and soloist with the big American orchestras did not materialize, the pianist continued to be regarded as a Mozart specialist. This reputa-tion was based primarily on his recordings and some published articles.

Recordings have worked comparable wonders for other such "sleepers," miraculously transforming them into international experts on Vivaldi, Albinoni, Bononcini, Handel, and more baroque composers than I can name. A former section leader of a London orchestra once toured Europe like a musician of the eighteenth century, leading a small chamber orchestra in "Brandenburg" Concertos and other masterpieces, and effectively selling the growing library of his recordings. This tech-nique won him considerable acclaim until—in the best traditions of the

Peter Principle—he received an assignment for which he was really not suited. His reputation, which had been won by playing a vast repertoire of old music, led to his appointment as music director of a major American symphony orchestra. Even the management of that orchestra openly admitted that the incumbency of this excellent exponent of baroque music was little short of disastrous.

There is no fundamental reason why a good violinist with leadership qualities should not be equally successful as leader of a hundred-piece orchestra. Nonetheless, in this instance certain crucial factors had either been overlooked or disregarded. The success of his recorded repertory had been achieved mainly with that vast mass of thoroughly pleasant, yet virtually meaningless eighteenth-century music for strings (plus the occasional wind orchestration that was unproblematic and devoid of tension or problems of interpretation). Not one of those responsible for finding a new music director was sufficiently musical for the task, and not one seemed to realize that a coach who helps a tennis player to win the Wimbledon singles title may not necessarily be able also to produce a champion basketball team. A successful recording artist will not automatically be similarly successful as a conductor.

In the case of the Mozart pianist the discrepancy between the studio artist and live performer became evident when his technical fallibility was exposed on stage. He had doubtless needed several retakes to produce one publishable recorded version of the same pieces. Conducting is slightly different, in that there are rarely any clearly audible wrong notes by which to judge a conductor, but there is a tremendous difference between handling a group of performers in the studio and handling the same group in front of a live audience. Incidents such as these reinforce my concerns about the lack of musical expertise among lay boards, and they also reflect the extraordinary influence of the international recording business.

Herbert von Karajan

Herbert von Karajan understood earlier and better than anyone else in the industry how the miracle of recording technology could be turned

from master into servant. I should therefore like to devote a few paragraphs to his remarkable career. My remarks are based primarily on first-
hand knowledge and not on documentary research.

In 1930 I attended summer courses at the Mozarteum in Salzburg.
This was the local conservatory, under the direction of Bernhard
Paumgartner (a Mozart expert like virtually every citizen of Salzburg). It
offered summer courses running from the beginning of July to the end of
the Salzburg Festival (which was some weeks shorter in duration than the
courses). The summer in Salzburg was the classic graduation trip for
aspiring young musicians. One of the instructors of the conducting class
was the twenty-two-year-old Karajan. It seems to me now, looking back,
that even in those very early days his basic interpretive approach gave
priority to sound.

He was also, I might add, a thoroughly prepared and serious musician
even then. This may seem a superfluous statement considering Karajan's
remarkable career, but I make it nonetheless because over the years his
detractors often tried to dismiss him as a mere showman. The same was
said about Leopold Stokowski, and in my view the accusation is as
groundless in his case as it is in Karajan's (although it is true that
Stokowski, unlike Karajan, sometimes made some unorthodox musical
choices). A musician friend of mine once observed Karajan giving a master class to a student orchestra. Karajan, my friend told me, got straight
down to business and rehearsed the students in exemplary fashion. I
gained a very similar impression during the classes at the Mozarteum—
that of a perfectly well-prepared and enthusiastic young conductor whose
personality and tastes were already formed. I recall in particular his
spirited discussion of Richard Strauss's *Tod und Verklärung*. Besides teaching classes, he also led rehearsals for Puccini's *Tosca* at the local State
Theater. During those rehearsals he was coached by an older conductor,
Meinhard von Zallinger. Of course, this will sound like the wisdom of
hindsight, but it seems to me now that even in those days a gambler
would happily have staked much money on the young Karajan.

Around 1950 the multitalented Walter Legge founded an elite
orchestra in London for recording purposes. The English do not support
their London-based orchestras although the Royal College produces

superlative musicians. It is therefore relatively easy to form an ad hoc orchestra in London that is technically superb and able to render difficult brass passages—in other words, an orchestra that is ideally suited to a tightly budgeted undertaking such as the recording of music. Walter Legge was a good headhunter and had a keen musical ear. He found technicians who could make good records and, with an uncanny instinct, picked Karajan for his large recording projects. The great soprano Elisabeth Schwarzkopf, who had sung with Karajan previously, also became involved. Legge subsequently married Schwarzkopf, who went on to record as much music for the female voice as Dietrich Fischer-Dieskau recorded for the male baritone.

In 1954 Karajan succeeded Wilhelm Furtwängler as conductor-in-chief of the Berlin Philharmonic Orchestra. The forty-six-year-old Karajan, long acknowledged as the natural successor to Furtwängler, then proceeded to build a veritable music empire by assuming the direction of the Vienna Opera. Like every talented musician before him he gave up this post after a few seasons, but he remained on very good terms with the Opera. Subsequently he became head of the Salzburg Festival.

Karajan's great discovery was that the recording could take precedence over the live performance. He may have learned this fact from the world of pop music or he may have discovered it independently. Everybody else in the profession first rehearsed the repertory, then performed it, and then (when it had become second nature to the ensemble) recorded it. Karajan had learned (perhaps in London) that an orchestra could, if its members were good at sight reading, prepare a piece for a recording session without ever having performed it in public. Karajan used this technique to great advantage in his opera productions for the Salzburg Festival. At the numerous staging rehearsals required for each opera, musical accompaniment was furnished by recorded tapes. This technique protected the singers' voices—since they could rehearse staging to the background of their recorded voices—and spared everybody the often laborious instructions that typically need to be made to an accompanist. Karajan also understood the crucial importance of the Artists and Repertory person who (as I can attest) can either be extremely helpful toward producing good results or quite the opposite if he is out-of-tune with the performers, the music, or the recording location. Karajan selected his own person for this role—an individual who was not furnished by any record company, who never became a producer for anybody else, and whose ear was evidently in tune with Karajan's own.

So Karajan was both aware of the potential of recorded music and well able to keep control of his circle. Other artists (I cannot say all or most, since I have no statistics) made their recordings under the watchful eye of the recording company (and especially of its Artists and Repertory people). Karajan was certainly talented enough not to need "plastic surgery" (my euphemism for the doctoring techniques employed with second-grade performers), but I would guess that he was forced to use it sometimes since certain soloists who recorded repeatedly under his direction did not attain comparable success in personal appearances.

The clarity of sound recordings is not always repeated on film or video. When Karajan led the opening celebrations of the newly built chamber hall adjoining the Berlin Philharmonic, he was wise enough to choose a major work (Vivaldi's *Four Seasons*) and one of the prettiest violinists (Anne-Sophie Mutter) to share the spotlight (on that occasion, hunger for the spotlight certainly took precedence over authenticity). The great financial success of Karajan's audio recordings was not repeated with his tapes for television, but that had rather more to do with the nature of home entertainment. Karajan's mastery of the world of sound recording has yet to be emulated by anybody else—perhaps it will prove to be his most lasting contribution to the world of music.

Arturo Toscanini

The compliment I like best of all is when a musician says of me: "He lets us play." I am not alone in this. The "dictatorial," "note-perfect," "temperamental" Arturo Toscanini once said to me words to the following effect: "I start rehearsing, say, the first symphony of Brahms. When we get to the second movement the oboist plays his solo passage. Perhaps he does not do it quite as I would, but what he does is carried by conviction and experience. I say nothing and let him be."

The first time I played at a rehearsal for Toscanini it was for the solo quartet of the Ninth Symphony, in Vienna. When I arrived at the rehearsal room, the bass soloist, Richard Mayr, was already there, nervous as a cat. He was one of Vienna's greatest favorites in all the fine bass parts, but now here he was, about to meet the much-vaunted "musical Mussolini." While we were still waiting there alone, Mayr said to me: "I've sung that thing now for thirty years and I can't change; if he doesn't like it, then . . ."

When Toscanini and the other musicians arrived, we started. Mayr sang the great recitative, making a few tiny, typically Viennese errors that were not commented upon. Toscanini had understood within a few moments of the first solo passage that Mayr was an extraordinary artist, so why bother being *pignolo* [fussy]? He watched Mayr's face while he sang, said simply "bravo, bene," after the solo, and that was that. We went on through the quartet and Toscanini let him sing it just as he had sung it for thirty years. He, like everybody else in Vienna, loved it. Singing, dancing, and playing should be right and should also reflect the wishes of the composer. They need not, however, be so correct that their artistry degenerates into little more than meticulous work.

Given the resurgence of interest in Toscanini, I sense the impending arrival of a whole series of learned deductions by pundits who will compare the conductor's reissued records with each other, with those of later followers, and with those of would-be imitators. There will, I guarantee, be but one outcome of their comparisons: they will make nobody a better musician or a more perceptive interpreter. It is still possible, however, to make one's way by publicizing oneself as a follower of the late maestro. I know of at least one conductor who has made a world career out of that. If my recollection is worth anything, please be assured that any extant sketches of Toscanini's musicianship and music personality are largely influenced by publicity of his invention, distributed obediently by a band of thurifers who mostly could not read a note.

One of the more prominent of these sketches asserts his apparent fidelity to the printed page of the score. Had he really been as faithful as is generally supposed, he could never have become as effective and overwhelming as he did. In fact, he edited any, and every, score whenever he felt it was necessary for the accomplishment of his reading. If it should not be clear why I choose to write a profile of Toscanini, let me say that my reasons are similar to those that have also prompted me to write a brief profile of Herbert von Karajan: it is necessary to put their recordings into a proper context.

I know Joseph Horowitz and I can vouch for his honorable intentions in writing his book *Understanding Toscanini* (1987). The thesis developed in that book suggests that Toscanini was somehow prominently involved in the ostracism of modern composers by those glamorous, all-powerful recording enterprises. Like every prominent performer, Toscanini was a beneficiary of American-style music fashions of the 1930s. I would guess he never set much store by Felix Weingartner's book *On Conducting* (1920) in which a music director is charged with the task of improving the taste of the public. Toscanini was no different from anyone else whose ambition is to parlay a talent into career, fame, and fortune.

I had already concluded in the 1940s that he never made any mental connection between a musician and the social conditions of music and music institutions. His dislike of making recordings was not, I would suggest, based on any personal philosophy. It might well have been instinctual, since he had a fantastic instinct for all artists and their abilities and limitations (including his own). He perhaps felt that one of his greatest assets, his image as a firebrand musician, would not come across well in an enduring document such as a recording—if so, I believe he was right.

On several occasions he told me which music he did not identify with. Sometimes his arguments seemed merely to be confirming a personal dislike; at other times he would declare a certain composition to be out of his range (almost as a singer might say that the role of Sarastro is "too low" for him). He knew that the thrills expected of him could not be delivered with Hindemith or Stravinsky, so he left those composers to Guido Cantelli and Ernest Ansermet. In this respect, though, he was no different from several dozen other conductors, pianists, violinists, and general virtuosos, who are all well aware that what is expected of them can be delivered only on the backs of certain horses. Toscanini, like every successful musician, was mortally afraid of being found out.

The refusal to risk, to dare, to experiment, and to expand the repertoire stems, in this sense, from the inflated expectations of those who own the franchise or who, like Sol Hurok, present performers. Racing fans will only fill the stands if they know the rider will be sitting on the right horse. Just as race-course administrators will ensure that the right person is in the saddle, so our music impresarios are only too happy to serve the public by matching the popular performer with the popular music.

Eight

The Orchestra, the Analyst, and the Timekeeper: Sketches from a Musical Life

The Personality of Orchestras

American music reviewers have become increasingly insistent that European orchestras possess more collective personality than their American counterparts, and that the latter are, moreover, cultivating a more neutral kind of sound. The word *neutral* might here be easily translated as international, virtuosic, impersonal, and so forth.

The orchestra does not need a personality, even if its soloists certainly do. The *ripieno* (those who make up the string choirs or the second wind desks) need uniform training to enable them to mesh with the others into what is known as the ensemble. Whenever an orchestra that is genuinely together musically plays a popular piece by Ravel, it usually must still hire an extra percussion player, who is generally assigned to the bass drum.

On many occasions (from my experience I might cite the Vienna Opera's production of Ernst Krenek's *Karl V* or the Philadelphia Orchestra's rendition of Ravel's *La Valse*), I have noticed a certain lack of unanimity with such pieces and it has generally proven to be the case that the bass drummer is an outsider. American orchestras and good European orchestras have always, of course, possessed that personality that emanates from the score, the composer, and the ethnic and stylistic means of communication. That personality must be drawn out by the leader (the chorus master in a large vocal ensemble, the first violin in a string quartet, the conductor in an orchestra, and—unfortunately for this generation—hardly anybody in opera). This kind of personality is entirely distinct from that personality that concerns the issue of internationalism alluded to by the American critics.

It is the conductor who is at fault if an orchestra sounds too neutral, too international, or even too personal. In my view an actor who is always wholly recognizable can be a useful and flexible member of a drama company, but the truly outstanding actor is able to make himself unrecognizable even to the extent of changing voice and posture. Just as an actor's makeup is only helpful to a certain degree, so too the external sound aids are only of limited help to the orchestra. A harpsichord and a viola da gamba will be an asset for a Bach rendition, but they will not replace the leader's sense of style, manner, or meaning.

There is a suite for orchestra extracted from Zoltán Kodály's *Háry János* that includes a short, very simple piece called "Song." It begins with a viola solo. Most students of the viola can read the few notes on sight, but in most cases their renditions will be faulty because they will not be idiomatic. I cite this particular case because I conducted that solo in rehearsal with one of the finest orchestras in Europe—or indeed anywhere—Amsterdam's Concertgebouw Orkest. The viola player played the piece as any musician with a good rhythmic solfège background would, but this made it sound unidiomatic. The song was jotted down by Kodály from a folk melody he had heard sung by peasants, and the opening rhythm in the score was merely an approximation of the accentuated first syllable of the Hungarian language. That rhythm is as impossible to render in musical notation as the M-TA-TA accompaniment in a Viennese waltz. The Dutch viola player, by the way, firmly rejected my explanation that this first phrase could not and should not be played as printed, so ingrained was his habit of trusting blindly in the written instructions of the composer. He simply could not comprehend that, as long as it had to be done in the language that Western composers have at their disposal (traditional musical notation), neither Kodály nor anyone else in the world could write down that Hungarian accent.

Writing down pitch can present similar problems. For example, since "art" music, unlike traditional music, does not use quarter tones (staves or spaces were not foreseen for them), Bartók was obliged to make up his own device for writing down quarter tones. These are extreme examples of a kind of music that might be described as parochial or noninternational. They are indeed so extreme that the composers in question could do little more than approximate pitch, inflection, or rhythm.

Hungary's culture has long been familiar to the Viennese, and our comprehension was helped by hearing the Hungarian language spoken. This meant that hearing the accented first syllable (saying "hottel" instead of "hotèl") was a common experience for us. I later married a lady who not only played the violin but was also of Hungarian parents. I am quite certain that my understanding of Bartók's and Kodály's music was helped considerably by the fact that my wife speaks the Hungarian language. There is a great divide separating the native from the person who is not deeply familiar with the whole cultural orbit of the music's background, and that divide is not easily bridged.

The deepest folkloric traditions and the very essence of ethnic *melos* sometimes remain impenetrable even to very fine and well-trained musicians. Some of the best-known works of nationalist composers—a term commonly used for many of the Slavic masters—have turns, themes, rhythms, and lilts that are usually lost after they have been played abroad for many years and become "world property." Like many a *vin du pays*, they do not travel well.

Far more complex is the case of Beethoven's Sixth Symphony. Beethoven was a master composer whose work became truly international without the need for compromise by interpreter or listener (but who also wrote one or two major pieces that do not travel well). The four complete cycles of Beethoven's symphonies led by Herbert von Karajan received almost universal acclaim, and yet there were reservations about his performance of this Sixth, "Pastoral" Symphony. I personally have never heard this particular work performed by Karajan, either recorded or live, but it is of more than specialized interest to ask why a conductor such as Karajan or other fine Beethoven conductors should have difficulties with this one work. Why is this score different from other scores? A brief look at this puzzle may help us understand a little more about the question of the orchestral personality and the notion of internationalism in music.

Beethoven's Sixth is the only classical symphony that is in five, not four, movements, the only one that ends softly, and the only one that gives subtitles for each movement. These subtitles are "Pleasing Emotions on Arriving in the Country," "Scenes at the Side of a Brook," "At a Village Dance," "The Coming and Passing of a Storm," and "The Thanksgiving Song of the Shepherds." All five movements are in perfect classical form. The fourth movement (an addition) might easily be filed away into a specific category by academic analysts, but there is also a cautionary note from Beethoven: "Mehr Empfindung als Tonmalerei" (More emotions than tone-painting)—not a symphonic poem, as a contemporary of Liszt might have said.

The opening section is, as explicitly stated by Beethoven, about emotions. The dances of the third movement are also clear as to their purpose and meaning. The fourth "storm" movement and the finale, however, go much deeper than their subtitles indicate. Nature was very close to Vienna's urban center even in the early 1800s, and nature was also very close to Beethoven, who used to spend time in nearby Heiligenstadt just as present-day city dwellers spend time at their weekend cottages. Nature was also very close to the poets of Germany's *Sturm und Drang* period, during which the Sixth Symphony was written. The term *pastoral* does not refer to the duties of the clergy, but to those of the shepherd. It is not, though, to be confused with the Watteau images of shepherdesses flirting with gentlemen in hunting attire.

The final movement, which is in perfect rondo form, is addressed to the same deity described by Goethe in his poem *Grenzen der Menschheit* (The Limitations of Mankind), in which the "holy father of all the ages dispatches blessed lightning over the thirsty earth." The lightning is there portrayed as a blessing because it is followed by the life-giving rain that enables grass and wheat to grow and nourishes the sheep needed for clothing and nourishment. The storm passes and the shepherds offer their thanks in a song that "has no end." Since any piece of music must have an ending, there are two chords marking the limitations of mankind or the finite life that may be terminated suddenly.

In other words Beethoven, in this work, goes beyond the horizons of his other symphonies—the jolly, buoyant First and Second, the breakthrough to previously unknown grandeur in the Third, the wit and bravura of the Fourth, the drama, hymns, and apotheosis of the dance in the Fifth and the Seventh, the boisterousness and gaudiness of the Eighth, and the march of mankind to brotherhood in the Ninth. Each is different, each is masterful. All are of human, earthly dimensions, and travel quite effortlessly beyond time and space, beyond Vienna, the Habsburg enclave, Central Europe, and Western Europe, over the oceans and over the decades. They may be given a respectable rendition by orchestras whose half-attentive conductors simply listen to a Karajan recording on the blissful assumption that Karajan "can't go wrong."

The Sixth, though, is different. The Sixth ventures into realms otherwise reserved for the composer's final phase (including the last five piano sonatas, and the five string quartets, and the *Missa Solemnis*, which may be considered the piece that explains and opens up the Sixth Symphony). Neither the *Missa Solemnis* nor the Sixth is susceptible to the kind of "international" treatment that merely requires the notes to be played. Like the Sixth, the final section of the *Missa* is in $\frac{6}{8}$ time. It also breaks off suddenly for the same reason as the finale in the symphony breaks off suddenly: there is no real end, there is merely a human final chord. Just as with the Sixth, there is no final cadence. Whereas here this lack of cadence signifies an expression of man's eternal gratitude to the deity, in the *Missa* its place is taken by the prayer for peace.

I have not forgotten the second section of the symphony, "Scenes at the Side of a Brook." To do it justice I must recall performances by two eminent conductors, Arturo Toscanini and, much later, Carlo Maria Giulini. Toscanini gave us a delightful brook that rolled merrily along without anything missing (I and millions of others simply did not question that every note of Beethoven had to be done just as Toscanini said it should). In the 1970s, when I had been conducting symphonies for a quarter of a century, I heard a performance that—like everything by Giulini—sought to probe the depths of the music. This was no glib, note-perfect, technically unblemished, brilliant international exposé. Giulini made of movements one and two a continuous whole, almost equalizing the tempos and making the two sections into one half-hour long andante—equivalent perhaps to a leisurely walk by a brook in Heiligenstadt.

I confess I found Giulini's approach to be undifferentiated and quite dull—so much so indeed that I have lost all memory of the other three sections of that performance. What this second movement shows at the start would not please the wise writer of the record magazine who is convinced that Beethoven's metronome marks are wrong. It is a perfect metronome figure that is nonetheless always replaced by considerably more fluid tempos on the perfectly logical assumption that since brooks are quite speedy Beethoven's metronome figure must be wrong again. Yet, the scene at the brook is not about the "flowing of the brook" at all, it is about the emotions of the nature-lover who listens to the bird song as he beholds the brook. Those emotions have been expressed in a perfect classical slow movement—a movement in which time does not move.

Here again there is a startling resemblance to the *Missa*. The symphony's movement is in $\frac{12}{8}$ meter; in the *Missa* there is also a $\frac{12}{8}$ movement that accompanies the text "Benedictus qui venit in nomine Domini" (Who comes in the name of God?). A solo violin descending, not too slowly, from heaven, like the Dove, the Holy Ghost, or Inspiration. Nobody profits from being told to "do it a little slower," because that amounts merely to using an international symbol for something that is untranslatable.

There is so much more in these relationships that can be understood by listeners in any part of the world, but those listeners must somehow acquire an understanding of that imperceptible spirit that goes into a work of such genius.

Thus far my distinction between international and parochial music has concerned the interpretation of older music only. Theater people can point to many illustrations of what is and what is not international. A show that is a hit in London's West End will not necessarily succeed on Broadway, and vice versa. This is the case although in both theater districts everything is done in English. (I do not include here the distinction between Cockney and American dialects, since dialect in language is similar to folklore, which also cannot be written down.) We must thus interpret the word *international* in the sense of intercultural.

Narrower, more parochial cultures will mostly produce art that has the narrow perimeters of folklore. Music *qua* music, such as that of Vivaldi, Paganini, or everything based on the virtuosity of instrumentalists or coloratura singing, becomes international almost by itself. Karajan set himself up as an intercontinental musician from his twenties onward, but this drive to be a world citizen in music limited his potential to fully identify with those musical works that are tied to the world of the composer and to his time. In my defense (lest I be indicted of *lèse Karajan*) I would state that even the most ardent admirers of the late maestro always conceded that his performances of Bach's music, such as one fully staged *St. Matthew Passion,* were an embarrassment.

My interest in the notion of language as applied to music is tied up with the exploration of the international dimension of music. Intentional internationalism in contemporary music is equivalent to commercialism. Schoenberg's avowed pursuit of autonomous musical composition was the archetype of music that is noncommercial (meaning that it cannot be sold in sufficient quantities to allow the composer a decent income on which to live and pay his bills). No matter how difficult it may be to liberate oneself from the vast labyrinth of old connotations and associations, we have to separate the concept of international/commercial from any a priori connection with artistic quality. International/commercial may well refer to the greatest masterpieces of the past, present, and future, but it may also refer to tripe, hackwork, and the meaningless manipulation of the notes.

An excellent illustration of the difference between an international composer and a "compositeur du pays" is the odd couple Ravel and Debussy. Among musicians there is little doubt that Debussy is the greater composer of the two. Ravel is often mentioned in tandem with Debussy, but he is no more a matching piece on the other end of the mantelpiece than Bruckner is for Mahler. Ravel is, however, the greatest "international" composer of the twentieth century. His entire output is guided by an elegant, urbane mastery that is equally appealing to audiences in Turin, Tokyo, Berlin, or Moscow. Debussy's great works, on the other hand, are probably still relatively little known in such places.

If listeners in those cities were to be confronted with his late duo sonatas, his early *La Damoiselle élue*, or his song cycles, they would politely applaud the mastery of the performers without having the slightest notion of what the music was all about.

These pieces are not international, nor can they even be sold at home in France as easily as Ravel's works. As for his opera, *Pelléas et Mélisande*, not only is it being swallowed up among the coughing and sneezing of houses that are too large, it is also severely handicapped by its being in French (not the great favorite among opera singers). It is quite common to find the twenty-four preludes by Chopin in recital announcements, but I have yet to see a single recital featuring the twenty-four preludes by Debussy. Both Ravel and Debussy are unquestioned masters, and I would not hesitate to bestow on both composers the kudos bestowed by Haydn upon Mozart when he said to Father Mozart, "Your son has taste and the greatest knowledge of composition." I own that I did omit the first part of Haydn's sentence, but there is no doubt that both composers have an utterly refined taste and are able to make the notes do exactly what they wished—the definition of "knowledge of composition."

A different and equally enlightening example is furnished by the American composer Aaron Copland. On the occasion of Copland's eightieth birthday, in 1980, a colleague of his wrote an essay that was respectful in a manner befitting the composer who was the archetype of the successful American musician. The halo over Copland's noble head owed much to his shrewdness in combining well-known musical formulae from Western folklore with a rather simplistic style. This combination was a speculative attempt to please a large constituency. According to the birthday essayist, Copland was quite aware of this popular style, since he also opted, in his Symphony, his Variations, and in a twelve-tone experimental piece, to demonstrate that he knew how to be "serious."

Copland's longevity undoubtedly nudged performers toward a patriotic assessment of his overall *oeuvre*. Nonetheless, this cannot, surely, alter the inevitable verdict of even the friendliest juror, namely, that only the skillfully planned "populist" works made their mark, while the "serious" and "serial" are little more than hobbies for loyalists to cherish. Intended as boulders, those works were mere pebbles. By more rigorous standards of composition, they have produced barely a circle in the water. Why is this so, and why could this able composer not come up with a symphony equal to his *El Salón México* or other works of that order? For the reason that Andrew Lloyd Webber has not been able to deploy his veritable armada of highly useable and acclaimed show scores to establish a beachhead in the field of sacred music: the public of Webber and Copland does not require requiems or symphonies.

At the 1987 International Music Festival in Lucerne, the opening concert was a performance of Copland's *Lincoln Portrait*. I was listening on the radio, and well recall the radio announcer's saying that Copland "was not a known composer" in Europe. Copland was able to develop a style of composition that was popular in the United States but not abroad, although many American conductors perform regularly in European cities with European orchestras. The Lucerne performance was conducted by Herbert Blomstedt, the Swedish music director of the San Francisco symphony. Perhaps Blomstedt felt he ought to acknowledge the American city where he is responsible for looking after music (in a highly responsible manner moreover); perhaps he was asked by the festival direction to include the *Lincoln Portrait* for political reasons. The performance did, however, feature the festival orchestra, which is formed each year ad hoc for the solemn opening concert. It is doubtless true that wherever American music is performed today there is generally more to its selection than simply the conductor's preference for that particular work.

Nobody in music, even the composer's most ardent admirers, will call Copland's *Lincoln Portrait* great music. It is a serviceable piece that is entirely suitable for a patriotic holiday, a children's concert, or a political gathering. There is nothing wrong with it, just as there is nothing wrong with Benjamin Britten's *Glorianna*. Just as *Glorianna* is not among the better compositions of a very fine composer, *Lincoln Portrait* is not the worst of Copland's (although it is rather near his low point). As part of the campaign to create a genuinely American school of composition, Copland has made it into the symphony orchestra's regular programs, mostly with his populist pieces, sometimes with his more serious music.

At the heart of the matter, though, is the delicate state of an American culture in which the composition of any music other than jazz is fraught with problems. One might even shrink these vast cultural and political trends into a neat little scenario. Uncle Sam's great-grandson has begun to tire of imported music and wants to make his own. He copies assiduously the central European composers of the 1860s, then the 1870s, and then the 1880s, but progresses no further because the *fin-de-siècle* neurotics give him a terrible headache. His son (Uncle Sam's great-great-grandson), sickened by the war of 1914–18, turns instead to France, where he finds that a delicious cocktail of Dada and learned primitivism, enlivened by a dash of popular themes, can be made into a reasonable facsimile of sophistication-cum-residuals. The resulting music is not, however, indigenous to the United States. So neither "international" nor "parochial" may be equated, then, with relative merit, just as merit has little to do with duration. Those composers who write longer works (Olivier Messiaen, who wrote a main work for an entire evening; Karlheinz Stockhausen, who wrote an opera for several full evenings) are at fault if the topic (in words) or the thematic development (in music) can be done in less time. Minimalist scores of forty minutes or so might be useful as a nonaddictive soporific medicine, but for longer pieces themes really are necessary. A long speech without a proper subject may serve as a harangue, but not as an oration. In other words, whether Bruckner's Eighth Symphony is or is not a masterpiece has nothing to do with its duration.

Richard Strauss's *Till Eulenspiegel* can be played as a romp without knowing who Till was or what his pranks were. The rapidly descending passage for the solo violin will be played by many a splendid concertmaster who knoweth not that the passage represents Eulenspiegel's urinating onto the crowd from up on the roof. Whereas that work is adaptable to any bland virtuosic internationalism, the solo violin Rondo of Mozart's "Haffner" Serenade is ruined by such a virtuosic approach. This has been demonstrated, both on television and for a live audience, by one of the current generation's super-violinists. Composers prior to Schoenberg were writing their scores with one element in common: tonality in the broad sense of the term plus metric and rhythmic patterns that enabled listeners and amateur players and singers alike to associate their new experiences with previous auditory impressions.

So music is a language that is still recognizable many generations after the originals were created and to people who habitually speak and read different languages. Pierre Boulez wrote an essay entitled "Schoenberg est mort" as a musical obituary to mark the end of the "affair" (the cohabitation of composers with serialism). It is my impression—and this may not reflect the views of Boulez or his followers—that the new music is essentially an exploration of sonic sensations that, given the essential sameness of human auditory equipment, should qualify as internationally digestible music. Perhaps.

For the time being there is no sign that composition on five staffs in metric and rhythmic patterns, prefaced by numerals such as $\frac{4}{4}$, $\frac{5}{8}$, and so forth, has yielded center stage. The occupants of center stage, particularly the symphony orchestras, are severely disadvantaged by the poverty of new music and by the geriatric element among the public patrons. These are peculiarly American crises.

International Music

Is music really an international language? My instinctive answer would be "yes and no," and I suppose you will tell me that is really no answer at all.

What we have today is a thriving international exchange of performers combined with a rather less than thriving international exchange of compositions. There was a time when the elegant world spoke French, but there is little doubt that English is now the international language for the technological elite who fly across continents and oceans. For that class of people music has also been, in a sense, "international," and yet I hesitate to add the word *language* because I am just not sure, for example, whether the message intended by Mahler in his Ninth Symphony will be entirely appreciated in certain cities of the non-English-speaking world.

Most casual concertgoers in the United States believe that the widespread popularity of Mahler's music today has been caused by the pioneering of Leonard Bernstein. Not to take away an ounce of credit from Bernstein, it might be fairly said that the same efforts by that deeply committed artist would not have had the same effect without the earlier efforts of refugees who fled to the United States to escape the Nazis. One might say that the language of Gustav Mahler may always be alien to those who have never read anything by Franz Kafka, but to what extent is music really "language"?

A former prominent American music critic, who is very learned and surely not a superficial listener, considered Mahler's orchestral work latter-day Tchaikovsky, by which he meant it was bombast alternating with sentimentality, with kitsch never far behind. Knowing the educational and ethnic background of that critic I can understand what he meant. By temperament Mahler was a virtuoso, and his best writing was focused on virtuosity. I, an orchestra conductor, know that in Mahler's orchestration there is a large element of virtuosity, which gets across to people who need not comprehend anything of Mahler's angst, neurosis, and Weltschmerz to enjoy his music quite sincerely.

Music that allows performers to shine brilliantly seems to have an easy time traveling across space *and* time. Paganini, in the hands of a fine player, is neither Italian, European, nor nineteenth century. Even those who have no idea how difficult it is to play the violin can be speechless when observing the little miracle that can be produced by two hands and arms armed with a small wooden box and a stick with hair attached to it. The appeal is as international as that of the trapeze artist who is greeted around the world by the same expressions of wonder and admiration. It is quite logical to suppose that this is because nobody in a circus needs to say anything, but is it not rather because the medium *is* the message? This is surely the case with strictly virtuoso compositions—music written by and for virtuoso practitioners of an instrument.

A transcription by Liszt of a Schubert lied makes little or no effort to retain the message contained in the original for voice and piano. A melody by Schubert, with a text by Goethe, sung by Dietrich Fischer-Dieskau, will not mean much to an audience in Palermo. If in the same program the accompanist plays that lied's virtuoso version by Liszt, the audience will cheer until the rafters shake. This is the basis of internationalism in music. The current vogue for old instruments and so-called authentic performance practices has, perhaps inadvertently, the same type of appeal: internationalism through virtuosity. For at least fifty years we have been told that Felix Mendelssohn's revival performance of Bach's *St. Matthew Passion* heralded a century of misinterpreting Bach's music.

If we all agreed that documentary accuracy was paramount, this might be true, but should documentary accuracy really be our primary concern? In my view this approach runs the risk of neutralizing (or, in my dictionary, "internationalizing") the sense and message of Bach's music. Notwithstanding certain innovative interpretations of his music (such as a delightful "Brandenburg" Concerto for Moog synthesizer, which I enjoyed immensely), Bach, in his cantatas, passions, masses, and motets, is a parochial composer whose spirit is essentially bound to a cultural orbit in which Luther and the incarnation of God are realities. All this is valid, by the way, for first-rate compositions only—a point to be remembered by those contemporary composers who attempt to parlay their music into an international orbit with program notes and other similar verbal propaganda.

Such composers also frequently employ the seemingly simple device of giving it an attention-seeking title. One example of an instrumental composition with an "honest" title is Liszt's short symphonic poem *Orpheus*. The symbolism of that piece is apparently quite evident in the title, but then this is only true for those who are at least somewhat acquainted with Greek legends and mythology. In my experience as a conductor I have noted that few, if any, of my professional colleagues explain such poetic content and backgrounds to players, either assuming that they know it already (alas, not the case) or not even finding it necessary. Frankly, if they were to follow Schoenberg's analysis of the aforementioned Brahms lied, they might well conclude that references to poetic content are superfluous, if not detrimental. Richard Strauss, who also composed symphonic poems, was one who felt that it was essential to acquaint players with poetic associations by making them manifest in titles and prefaces.

The international success of symphonic poems—be they by Liszt, Strauss, or anyone else—is due to their virtuosic elements. If Richard Strauss's symphonic poem *Ein Heldenleben* is still performed in response to public demand, it is because of the brilliance of its orchestration, a wonderful solo for first violin, and a truly moving final section in which the solo fiddle is matched by a horn solo. Because of an absurd, self-inflating "autobiographical program," the piece is so embarrassing it is played less in Germany than abroad.

Stage Fright

As I was growing up in Vienna, my father's sheet music and my mother's life-long love of theater instilled in me an instinctive yearning for music and the stage. I often wonder why it is that some of our most talented performers tend to cancel their performances at the drop of a hat without really being ill. I believe it is because they simply do not feel at home on stage or on a platform.

Whereas many artists learn to control this stage fright sufficiently to function for many years, others do not. Some (those two wonderful singers, Rosa Ponselle and Franco Corelli, are prime examples) gave up glorious careers simply because of these nerves. Artists such as Vladimir Horowitz and Van Cliburn have chosen temporary retirement followed by comebacks. Glenn Gould, perhaps one of the all-time greatest (and in view perhaps also the kindest and gentlest) artists, preferred to do his playing in a recording studio.

There are many theories as to the psychological causes of stage fright. I certainly would not claim to know any better than the experts, but I have developed my conclusions over the years after studying some of these personalities and working with them. They all seem to share one common trait: a lack of obligation to their talent. Not only do these people not feel *at home* when they reach the platform, they also appear not to understand that their talent is both a gift and a debt to be paid to the patrons. In my early outings I was as nervous as anybody, but as I gradually gained command of the material, all the unnecessary nervousness vanished. By unnecessary nervousness I refer to those nerves that do not contribute toward better performance. This has nothing to do with that necessary tingling of the nerves that one might call concentration, expectation, or quickening pulse—the nerves that heighten vitality while leaving the brain in control.

The great pianist Arturo Michelangeli is very precise about what kind of instrument he will and will not use in public concert. That is a standard trait for every serious pianist, but with Michelangeli it sometimes reached quite amazing proportions. On one occasion, at a Zurich recital, he inspected his two instruments (which had been sent on ahead of him) and found that one had quite frankly "caught a cold" and the other would be acceptable for only half his recital. He declared that he wished to cancel the second half and an announcement was duly made. It was only after a certain gentleman had walked into his dressing room and rather forcefully assured him, in German, that the audience had "not paid good money only to be sent home with half a loaf" (or words to that effect) that he decided to play the whole recital after all.

I am sure that with some of these pianists there is a certain element of paranoia about perceived public hostility. (There is altogether too much backstage talk about enemies; it is curious that one hears so little about friends!) Another great pianist, Artur Rubinstein, put the whole thing into words one day as I drove him back to his hotel in Boston, after a recording session. Musing about Vladimir Horowitz and his habit of canceling at the drop of a hat, he said: "I played recitals when I had a fever of over one-hundred degrees. I may not have been at my best, but it is still better than sending the public home."

Time to Rehearse

In the manifesto written for the inauguration of Schoenberg's Society for the Private Performances of Contemporary Music, Alban Berg lamented the "insufficient rehearsal time" in the Vienna of 1918. This lack of rehearsal time has been loudly lamented by countless frustrated and otherwise badly treated composers ever since, and is often used by conductors as an excuse if things go badly.

In fact, this complaint has been uttered so often that it has now become accepted wisdom. In my experience there can be no arguing with composers over "difficult" passages in their works, even if such passages require extra time for preparation. I suspect that every great composition throughout history was judged difficult at first, but any complexities were generally overcome by the composers themselves, who understood that solutions were to be found that would not compromise their intentions.

The theories of Theodor Adorno—chief publicist, philosopher, and *chef d'attaque* for the Second Viennese School—certainly support the view that some modern composers may have been suffering from a touch of hidden paranoia. Certain compositions from the early twentieth century (and particularly those of the Schoenberg group) often seem so strewn with hurdles that one wonders whether they were placed there intentionally. They certainly require more rehearsal time. Then there is the case of Milton Babbitt. I have no reason to doubt the honesty of a composer who is as intransigent as Arnold Schoenberg and revered for his unyielding stance in all matters affecting modern music. Nevertheless, when a musician writes—for one of the finest string sections in the United States—a piece that proves to be unplayable, there must be a good reason. How then should we explain the debacle surrounding Babbitt's *Transfigured Notes* (his 1987 commission from the Philadelphia Orchestra)?

Babbitt is an avant-garde composer who for much of his life has accused orchestral associations of being too conservative in their programming. It is perfectly imaginable that he used the Philadelphia commission—awarded to him by one of America's most conservative musical institutions—to prove to the world just how conservative they were. Let us suppose that this was the case. Babbitt guessed correctly that in 1987 the vast majority of competent music critics, music judges, and commission distributors would be too scared to suggest (as I suggested privately to my wife) that the piece could not be performed.

I should also like to cite just one of Schoenberg's compositions: his *Herzgewächse* for soprano with three instruments, Op. 20. The three instruments in question are celesta, harp, and harmonium. Nothing too problematic there, it would seem, but one would be hard pressed to find any ensemble—large or small—in which these three instruments and their players were regulars. Of course, the soprano is hardly an endangered species. Our Schoenberg soprano must have a G below middle C and an F above high C—namely, a three-octave range. A voice like that is, to put it mildly, very hard to find. The low G is difficult even for mezzo-sopranos, the high F similarly taxing. To require a singer to give you both those extremes, together with all the other notes in between, is asking a good deal indeed.

If this work were a major essay in composition, it might be churlish to mention all this, but if you take the composer's tempos at face value (and those tempos are certainly what Schoenberg would have insisted upon), the whole piece lasts about three-and-a-half minutes. Again, one might argue that nobody should make a case out of so short a piece, but I do sometimes wonder why a composer would place hurdles across his or her path toward acceptance. It just happens that this piece demonstrates the phenomenon more overtly than, for instance, the eight flutes in the *Gurre-Lieder* or the six clarinets in the Four Songs, Op. 22.

The issue of insufficient rehearsal time is as much publicized in 1990 as it was in the Vienna of 1904, when Richard Strauss reported from New York that he had managed to achieve a satisfactory rendition of his *Sinfonia Domestica* only after fifteen rehearsals with the musicians. Those fifteen rehearsals were probably made necessary by the newness of the instrumental demands made by Strauss. Many stories testify to the difficulties encountered in his orchestrations by orchestras from Milan to Paris.

Those difficulties were largely because, in 1904, conservatories in Milan, Paris, and New York were teaching with an outmoded syllabus (some were continuing to do so in 1960). They were still giving instruction in wind and brass instruments according to standards current around the year 1875. Indeed, one major American symphony orchestra, which performed very little contemporary music during the tenure of a certain venerable and conservative director, is still today slowed by a percussion section that is not at home with the more intricate sonic and rhythmic problems of modernism.

At the Vienna Opera we once rehearsed Ernst Krenek's opera *Karl V* (a dodecaphonic composition). For this I also required a very large number of rehearsals—I did not count how many. One reason for this was simply that the entire crew of musicians (about twice the number of bodies in a traditional orchestra) had to learn the work. Because of the rotation system, an orchestra can perform, for three hundred nights each year, a repertoire that often consists of forty or fifty operas. That system can only work if all alternate and substitute players are fully conversant with every item on the schedule. With only one crew of the seventy-strong orchestra called for by Krenek, half the number of rehearsals should have sufficed, but since everybody had to learn the piece, one might argue that my sixteen or twenty rehearsals were really serving two orchestras.

Another version of the conductor's lament was once voiced by the Romanian conductor Sergiu Celibidache, who protested that he must have extra rehearsal time to accomplish the deep metaphysical, transcendental, Zoroastrian, theosophist, or Buchmanite philosophy that he appeared to sense in every piece of music, including Ravel's *Rhapsodie Espagnole*.

So there are three principal reasons why there never seems to be enough rehearsal time: the need to educate players who have remained decades behind the times, the need to allow for personnel doubling and changing, and simple self-aggrandizement. The third category, unfortunately, includes cases in which very good composers have created unnecessary difficulties.

Selling Out

The word *commercial* has no place in the vocabulary of music and has generally been used with scant regard for its true meaning. When Beethoven's secretary asked the composer to lend the four parts of one string quartet to a group of players, the composer asked for forty florins. Was Beethoven at that moment a commercial composer? When Virgil Thomson wrote the film score *The Plow that Broke the Plains* did he demean himself by accepting a big fee? When Andrew Lloyd Webber took a break from Broadway to compose a requiem, did he betray his success in doing something that will probably not pay too many residuals? Was he thereby transformed from a commercial into a noncommercial composer?

All composers—even "academic" composers—begin composing with the intention of selling (yes, *selling*) their compositions. Selling equals commerce. If commerce is to be equated with corruption, then every artist might justifiably be considered a member of some vast crime syndicate. I have always believed professional musicians (including composers) to be honest. That does not mean that they cannot use their talents to make a better life for themselves.

Consider the following remark: "We think it's just too bad that Bob's boy went to Hollywood and sold out. He was such a favorite at Juilliard, and everyone there predicted a great future for him."

So it goes.

Such remarks, familiar enough in the private sphere, also abound in "serious" biographical writing. Take, for example, the tribute written by Arthur Berger for Aaron Copland's eighty-fifth birthday. Berger identifies two groups of works by the composer. The first, he says, is typified by works such as *Rodeo*, *El Salón México*, the *Lincoln Portrait*, and other scores that clearly demonstrate Copland's desire to be understood and widely performed. The second, which includes pieces such as the Piano Variations and the Third Symphony, were, says Berger, "made for the ages." Such a distinction is nonsense and cannot withstand any thorough analysis of the work of Copland, who, like any honest composer, always affixed a recognizable signature to his works. Mozart once wrote several dances simply because he was in urgent need of instant cash, but nobody ever regards those occasional pieces as commercial. Similarly, nobody ever calls Beethoven a commercial composer just because he asked for a fee whenever a publisher made a suggestion to him.

A composer, like any other human being, needs money to live. Few composers ever enjoyed a private source of income that would have allowed them to compose without any thought of their remuneration. Copland may well have loaded his Third Symphony with notes that he kept out of *Rodeo* for fear of making the latter work too complex for the wider audiences he had in mind. Does that make Copland a two-tier composer? Beethoven explicitly stated, in his forward to his "Eroica" score, that he made that symphony deliberately longer than usual. Does that statement, or works such as his Variations on popular Ariettas or the "Schneider Kakadu" trio, imply that Beethoven is a two-tier composer? Of course not.

In our age it has become almost compulsory for those musicians who choose (quite rightly) to earn money, to head for the analyst's couch to expiate their perceived sin. How they beat their chests in repentance for having sold out their genius to the vile demands of movie studio, director, or producer! I have known several composers who flourished in the movie world, earning handsome salaries that should have allowed them at some point to "head back East." Instead they quite naturally found it more agreeable to live in an expensive house, drive two or more expensive cars, dine in expensive, fashionable restaurants, and seek the aforementioned expensive atonement on the analyst's couch. How they would rue those wasted years, which should have been spent writing the great symphony instead of scoring and recording music that nobody listened to! This is bunk, but even if the hypocrisy of such behavior is well understood, the notion of the composer's selling out to commercial interests persists. I believe that this is wrong, and I do not accept the term *commercial* for the type of musical score commissioned by film makers. I do not personally like most film music, because I find the constant addition of meaningless sound that has no connection with the action on the screen to be rather disturbing, but then, if the movie industry depended on my patronage, there would be no movie industry.

Let us consider the relationship between the commissions of symphony orchestras and the commissions of film producers. I have examined many of the former and none of the latter, but I am willing to bet that no film producer would consider the works written for symphony orchestras to be good enough for a movie soundtrack. Their rejection of such works would not be a rejection of their complexities or dissonances, but rather of the uncertainties surrounding most new scores submitted in competitions and for commissions. The word *uncertainties* should be read as something of a euphemism, expressing in the gentlest manner those elements of contemporary music that characterize its relationship with the wider musical public. *Incompetence* is another word that springs to mind.

Do we not need an occasional child to cry out the words: "This fellow simply does not know how to compose"? Composers who do not know how to compose will just not do for film scores. In the movie world, split-second, stopwatch timing of a musical passage and phenomenal speed of execution are essential—there is a great deal of money involved (wildly excessive amounts by the standards of the musical non-profit world). Of course, the composer's ability to cope with these demands is not necessarily a sign of creative originality (which is low on the list of requirements of most filmmakers). I may be a Philm-Philistine, but I fail to see how the creative qualities of a score for a *Rambo* movie can make much difference to the response of the public or to the box-office receipts.

Without wishing to discourse at length here upon the essence of composition, I should like to stress that writing down music on paper is a craft. Even if the resulting stack of manuscript pages does not "take flight" in actual performance (and I suspect that no one will ever be able to predict whether or not this will happen), the musician who can write sequences of musical ideas on score paper, and who also knows how it will sound, is a competent composer who (if he is also efficient and fast) will find jobs writing film scores.

Writing movie scores is a perfectly honorable way for an artisan to make the most of what he or she has learned. To underline my objection to the expression *selling out*, it seems to me that one can sell only what one owns. Those good people who believe that "Bob's boy has sold out" by writing for Hollywood assume, by implication, that he had something to sell. It is curious that whenever this cliché is used nobody ever stops to ask what exactly it was that Bob had to sell. If Stravinsky, during his residence in Hollywood, had submitted to the demands of a movie director, he would indeed have been selling out, because by that time he already had a long and distinguished record of writing down symbols that, when heard, "took flight."

A fine example of a composer who went to Hollywood and never sold out was Erich Wolfgang Korngold. He made a tremendous impact on the standards of film music, simply by never departing from the style of his earlier opera compositions. He may have done this even though he realized that the fabric of his music had become obsolete. To those of us who, as students, used to do battle with the conservative Viennese establishment, his scores were a throwback to those musicians who sought ever more perverse themes to match Strauss's *Salome* and *Elektra*. Even though I enjoyed only a fleeting acquaintance with Erich Wolfgang Korngold, I became very friendly with his son. If his father ever did believe that he had sold out to Hollywood, I am certain I should have been aware of it.

One observes a similar phenomenon among the many conductors who made careers and fortunes specializing in "pop" classical music. The few I have known personally acted as suitors rejected by a capricious lady—destined to be masters of the classic and romantic repertoire, they had subsequently found themselves cruelly spurned. There are also certain psychological similarities between the role of the film composer and that of the pop conductor—not least because each is the most lucrative branch of its respective discipline.

Popular classical music, whether recorded or played to mass audiences, should not be seen as commercial purely because it earns more money than so-called serious classical music. The ability to write music with a broader public appeal is a rare and special talent. Composers such as Johann Strauss Jr., Franz Lehár, Jacques Offenbach, and George Gershwin represent the light muse of music just as the farces of the Austrian writer Johann Nestroy represent the lighter side of human comedy.

Now for an example of what I regard as commercialism in music: the use, in television commercials, of snippets from the best-known scores of the great classical repertoire. This represents vandalism and a display of scandalous disrespect by the advertising agencies, who seem perfectly happy to force music of nobility and refinement into a kind of symbolic prostitution. The musical signature tunes of radio and television programs rightly pay residuals to those who compose them, but the criminal abuse of the final page of Beethoven's Ninth is allowed to proceed free of charge because that music is deemed to be "in the public domain." This curious expression might be more clearly defined thus: "Any huckster may freely dismantle, dismember, or distort any immortal masterpiece of his or her choosing to sell any type of merchandise he or she is contracted to sell."

A "creative" advertising executive might argue that the exposure given to these snippets promotes wider public appreciation of immortal music. Such an argument only adds insult to injury. The repertoire of concertos, symphonies, quartets, and other chamber music combinations is defined only because of its totality—from the first measure to the last. Imagine a picture of St. Peter's Square in Rome, showing only one segment, two pillars, and the intervening space. The caption reads: "Here is what Michelangelo built on two sides of St. Peter's square." Just as those colonnades can be appreciated only when one sees and understands the overall intentions of their architect, so it is with a symphonic work. No one, surely, can believe that the final few seconds of the Ninth enable the listener to understand a work that lasts around seventy minutes? There must be many others who feel as grossly offended by this practice as I do. Of course, one can have a bit of fun, but it should be done within the confines of good taste—an increasingly obsolete commodity, it would seem.

It is essential to define clearly the language used to define the arts. Without needing to open one's dictionary, one might easily define the word *commercial* as "to do with commerce" or "related to trade." Now one fundamental element of commerce appears to be that one party should manufacture, or buy, for a certain price, something which is subsequently sold, hopefully at a profit. If that profit is smaller than reasonably anticipated, the sale is deemed not to have been a commercial success. By this or any similar definition, the term *commercial* will never be appropriate to music because composition and performance are both services. The notion of commerce should not be confused with that of service.

Much has been said and written about our transformation from a manufacturing to a service economy. What musicians do has always been considered a service by those who fully understand this term. When a commercial enterprise prepares itself for an Internal Revenue Service review, its bookkeeper will know the cost of buildings, borrowings, investments, and so on, but the individual artist, musician, or actor—the provider of a service—will never be able to calculate the cost of his or her years of study or how to project such cost as the commercial seller does.

In Vienna, prior to the First World War, many professionals such as businesspersons, bankers, manufacturers, doctors, and lawyers not only subscribed to theaters, operas, and concerts but also themselves played an instrument. In many houses there were regular chamber music evenings featuring several works, and participants practiced hard to keep themselves in form. A missing instrument might be found by hiring an off-duty member of the Vienna Philharmonic (whose musicians would often be glad for a chance of extra income, especially if the hostess was known to offer a splendid buffet supper). The devotion and enthusiasm of these prosperous bourgeois could not be questioned, and several amateur groups played at a level not far removed from that of the Philharmonic.

Yet, most of them forbade their sons to prepare for a career in music. Instead they engaged fine teachers so that their sons could master a string instrument sufficiently to serve as fourth player at a quartet evening. If any son were to find making music so pleasurable that he asked to become a professional (that is skip university, law, or medical school), the music-loving pater would swiftly exercise his parental veto, thus nipping his son's musical aspirations in the bud. The same father would have said yes to his son if he had been given a notarized guarantee that his career would produce another Piatigorsky or Huberman.

Nobody has ever been able to say exactly why one musician is elevated to stardom while another ends up playing fiddle on the pier. Perhaps the son might have made a good career composing advertising jingles. He might have been happier doing that than sitting in a law office or practicing surgery. It is too easy to be as blunt as those who commiserated with poor Bob, who "sold out" to Hollywood. Even if Bob had to abandon his dream of composing the great American symphony, he may still have preferred to remain in some other form of music.

Parents, relatives, and friends appear to be aware only of the contemptuous slant of the word "commercial" when it is associated with music. Unlike France, the United States apparently has no academy at which linguists and philosophers debate and consider words and their meaning. My acquaintance with film writers and composers taught me that the contemptuous slant given to the words *commercial* and *selling out* originated with those who had been obliged to abandon their grand illusions. Like the splendid neurotics that they were, they would apologize for their perfectly honorable occupation with the kind of self-loathing that has poisoned the language.

Music is an essential part of social services. Some music has always been possible only through the generosity of patrons. Today such generosity is labeled "subsidy"—mostly governmental subsidy in Europe, mostly private in America. Some music has always been associated with other arts and forms of entertainment, such as dance, opera, film, religious rites, or military parade accompaniment. Perhaps one might draw a clearer distinction between these artists and the "commercial artist" who works for advertising agencies, but that distinction is not always so clear-cut.

In any case, the snippet of the Ninth that is used (or abused) in a meat commercial—accompanied by a clown swinging a shashlik like a conductor's baton—may not be called commercial music. Similarly, the artist may not be called "commercial." The artist merely works for the firm or individual who is "commercial."

Achilles' Heel

Anyone wishing to be informed, amused, or uplifted by a new text must be able to read. It is generally accepted, I believe, that the eye is a more reliable recipient and retaining agent than the ear, and this is certainly the case in music.

Many documents, such as Mozart's letters, show clearly that sight reading was formerly regarded as essential for anyone making music. In fact, one reason why performers in the classical era needed few rehearsals is that their sight-reading skills were high. It is wrong, by the way, to conclude that standards of performance were low because there were few rehearsals.

It should be clear from any comparison of past and present that the skill of "instant recognition" was formerly very common, and that it was often sufficient to look at a sheet of music to be able to play it *a vista* (on sight) or, in other words, without having to practice it. How else, for example, could Beethoven's Violin Concerto have been performed in public a couple of days after the score had left the composer's desk? We do not know how early the soloist received his part, but we do know with certainty that he was not given nearly as long to prepare it as present-day violinists.

There are many reasons for this. Since most music was new, musicians in those days were not confronted with the stylistic questions that bedevil modern musicians (who have to struggle through three hundred years of repertoire). We can be sure that musicians active in the world of composed music (as distinct from traditional folk music) knew how to sight-read. Today this is not the case (and this includes some professionals).

Anyone who has attended an audition for a vacancy in a professional ensemble knows that many excellent string players begin to stumble when a chromatic passage is laid before them (that is, unless they know it and have rehearsed and practiced it). As composers began to depart from the classic tradition of retaining the best tonalities for respective instruments, they wrote pieces in E-flat minor (such as Prokofiev's Sixth Symphony) and used enharmonic changes (as early as Bruckner). String instrument instruction did not keep up with the pace. Consequently—

except in the cases of rare and bright individuals—one can swiftly find the Achilles' heel of otherwise fine musicians by merely picking an unknown piece with some degree of chromaticism.

This is damaging to modern composition. All statistics based on averages are of doubtful value, but it is probably safe to say that the reading of new music declined in inverse proportion to the growing chromaticism of Western composers.

The Devaluation of Masterpieces

Having at one time been ordered to stay in bed for a few days, I took advantage of the chance to have a radio at my side broadcasting several hours of music each day. There was an irresistible ninety minutes of the finest jazz during the cocktail hour, and other periods were devoted to mixed classical selections. After ten days of this I confess I was left feeling rather like the guest who indulged himself at the banquet with a good deal too much eating and drinking. I was also struck by the fact that the current much-publicized crises in the worlds of opera and the symphony are more than merely economic or creative in origin. The crises were caused by our having made too much music too easily available. The result is the same as that seen in any other field: devaluation.

Devaluation is not exclusively a monetary term—it can refer to all those values, concrete and spiritual, which encompass artistic endeavor. In the general human perception of values the factor of rarity plays an important role. Whether it is caviar or Bach's *St. Matthew Passion*, the premise is the same. When a rarity is transformed into a routine experience—whether one eats caviar three times a week or hears the *St. Matthew Passion* four times every three months—one essential value is lost. Beethoven's Ninth Symphony is a prime example of a musical masterpiece that has been used, overused, and abused in misguided efforts to ensure that there is appropriate music at political events. It is far from being the only musical milestone thus abused, but it is the outstanding example. During my enforced rest with regular daily programs from my excellent local radio station, I realized, perhaps for the first time, that there are not as many masterpieces as I had always thought. Or is it that after decades of intensive occupation with such scores one gradually loses the wonder and awe of earlier encounters?

There is no doubt that overuse diminishes the thrill, the excitement, the wonder, and all the other common responses to the extraordinary. Countless analyses, each more thorough than the next, have sought to explore the ill effects of scarce funding and aging audiences, and there has been an all-too evident reliance on hyperbole. My task is to find repertoire patterns that will breathe new life into the music establishments of many hundreds of towns in Europe and North America. During an American Symphony Orchestra League conference in Washington, D.C., attended by two thousand delegates from several continents, one particular newspaper headline caught my eye: "Trouble Is the Public: Rich, White, and Nearly Dead." We know this is so, and we wish it were not, but I suspect that even if the public were impecunious, non-White, and wide awake, something radical would have to be done.

A list of every program played by the Berlin Philharmonic Orchestra in their main subscription concerts from 1895 to 1920 (chief conductor Arthur Nikisch) reveals that there were ten programs seasonally (during the war years only six), with the vast majority of scores belonging to the classical hit repertory (or, put more politely, masterpieces). From my student years in Vienna I recall similar series of ten subscription matinee concerts, given by the Vienna Philharmonic and with even more concentration on unquestioned masterpieces. If in those decades a wit had answered a quiz about great composers, he might have stated that Tchaikovsky wrote three symphonies, (IV, V, and VI), Mozart six (Nos. 35, 36, 38, 39, 40, and 41), and Mahler five (I, II, IV, VIII, and *Das Lied von der Erde*). Those numbers were the "hits" of the day, and were all that were needed for a great series by a great orchestra conducted by a great personality. (Today Tchaikovsky has six symphonies, Mozart forty-one, and Mahler ten plus *Das Lied von der Erde*.)

Today's great symphony orchestras play not ten, but up to forty programs annually, and I do not know any knowledgeable musician who would state that one can fill that many programs with masterpieces. Regardless of one's standards or individual tastes, it may be confidently stated that there are standards that lie beyond the vagaries of fashion. Verdi, who was a singularly secure composer and who never deceived himself about success, wrote two letters that give us an excellent picture of what a masterpiece is. The following are (my) translations of letters written after the Parisian first night of *Don Carlos*:

To Opprandino Arrivabene, Paris, 12 March 1867.

Dear Arrivabene: Last night *Don Carlos*. It was not a success! I don't know what will happen later and I wouldn't be surprised if things change. This evening I leave for Genoa.

To Léon Escudier, Genoa, 1 April 1867.

My dear Léon: . . . In Ricordi's *Gazetta* I read the summary report from the more important French papers about *Don Carlos*. In short, I am a near-perfect Wagnerite. But if the critics had been a little more attentive they might have noticed that one finds the same intentions in the trio from *Ernani*, the sleepwalking scene from *Macbeth*, and in many other pieces. . . . The question is not to know whether *Don Carlos* belongs to a trend but to know whether the music is good or bad. That question is clear, simple, and fully justified.

Musicians and serious students of opera by now fairly unanimously agree that the score of *Don Carlos* belongs up on the highest shelf with the composer's highest achievements, *Otello* and *Falstaff*. Questions of standards and evaluation (good or bad music) enter into the debate whenever musicians and scholars believe their admiration of *Don Carlos* must imply raised eyebrows about *Rigoletto* and its hit tunes (which *Don Carlos* obviously does not feature).

This seems to me an arbitrary (if not to say snobbish) attitude, promoted by those who claim that only polyphonic music from Bach to Schoenberg is of value and that all else belongs "on the trash heap of history" (Dahlhaus). Adorno goes further, saying that the hit tune is a hit only because it can be recognized readily! Countering that notion, however, is the story (whether true or not, I cannot say) that Gershwin, wishing to achieve greater mastery of composition, once went to see

Schoenberg (who then lived in Hollywood) and that Schoenberg told him, "It is I, perhaps, who should take lessons from you." There seems little doubt that Gershwin invented better tunes than Schoenberg.

The Hour of the Stopwatch

Allow me to offer the following brief excerpt from the *New York Times* of 8 March 1990 (taken from a review by the paper's senior music critic on the subject of the final section of Mahler's Third Symphony):

> Mr. Levine outdid even Mr. Bernstein in stretching the heart-breaking finale out to twenty-seven minutes, which, if not a record must be close to one. At the other extreme, Sir Georg Solti has zipped through the movement in a bit over nineteen minutes.

This is not the first time that I have seen a music reviewer use the stopwatch. The descriptive method, it seems to me, is not unlike that of the sports columnist. In 1937, a day after the new NBC orchestra opened a series of concerts with Toscanini conducting, Mr. Francis Perkins, a critic of the *New York Herald Tribune*, came dashing into the Met's press office on 39th Street to declare that he had evidence that Toscanini was getting older: the maestro's performance of Brahms's First, he said, had lasted at least a minute longer than when he last played it at Carnegie Hall with the Philharmonic. In fact, a difference of one minute for a piece lasting around forty minutes is negligible, but it was clear to me even then that the hour of the stopwatch, as it were, was nigh. When, as in the case of the Mahler piece, the difference is fifty percent of the overall time, the critic is certainly justified in asking what went wrong. In this case he did it in somewhat elliptical fashion by calling the music "heartbreaking" and saying that Solti had "zipped" through in nineteen minutes (thereby implying that the quick version had not been to his taste).

Note the phrase "outdid even Mr. Bernstein in stretching," which goes further in suggesting that the final section was artificially slowed down. This goes to the heart of a little game familiar only to musical insiders. Allow me to elucidate. The final movement of Mahler's Third has a replica in the composer's Ninth, which also ends with a very slow (in fact slower) Adagio. These two movements are among the key test pieces in a contest known as the Tortoise Race—an open competition designed to find the slowest conductor in the land.

When Sergiu Celibidache came to New York with his Munich Philharmonic, his rendition of Bruckner's Fourth Symphony was clocked at eighty-five minutes, compared with Klemperer's sixty-one minutes for the same piece. One day after the March 1990 Mahler review quoted above, Leonard Bernstein's performance of Bruckner's Ninth was timed by another reviewer at three minutes longer than the same conductor's recording of twenty years before. Knowing that particular reviewer's boundless admiration for Bernstein, I assume that the slowing down by three minutes over more than two decades was interpreted as a symbol of that artist's stability.

Timing has not been of any practical significance since we stopped making recordings on 78s. For planning modern concert programs, however, no meticulous timekeeping is needed since there are many listings of performance times that enable even an inexperienced music director to do the job with a fair degree of accuracy, and a difference of a few minutes here or there has never been a significant issue anyway. Not that this fact stops people from using their stopwatches. In Chicago the stage manager operated an electronic timing device (perhaps because of union regulations) that was set in motion at the first note of each piece and stopped at the last. If I performed the same piece twice in exactly the same time, the stage crew would treat me to a free pizza. I managed this feat on only three occasions in twenty years of annual appearances. Since I do not eat pizza, by the way, we played it for the honor. I once missed out by one second with Debussy's *The Martyrdom of St. Sebastian*, but I still had to do without my pizza.

The Triumphs of Technology

Advances in technology have brought inestimable benefits to the world of music. I should therefore like to offer this modest tribute to their magnificence.

The ubiquitous fax machine is quite rightly regarded as a great wonder of our time. As a conductor I find it extremely helpful in my professional and business affairs. There are occasional problems (sometimes a musical text, such as an alternative version of a passage in a score, does not arrive in time), but in general the machine is an extremely useful device. If the original copy of a score is in New York, for example, and you need it urgently in Munich, the librarian can send you the original within minutes of receiving the request.

Then there is the photocopier. This machine is useful in so many ways that it is now almost impossible to imagine how the music library of a major orchestra (or any similar performing organization) could have operated efficiently before its invention. Imagine, for instance, a situation in which a certain composition contains a significant number of technical problems for string players. Since string players sit in pairs at their desks, the library will typically make only nine parts of printed music available for eighteen violins. To enable every player to have a part of his own (or at least the passage containing the problem spots), photocopies are made and distributed in a matter of minutes.

The modern music librarian also has a computer programmed to reveal not only what composition has been played but also when, how often, and under whose leadership. This information is of incalculable service to the planners of future seasons, in helping to avoid duplication and enabling marketing officials to state, for example, exactly how long it has been since their orchestra played a particular piece.

Then there is the good old telephone. I should like to cite a rather entertaining example of its continued usefulness. It is Vienna, in the fall of 1987. On a Thursday morning, at 10:15, a singer's agent calls the casting director of the opera house to announce that his client is indisposed and cannot sing the role of the Countess at that evening's performance of *Figaro* (scheduled to begin at seven o'clock). The casting director consults his computer to find out who, in the dozens of opera companies within flying distance, sings the role in question. Phone calls are then made to track down those singers identified by the computer, but these singers appear to be either already engaged to sing that night, indisposed, or traveling.

At last, a willing and able soprano is located in Düsseldorf. Alas, the hoped-for connecting flights are not forthcoming. It is now past 11:00.

After several more calls our lady is hunted down. Shortly after six o'clock she is "whisked" (as the newspapers always so splendidly put it) to the opera house. I arrive to find her endeavoring to have her second-act gown taken in from "very fat" to "well proportioned." I have just enough time to inquire whether she knows all the *secco* recitatives (a fact never to be taken for granted these days) before the stage manager is bellowing "Bitte Herr Professor!" (the Viennese title automatically bestowed on anyone wearing glasses). We begin. All is well. I am eternally grateful to Ms. Sentai, who gave us a superb countess. Should any musically inclined reader doubt my point about recitatives, by the way, I can assure them that Ms. Sentai, notwithstanding her most cultured style of delivery and her spirited acting, sang the entire role without appoggiaturas. So much for the musical technicalities, now back to the technological miracles. The main point of the story is that our performance of *Figaro* simply would not have gone ahead in the days before the telephone and the airplane.

Even the most ardent purist would have sat as happily through that *Figaro* as if he were an automobile enthusiast in the back seat of a slightly dented Rolls Royce. If that *Figaro* had been scheduled for recording over the following days, our savior, Ms. Sentai, would certainly have been asked to learn her appoggiaturas. No Artists and Repertory man worth his salt would ever have accepted even slightly damaged goods. Why should a record producer be more concerned with perfection than the direction of the Vienna Opera? Because . . . well, because a recording is a document, not a performance.

When Walter Legge asked Elisabeth Schwarzkopf to supply the high C for a recording by Kirsten Flagstad, he sought neither to offend Flagstad nor to win cheap publicity, nor to draw the public's attention to the bravura of the technicians. Legge had merely found that the recording of the great Tristan-Isolde duet was missing a true high C. It just so happens that a voice as that of Flagstad is never comfortable above B-flat. He called upon Schwarzkopf because in the recording world the dented Rolls Royce just will not do. A recording is listened to repeatedly by admirers around the world, and the modern singing superstar cannot afford to be associated with a bad note.

How exactly Legge accomplished his feat I have no idea. The nearest I came to such technological wizardry was in 1974, when I recorded

Erich Wolfgang Korngold's *Die Tote Stadt* in Munich. The role of Paul was sung by the tenor René Kollo, who was also commuting between Munich and Bayreuth to sing *Parsifal*. The dramatic passages went well but the lyric bel canto sections of his part showed the effects of his Wagner performances. Parsifal has a *tessitura* (medium pitch) that is lower than Paul's, and a voice like Kollo's changes more naturally from high to low than it does from low to high.

After several days of recording we still had not achieved an acceptable take of Kollo's lyric passages, so the producer asked me to play through these passages with the orchestra alone. Much later, perhaps a month or two after the Munich sessions, Kollo went to London, where the studios of that particular recording company were located, to do a voice-over. Kollo put on his earphones, the studio engineer ran the tape of the orchestral music, and Kollo sang the requisite passages. My presence as conductor was quite unnecessary to these proceedings, and when I later heard the finished product I marveled at everybody's skill. I am quite sure that if I had not been personally involved I would have noticed nothing untoward. There was no break in any continuity, save perhaps the inevitable faint difference between the acoustics of the large Munich studio and orchestra and those of the smaller London studio occupied by the singer alone.

I recorded twice for a Los Angeles company on a recording system called "Direct to disc." The advantage of this system was that the balance of sound was not constantly manipulated, but set for an entire selection. We therefore achieved a more honest replica of live sound balances. The great flaw in the system, however, was that we needed to play for eighteen minutes at a stretch without being able to splice later to correct errors. In the old days, a similar flaw had plagued the world of 78s, but at least then the required interval had been a mere four minutes and twenty seconds maximum. The eighteen-minute stretch was an almost unbearable strain on the nerves, but then a record is a document, and a document cannot tolerate fallibility.

Technology is indeed a wonderful thing.

Nine

A Musical World in Crisis

The Crisis Defined

The world of music is beset by several crises, and in this chapter I should like to discuss some possible solutions. Global economic crisis certainly has a dramatic effect upon the world of music, because it undermines the deficit financing that plays such a significant part in our musical world (whether as official subsidies or private donations). Paradoxically, the great economic squeeze may ultimately prove a blessing. As many musicians have long been aware, there are several other crises looming on the horizon, and the musical establishment has been able to ignore those crises only so long as the money problem could be resolved. Now the game is up.

The most visible manifestation of these crises has been the reluctance of the so-called mainstream (subscription) public to accept anything new (whether it be a modern work or not). A second manifestation—and one that has been largely ignored—is the obsolescence of the symphonic form. In 1907 Arnold Schoenberg gave notice that the public no longer played any part in his plans. Since then many composers, critics, and writers have apparently been addressing nobody in particular, and this new independence has, notably, created considerable problems at first performances. Similarly, the major recording companies will risk no money on projects with doubtful sales potential, no matter how high their respect for the orchestra.

Opera, which I have known intimately since I was sixteen, seems barely able to exist without its crises. There will never be a shortage of such crises as long as there are opera singers. In more recent times, however, the problems have stemmed from stage directors intent on producing provocative visual non sequiturs from the music of the great masters. There is frequently more to say about what precedes and what follows an opera production than about the work, and controversy often appears to be the main objective.

The case is somewhat different with music written for instruments alone. There are few scandals, and while there may be an intrigue here or there, the various philharmonics and symphonies serve up a comparatively lean diet of gossip. This difference is quite logical, since the dozen or more star singers of an opera company can never be matched by the one or two star conductors who constitute the entire scandal / tantrum potential of the symphony orchestra. The crises in opera and the symphony remind me of a joke very popular in Vienna during the economic upheaval of the 1920s. Question: What's the difference between Germany and Austria? Answer: In Germany the situation is serious but not hopeless; in Austria it is hopeless but never serious. For the word *Germany* one might easily read *symphony*, for *Austria*, one could substitute the word *opera*.

When Max Rudolf left the Metropolitan Opera in 1958, Rudolf Bing's management team suddenly found itself bereft of professional musicians. I therefore joined the team for a short while, combining my management duties with some opera conducting. The daily casting meetings were great fun, but the less attractive part was an institution known as stable watch. This task, which fell to each of us every fifth performance, entailed our being present from thirty minutes before curtain until the end of the evening (or matinee). We were required to say a decisive word if something went wrong, and we made the rounds of the dressing rooms to be sure that everyone was in condition to go on stage.

We also went backstage for the curtain calls to prevent little tricks of applause-stealing and similar magnanimous acts so popular among our colleagues of the lyric art.

Whenever my turn came, I would bring some reading. After the show had begun I would dine in a delightfully deserted first-rate restaurant in the Grand Foyer. I thus made the best of a free evening only slightly restricted by having to spend four hours inside the opera house. On one occasion I had just arrived at the Grand Foyer to pick my table for later, when a wardrobe man came running after me, begging me to come backstage to arbitrate a fight. The show was *Cavalleria* and *Pagliacci* and the tenor for Turridu was claiming the first-tenor dressing room (which had always been reserved for Canio). A cautious elder staff member had called Bing, who came very quickly and relieved me of the distasteful prospect of settling an infantile status question between two tenors. Thus were we all robbed of any chance of a fist fight or shouting match leading to double cancellation.

A lack of costumes provided by the company has always been the cause of much hilarity, certainly at the Met during the time I conducted there. Due to the economic depression no money was spent by management on anything but fees and salaries; there were no new productions and no full rehearsals, and the lead singers ordered their costumes.

I recall the time when Helen Traubel was advised to order costumes for her debut as *Lohengrin*'s Elsa from a famous fashion designer. Traubel had learned the Kirsten Flagstad repertoire after the Norwegian diva had left to join her husband. Lauritz Melchior, who was cast as Lohengrin, met with Traubel for a photo-session half an hour prior to curtain up. Mrs. Melchior, who had a rather pixyish personality, remarked to some people standing around that Helen looked not unlike the Archbishop of York. Her comment appeared verbatim the next morning in the *Herald Tribune*'s review of the performance, and nobody could convince either Traubel or her husband that this was coincidence (as Mrs. Melchior protested).

The absence of any real element of showmanship or color limits concert attendance to those who are truly devoted to the music performed. Opera audiences are interested in more than the substance of the artistic achievement, while one suspects that those who attend the concerts given by philharmonic orchestras or chamber ensembles do it to please a spouse, or to appear musically sophisticated, or perhaps in order simply to have a regular outing every first Tuesday of the month.

I have never sneered at such people, because without them—at least in the United States—the musical world would not be able to function at such a highly sophisticated level. At the same time, I have often felt that in the realms of the instrumental concert a minimum of showman-ship is missing. It could all be a little more colorful and less like a PTA meeting if every organization were to seek expert advice from people who know the entertainment business.

When I arrived in the United States, in 1937, I was told on many occasions that the American concert public was not too fond of vocal performance. Not only did this judgment appear to conflict with atti-tudes then prevailing in Europe, but it was shown much later to be quite wrong. Sometime in the early 1980s, I believe, the great Spanish soprano Montserrat Caballé incurred the wrath of the Met's manage-ment and was not reengaged. After her spell out in the cold, however, she was engaged by the New York Philharmonic as soloist. The music administrator, Frank Milburn, later told me that in all his thirty years with the New York Philharmonic he had never witnessed ovations such as those given to Caballé. This is just one among many such incidents that illustrate that symphonic organizations boycott vocalists at their peril.

It is not only star singers that appeal to the public of subscription concerts. I once built a New York program around Debussy's *La Damoiselle élue* and *Trois nocturnes*. Since both pieces require a small ensemble of women's voices, I hit on the idea of adding the Four Songs, Op. 17, by Brahms. Those songs were duly performed by twenty-four splendid professional ensemble singers, and yet I was quite amazed to find that the songs, unspectacular for effect, turned out to be the hit of the program (not once, but four times in New York and again four times in Chicago). So much for those who said that vocal music was not popular with symphony audiences. One reason why the participation of singers is not encouraged may seem incredible: lay directors frown at having to pay a small chorus when only three members of the band are in evidence. I experienced this type of mentality in the mid-1960s during my one (and only) appearance at a meeting of the board of trustees. Manager and trustees were quite adamant that we did not need to put on special events such as an opera in concert form.

In those days, every event was entered separately into the budget. I argued that our so-called normal concert programs, which offered overture, concerto, and symphony, did not draw a single media representative from the cities that furnished our public. Only a strategically placed special event, I told them, would give us the necessary shot of publicity for the summer season. We were allowed one such show each summer, but nobody among the trustees saw this as anything but humoring Erich Leinsdorf's nostalgia for his operatic past.

None of this is new, of course. When Virgil Thomson was music critic for the *Herald Tribune* in the early 1900s, he attacked the mismanagement of American music organizations, lamenting in particular the hegemony of German music philosophy and program ideas. Yet, no matter how eloquent his pleas for diversification and for more encyclopedic programming, he made no dent in the armor. Overture, concerto, and symphony remained our standard bill of fare.

Half a century later several major orchestras are led by middle-aged or older German conductors. This is an error, and one for which the managers are responsible. They made those appointments by recording opportunities and on the assumption that a combination of the "three Bs" (Beethoven, Brahms, and Bruckner) and Mahler would always guarantee a healthy future for nonprofit associations, even in a time of economic siege. Managements and boards have no taste for long-term policies.

Another major managerial miscalculation was to have paid no attention to the blossoming of chamber orchestras, academies, consorts, and other similar organizations that have succeeded in establishing a virtual monopoly of pre-1800 music. The death or resignation of several prominent and effective music directors at the great orchestras has created a calamitous situation. During the incumbencies of Koussevitzky, Ormandy, Szell, Bing, and so on, there was no question who decided what. It was conceded of these gentlemen by friend and foe alike that whatever one liked or disliked could fairly be credited (or debited) to one man at the head.

As for the economic crisis, it has always been taken for granted that opera and ballet companies, and the larger instrumental and vocal ensembles, have never been able to meet their costs without government subsidies or private donations. When I first came to the United States, as assistant conductor of the Met, I could not but be aware of the Great Depression. There were endless discussions (in the corridors of the opera house, between rehearsal calls, and elsewhere at private parties), on the deficit, on the lack of money for new sets and new costumes, on the sorry state of the Met's inventory, and so forth.

On one occasion, during a weekend spent at a Long Island home, I met a man in the clothing business who very patiently explained to me that anything aiming at quality was then considered a luxury item (or in our case a luxury service) and that luxury items should be priced high to allow the seller to make a fair profit. I do recall that popular concerts at popular prices were then given no more than one rehearsal, while regular concerts were given several rehearsals. Fifty years after the depression, American orchestras still give pop concerts with one rehearsal, while regular programs have four.

There are other expenditures that are considered irretrievable. The irreconcilable conflict lies in the universally accepted need to lure more young people such as students and young professionals, lest the disappearance of older subscribers should leave seats empty. Even as they try to fill seats, orchestral organizations raise admission prices. Every other argument urges the lowering of admissions. Basically the situation has always been similar to that of newspapers, which, no matter how large their circulation, must rely on advertisements that never seem to cover costs anyway. A program book or playbill is no medium for genuine commercial advertisers and is therefore unproductive in that respect. Subsidies have never amounted to much in the United States, and even in Europe their size is falling. Since mass dismissals are quite unthinkable, the only remedy is a drastic cutting of all fees and salaries (though nobody would ever dare admit as much).

I am also forced to conclude that stressing international values and publicity has had a negative effect overall because imported artists feel no loyalty to their American connections. The same is true of the sponsoring corporations that have taken the place formerly occupied by wealthy individuals. When a chairperson is transferred to another city—usually as a result of a merger that moves the company headquarters elsewhere— his or her obligation to support civic enterprises in the former home is removed. Add to this the wanderlust of ambitious conductors and orchestras (some with very distinguished pasts), and you have a situation that resembles a body devoid not only of a head but also a wallet.

The chronic lack of money and leadership is most apparent in cities that are not tourist attractions. Prominent orchestras used to make concert tours even before air travel became common, but the urge to travel to other continents has now become an obsession. Board members will not want to make a financial contribution if there are no European press reviews. In fact, my casual conversations with European journalists and my reading of the more voluble German newspapers have often shown just how negatively this or that American orchestra is reviewed. I have often wondered frankly how the hapless press agent in question ever comes out of it all alive.

There is a deeper and more obvious financial reason for these tours: most American cities simply cannot absorb the number of scheduled concerts to which the orchestral associations have been committed since the advent of the year-round contract. Their plight is much like that of the airline industry. When air traffic was buoyant because of soaring business profits, the airlines promptly bought or leased more planes; when the downturn came those planes were left sitting on the tarmac to pile up huge losses. Musicians who were being paid for not performing would be the musical version of that recession-hit air traffic (although it must be said that even in healthier economic times American orchestras have had too many scheduled concerts).

I have written the foregoing paragraphs because I am deeply concerned about the future of symphony orchestras. Most managers are keenly aware that, whereas quick remedies are politically impossible, long-term remedies may take too long. I certainly have no tricks to suggest. I do, however, believe that conductors and managers should radically alter their focus. Instead of concentrating their gaze on the distant horizons of internationalism, they should learn to concentrate more closely upon the needs of their local environment.

A Crisis of Responsibility

In September 1992 the *New York Review of Books* carried a splendid essay by Aileen Kelly on the Russian thinker, Mikhail Bakhtin. At one point Kelly quotes Bakhtin saying that in an age of ideological confusion there is a need for "new prophets and certainties."

Later Ms. Kelly cites Bakhtin's argument that moral responsibility was threatened by all forms of so-called theoretism—a way of thinking that sees all events as instances of universal rules or principles. Although rules can be helpful, Bakhtin maintains that we develop as moral beings by increasing our responsiveness to the irreducible particularities of each case.

Bakhtin's words illustrate perfectly the chaos prevailing in musical composition and in the work of stage directors who vandalize great (and less-than-great) operas. To make confusion total, the anarchist stage directors are paired with music directors who follow an older drummer, rehearsing orchestras until everybody is blue in the face to produce nuances that are eloquently contradicted by the visual goings-on. In my experience with famous international festivals I have observed that there has been an accelerated trend to disregard "irreducible particularities" and replace them with theories based on nothing but the stage director's misguided attempt to make an old drama or comedy relevant, although the drama or comedy had never lost its relevance in the first place. The great repertory of the lyric stage possesses an eternal relevance that derives from its preoccupation with unchanging human passions.

My one encounter with blatant disregard of an author's intentions occurred in Bayreuth in 1972, when I was engaged to conduct *Tannhäuser* with Götz Friedrich as stage director. I will confine myself simply to an account of one idea, which negated the entire religious foundation of the drama. In act 3, Tannhäuser returns from his journey to Rome where the Pope, after hearing of Tannhäuser's time spent with Venus, had declared, "Just as this staff in my hand will never again show blossoms, so will you never be redeemed from the fires of hell." This is reported in song by Tannhäuser to the horrified Wolfram. Now, Wagner's dramatic text was completed many years prior to 1870, the year of the Pope's declaration of infallibility in cases of dogma. In any case, that declaration would probably not have changed one word of Wagner even if he had written it after 1870.

Wagner's lifelong leitmotif of the redemption of the sinner had not ended with *Tannhäuser*, but it certainly did end with Götz Friedrich in 1972. In Friedrich's version we never saw the appearance of the group of young pilgrims carrying aloft in joyous triumph the blossoming staff of the Pope. In fact, we never saw the pilgrims at all because they sang backstage. Since very little choral singing can be understood even if the choir lines up along the footlights, it is quite reasonable to state that anything sung backstage by a chorus with a lively orchestral accompaniment might as well be in Urdu.

I had been to Wolfgang Wagner's office prior to the premiere, to inform him that after that summer's five performances somebody else would have to put up with that kind of festival. This was later considered decidedly unsporting of me, especially since the enthusiastic cognoscenti in the audience proved to be quite unaware of how they had been cheated. After this experience I conducted very little opera, and whenever I was asked to do it I opted for existing older productions to which there could be little objection.

I confess I had no stomach for the knowledge that the opera conductor had lost all rights to assume overall responsibility for a presentation. I have been dismayed to see how it is now virtually impossible to return to representational staging. The Met once tried it with the *Ring* cycle and it did not work. For one thing, the subscription public of the Met is accustomed to hearing Wagner with overwhelmingly powerful singers.

Such singers are, alas, no longer at hand. The old has been irretrievably lost, while the new has yet to be found. If I were ever to be interviewed under oath about where the responsibility for this loss lies, I fear I would have to point the finger at those notable conductors who have been content merely to complain at dinner parties while failing to take the one and only appropriate action—namely, to resign in protest. The power of the stage director is so firmly entrenched that the conductor has lost all his influence. In a telecast of a shameful production of Offenbach's *Tales of Hoffmann*, the name of the conductor was not to be found on the screen.

As far as conductors are concerned, it is possible to determine exactly when the crisis of responsibility set in: the moment when conductors first began to accept a second position as music director (generally on another continent). The advent of the jet aircraft made this possible, and the fat, so to speak, was in the fire. Managements, who are powerless to reverse the trend, must accept having their stars around for only half the time, but it is nonsense for them to protest that since they are continuously in touch with their star conductors via phone and fax everything is just fine. No telephonic description of a problem can ever equal personal observation.

On one occasion I found that, to rehearse a particular score, the assigned (second cast) woodwinds would not do. I duly informed the orchestra's general manager (this term today refers to the individual who is one rung beneath the manager, who is listed as executive vice-president or some such title). The general manager did not have the authority to settle a dispute involving the guest conductor, and so called the music director who was on tour with his "other" orchestra. A telephone connection to Taiwan was necessary to decide a very simple question which in more normal times would have been settled by an associate conductor (who nowadays does not exist anymore). It is rarely a question of malice or deliberate avoidance, but it all amounts to a chaotic situation for which nobody takes any responsibility.

If my memory serves me correctly, responsibility always used to lie on one side of the scale, with an equal weight in decision-making on the other side. Ideally, both sides would balance. From my experience as a music director I vouch that there is no longer any such balance. This is one very good reason why one should not blame conductors for acting like traveling salespersons instead of holding on to challenging positions.

Felix Weingartner, in his essay *On Conducting* (1920) stated that the conductor's role included the great task of "improving the musical taste of the community." Besides the basic condition that one must know a community in depth before one tries to improve its tastes, an individual seriously attempting to do that job today would meet immediate resistance from the bookkeepers of the organization headed by our enterprising would-be improver of tastes. The reason for this lies in the world of politics and particularly in post-1950 demographic developments. By

1950 there had been notable progress in the rebuilding of institutional activities following the ravages of war. The world of the performing arts—music, theater, opera, and ballet—had become increasingly democratic. In 1951 Bayreuth was reopened and Wieland Wagner took on the staging with the principal aim of doing away with all tendencies toward realistic, representational, or visual ideas.

Of course, some artists were politically very left-wing, but it might be argued in their defense that the political Right just does not produce attractive art. One need look only at cabaret, for example, to realize that first-class entertainment comes from the opposition and from the underdog. To keep pace with political developments and with improved social justice in Europe and in America, musical organizations, such as opera companies, ballet companies, orchestras, and professional choral groups, have witnessed a constant improvement in their collective contracts. More favorable working hours and improved wage conditions were accompanied by an ever-greater voice in matters artistic, the jurisdiction over which was gradually wrested from the hands of management (for the unions a conductor is, by definition, a member of management).

THE HAZARDS OF DEMOCRACY

The orchestra members have an important say in the casting process. There is undeniably some logic in this and in other questions where players' committees have taken over decision-making. Nonetheless, the overall responsibility of the music director has been thereby diluted and is going to be diluted even further. I swear the day is nigh when a committee will politely enter the conductor's dressing room before the start of rehearsal to admonish him for having "taken the slow movement of the symphony not as slowly as did Maestro Tortoisinovitch in a recent performance," or some such bitter reproof. Whereas I personally have been spared this dire circumstance, I did experience at two orchestras (Boston and Philadelphia) a major debate over the particular contractual clause that stipulates that there *will be* at every concert a fifteen-minute intermission.

In Boston the debate centered on plans for concert performances of the *early* version of Richard Strauss's *Ariadne auf Naxos*. A member of the committee who had played the opera raised the question in a visit to the manager's office. The manager promptly brought the problem to me, and despite my protestations that this was a one-act score with no possible point at which to break, I was reminded that there was a fifteen-minute intermission in the collective contract. To my delight, a post-Shakespearean Ariel came to my rescue, declaring that he would be willing to precede the opera by a suitable piece which, to give some kind of time balance should be not less than fifteen minutes. Our arguments, however, were to no avail.

The Philadelphia episode came out the other way. It happened at the summer pavilion in Saratoga, where I had programmed Mahler's Fifth Symphony. As those seventy minutes of music seemed quite sufficient for a warm summer night, this was the only piece planned. Despite management's earlier claim that its relations with the union and the in-house committees were excellent, the two top managers arrived in my dressing room ten minutes prior to the opening C-sharp minor, looking decidedly sheepish. They proceeded to impart the joyous tidings that the committee had paid a visit half an hour earlier and made the simple declarative statement that "they were in breach of contract" (no negotiations). Fortunately it is always a safe bet, if you have a great and experienced orchestra, to dig up the "Oberon" Overture. It can be played in between six and seven minutes, and you can then have your intermission. So much, however, for the excellent relations between the management and the players' committee.

It is possible to run an orchestra democratically but the cost has yet to be fully calculated. The experiences of an orchestra in Philadelphia are also rather different from those of less well-endowed groups. The Toronto Symphony, for example, delegated one junior executive to drive me from hotel to rehearsal and back again. This young executive explained to me during one of our drives that the orchestra wished to cut its rehearsal schedule and, more specifically, wanted the same timetable as the Chicago Symphony.

My suggestion was to tell the next meeting that management would gladly abide by this schedule when three programs had been played on the same level as the Chicago orchestra. It might even be argued, in fact, that Chicago does not rehearse enough—106 players need some rehearsing. No matter how correct it may have been to promote democracy in the world of music, no matter how logical to transfer *certain* decisions to the players, the end effect has been to destroy the notion of leadership. Let us not forget that in 1940, a music director was required to conduct, hire musicians, and select both repertoire and new compositions.

If my memory serves me right, it was in 1975 that six of the major US orchestras each commissioned a composer for an orchestral work, each with the understanding that the work of the other five composers would be performed by the other five orchestras after the premiere of each composition. Since I was a regular guest at the New York Philharmonic, I was asked to conduct the piece commissioned by the Chicago Symphony. The work in question was a score about Alice in Wonderland for voice and orchestra, by David del Tredici. I accepted the commission and duly received the score (a huge volume).

The del Tredici piece had, as its key motive, a morsel of a phrase that might be taken for *Tales from the Vienna Woods*. It was fifty-eight minutes long, and I confess that I was rather less than desperately committed to performing it. Then, one fine day (to quote from *Madama Butterfly*), George Solti called me from Chicago to report the enormous public success of the piece. Would I give him the pleasure of leaving the New York premier to him and the Chicago Symphony, for their forthcoming visit to Carnegie Hall? Overjoyed, I immediately said yes.

Solti was better informed than I, however, and said: "I knew that you would be kind and helpful, but I am afraid that Moseley [Carlos Moseley, president and manager of the New York Philharmonic], may never agree." I replied that I would try, and (still believing that there would be no hurdle) I jubilantly informed my wife that I was out of it. To my infinite surprise, however, I was called up by Pierre Boulez. He mentioned that the singer Barbara Hendrix was "charming" and that, after all, there was a contract that stipulated that each of six orchestras had to perform it and "sorry to Solti." Our performance, as it turned out, was greeted with lively Olés and Huzzas, and no further adverse effects were noticed.

It has never been my intention to show virtuous moral disapproval, since I am quite certain that there have been incidents in my career that I would have criticized strongly, had I learned of them from somebody else. Responsibility has become an endangered virtue for anyone in a leading position, and not just for those in the performing arts. For music directors, who must lead a musical organization with a hefty deficit budget and thousands of subscribers, truly free decisions are virtually impossible.

COMPOSERS

The acceptance and rejection of new music by an orchestra are these days extremely complex matters. Notwithstanding the functioning of several groups and ensembles who specialize in contemporary music, composers still swallow the bitter pill of compromise and compete eagerly for recognition by the major symphony orchestras. This is the case although many of our music directors are European and lack the ability (as, for example, Leopold Stokowski lacked it in 1942 in the case of Schoenberg) to immerse themselves in the true American spirit.

The Philadelphia Orchestra, wishing to celebrate the bicentennial of the signing of the US Constitution, awarded half a dozen commissions, which were to be delivered in time to prepare them for the orchestra's calendar year 1987 concerts (meaning winter/spring for the 1986–87 season and fall of the 1987–88 season). Having been a regular guest there, and being known for learning complex scores, I was asked by the judges if I would participate in the celebrations by taking on one of the six commissions—preferably the piece by Milton Babbitt, a much-revered teacher and composer. The score arrived six months prior to the planned performances. It was written for string orchestra (according to a footnote), it was nineteen minutes long, and it was entitled *Transfigured Notes*. After examining the score for several days I sent it back with regrets (but without adding, as I did to my wife, that the piece could not be played in that form).

The conductor Dennis Russell Davies was very generous, accepting the Babbitt and yielding to me "his" assignment: a piece for winds and percussion by Walton, which I performed. After a few rehearsals, however, Davies saw that it was impossible to produce a reasonably coherent rendition of the Babbitt and took it off. There was an enormous scandal with everybody attacking everybody else, except that for some reason nobody mentioned my name or that I had sent back the score. The point of this story is not to criticize Milton Babbitt, but to illustrate the point that a conductor must have the ability to read and assess a new score without ever having heard it played. It is an essential part of his responsibilities as conductor and musician that he should then be prepared to state his view about the work clearly. Alas, many conductors are either not able or not prepared to do this.

Two years later, the Dutch conductor Hans Vonk took the piece on and was given an unheard-of amount of rehearsal time. After many hours he also threw in the towel, and the orchestra released to the press a statement that the work would not be performed due to difficulties beyond the practicalities of a very busy season. In that press release I was mentioned as having been the first to send the piece back without trying it. Who shirked responsibility here?

The first obvious answer is the recipients of the press release, not one of whom—newspaper reporter, critic, or panelist—ever asked himself or herself "How come that Leinsdorf fellow sent it back before even trying it?" The composer dismissed the Philadelphia Orchestra as a nineteenth-century museum piece. Now this happened to be a nasty but not entirely false statement, since during Ormandy's tenure the Philadelphia repertoire was known as the most conservative among the big and great orchestras of the United States.

The second inexcusable lack of responsibility, however, I charge to Babbitt, who has taught and lived for many years in Princeton, New Jersey, which is near enough for him to know the strengths and weaknesses of the Philadelphia Orchestra. I think Babbitt must have known very well that what he put together would just not be right for that particular orchestra. For centuries the greatest composers have always written commissions *for* the person or group envisioned for performances of the piece. It is quite conceivable that Babbitt wanted the scandal. He knew very well how much complexity that particular ensemble could master within the allotted rehearsal time. If his invention ran away with him he could have notified the orchestra's management that he wished to be excused, or perhaps even asked to do another piece during a later season. The lack of curiosity by the militant *Garde Moderne*, not one of whom asked me a question, demonstrates to me a reluctance to come face-to-face with the realities of responsibility.

There is a thread, of eighty years' standing, connecting Arnold Schoenberg with Milton Babbitt. It is reported that Zemlinsky once suggested to Schoenberg that he make some abridgments in the tone poem *Pelleas und Melisande,* a work from Schoenberg's tonal style but one that is very prolix even by the standards of the sixty-and-more-minute symphonies of Bruckner and Mahler. The cuts were suggested "out of consideration for the public." To which suggestion Schoenberg replied that he would show as much consideration to the public as the public had shown him (that is, none whatsoever). In an interview approximately eighty years later Babbitt stated his attitude about the public: "Who cares if they listen?" There was also a Schoenberg project in Vienna, called the Association for the Performance of Contemporary Music, whose rules stated that only members of the association (that is, neither press nor stray visitors) were admitted. In other words, Schoenberg wanted in the audience only those who were committed in advance to a veneration of the master.

There is no doubt that Schoenberg was a great composer by any professional standards. When, however, he reached the point at which extended chromatic writing became atonality, even Theodor Adorno (who has few deities next to Bach and Schoenberg) wrote that the revered master had given notice to his compact with the public. A different writer might have said that Schoenberg could no longer be bothered with the listener, but Schoenberg's confrontational language was always used as a battle cry by anyone and everyone who did not have Schoenberg's skill but who used his irresponsible social stance to pass themselves off as "inspired artists" who could not be bothered with the public.

Composers have a fully conscious relationship with the public, and this is not to be confused with catering to low instincts or vulgar tastes. It is worth recalling Beethoven's words from the preface to the first edition of the "Eroica" symphony: this piece, longer than customary, should be placed toward the beginning of a concert, lest the public, fatigued by many numbers, lose the necessary attention later in the evening." Then there is the same composer's *Battle of Vittoria,* written for the newly invented metronome and very possibly his worst composition.

These two pieces should be instructive for those composers who prefer to follow Schoenberg and Babbitt in their disregard for the public. There have always been "art for art's sake" movements; such movements have always worked for artists who do not wish to venture outside a very limited circle. Any composer who writes for a symphony orchestra, however, knows that since 1950 audiences have craved "popular" music and that classic and romantic orchestral music has become more popular than it was in 1930.

MANAGEMENT

Management has the responsibility to make this preference for "popular" music clear whenever programs are planned or commissions awarded. In the case of Milton Babbitt's piece for the Philadelphia Orchestra, I am sure that the jury members intended to open new outlets for avant-garde modernism. They did not, however, achieve their objective; nor (to judge by subsequent conversations with a panel member) did they learn anything from the episode.

As for scolding management for avoiding its responsibilities, there are one or two difficulties involved. Management rarely includes staff members who are sufficiently able, willing, or courageous to speak candidly with music directors whose role has been transformed since it became physically possible for them to lead two orchestras. One ambitious conductor took on a third orchestra, and I believe this is frankly irresponsible. The case against the attempt to head several orchestras is, in my view, a compelling one.

The style of conductors such as Frederick Stock and Serge Koussevitzky has been described as dictatorial, and yet for such accomplished men that style was perhaps indispensable. A musicians' union might further argue that modern symphony concert audiences cannot tell the difference between the eloquent rendition achieved after three rehearsals and the perfectly etched and chiseled rendition produced after six rehearsals. I know one such etcher and detailed-nuance-hunter who will go on haggling until he is given a dozen rehearsals for a repertoire opera (even though when the show eventually opens everyone's attention is, unfortunately, focused on the dreadful mess produced by the stage director).

A music director should primarily be concerned with the organization of which he (or she) is head, and this notably means remaining with that organization for the major part of the season. I am quite aware, however, that this is nothing but a daydream, and it is that awareness that kept me working as a guest conductor for twenty-three seasons. One former music director used to spend less than one-fourth of the home season with his charges, so it seems that even spending half a season at home is now considered beyond the call of duty.

Since the situation is not likely to change soon, it is more imperative than ever that the permanently sitting management group should include one person with sufficient musical authority and with sufficient license to act as deputy music director when the celebrity is away. It might also be argued that the same person should check press reaction to soloists' debuts, conductors' debuts, first performances of modern works, the general level of performance during the music director's absence, and so forth.

It was helpful during my first few years at the Met. In those days New York published nine daily papers, most of which printed reviews of every cast change and some of which reviewed every performance. The position of deputy music director might be very similar to the Artists & Repertory position at a recording company.

It is odd that, whereas leadership is acknowledged as essential in the world of sports, boards of directors in the musical world appear not to understand that a large team producing musical performances has at least the same right and need for continued direction as a team playing baseball. This is a sign of the low esteem in which musical standards are held. When was the last time a soccer coach, baseball field manager, or football coach took six weeks off during a playing season to work as a guest coach in some far-off place?

These sports functionaries have the authority to decide, and they are quickly fired when the team loses more games than it wins. The difference between these responsible persons and the irresponsible masters of the baton lies partly in the area of public perception. There is no parallel, in music, to the notion of "games won and lost," and yet the ground rules for public relations and performance standards are very similar.

Although shocking for certain music connoisseurs, it is nonetheless a fact that both musical performances and sports contests belong to show business. This point should be intellectually accepted by all the establishments producing music, because orchestras can no longer survive by simply riding out the lean times in the hope that a better economic climate will come along soon.

When Rudolf Bing became manager of New York's Metropolitan Opera he brought with him several trusted collaborators from his previous posts. Among these was the conductor Max Rudolf, who combined the functions of artistic administrator and musical advisor to Bing on matters where only a trained musician could be a competent judge.

When Max left the Met for Cincinnati, Bing invited me into his circle of aides with the following phrase (typical of Bing's humor):

"I won't have a music director or people might think that I need musical advice. Since I in fact do need musical advice, however, I must have someone in Max's place, and as you continue to conduct a good deal at the Met you don't need a title."

This arrangement was perfectly fine by me, and I was also given no administrative duties (for which I had neither talent nor inclination).

THE ARTIST

Leadership can be exerted only when responsibility and decision-making are evenly balanced, and this fact is not limited to the more obvious fields of artistic management. It is, for example, increasingly significant in the matter of musical interpretation, where irresponsibility is most obviously manifested in the abuse of recorded music.

I object to the use of records to study Beethoven, Berg, or any composer. My objection is founded upon my conviction that a musician who wishes to appear before a paying public should have enough insight into the compositions of his (or her) choice, not to need any model. If this sounds arrogant or severe, it is neither of these things. The musical world is filled with talented people (I hesitate to say blessed, and I cannot say cursed).

After decades of searching for, accepting, and refusing proposed soloists—be it for voice or instrument—I would state under oath that there is a great deal of very serious and better-than-competent achievement. There are frighteningly few artists whom I would trust with the all-time masterpieces of their instrument or voice range, but I am always happy to give an off-center piece to a pianist who runs with the field. There are two reasons for doing this: first, it protects the artist from accusations that he lacks authority or maturity; and second, it protects the works themselves from one of the worst of contemporary phenomena, the trivializing of masterpieces.

I am unable to protect the Ninth Symphony of Beethoven from being abused in every possible manner, but when it is suggested to me that I consider an unknown pianist for the Piano Concerto No. 4, Op. 58, by Beethoven, I say, unhesitatingly, no. There are never more than a few pianists around who may touch that particular piece anyway, and it is certainly not a proper choice for a debut because a soloist does not drop in for a couple of rehearsals with an unfamiliar orchestra and an unfamiliar conductor to tackle this kind of work for the first time.

Whereas the great masterpieces are few, there are many concertos (for instrumentalists) and symphonies (for conductors) that will guarantee a fine reception. The latter are the responsible choices for the younger (or newer) generation of artists; concerts are not the same as competitions and artists' debuts are not auditions. The audience has the right to hear an artist performing to his or her strengths and should not be put into the position of a jury. A music director who acts otherwise is simply shirking his responsibility.

Why should a youngster on the podium or at the keyboard be prevented from stepping straight into Brahms's First Symphony, for example? Brahms's work is a milestone in composition and represents the composer at the acme of his creative powers. These two facts alone entitle this work to be handled exclusively by interpreters who are also at the acme of maturity and who do not need to show themselves off. I do not think this is unfair at all; after many encounters with young conductors (and indeed with young and not-so-young soloists) I would conclude that the general fashionable approach to great masterworks is irresponsible.

Readers of my earlier books will know that I do not consider the study of recordings adequate preparation for conducting a real orchestra. My generation, whose years of musical instruction predate the ubiquitous availability of recorded music, attended concerts armed with pocket scores. Some even took their pencils to underline or comment upon this or that passage. In Vienna I had the singular good fortune to observe Furtwängler, Walter, Klemperer, and a galaxy of other opera conductors, all of whom we, the students of the State Academy, would discuss before, during, and after each event. If I still recall much of what was said then, and who made the deepest impression on me, the transition from student to alumnus ensured that I swiftly forgot the detailed nuances and overall concepts of those gigantic figures.

I was, undeniably, an ungrateful student. I left both my private tutors precipitously, leaving behind a bad name that was fully justified according to the criteria and self-interest of both men (who had been generous and very good instructors). I fled when they became possessive of me, and my relationship with the great figures on the podium was quite similar (except that, since I did not then know any of them personally, there was no human dimension involved).

I mention this because there are musicians with considerable talent who cannot, or will not, wean their minds from a great model. I recall one conversation between the former concertmaster of the Boston Symphony Orchestra (BSO), now a very successful conductor, and one young musician, following a performance of Beethoven's Fifth. "You are so young, isn't it strange that you emulate Klemperer, who is so old?" asked the maestro. "No dear friend," was the reply, "I studied this symphony with Furtwängler." Since Furtwängler was then terminally ill, however, I suspect that the studying in question must have been undertaken with one of the great man's recordings.

The young man in question is now middle-aged and extremely successful, but still addicted to emulating the revered model of his younger days. Finely sensitized orchestra players, a few older critics, and some audience members realize, however, that the Furtwängler style was fine into the 1960s, but is no longer fine today. I am not one to change with the fashion to sell a few more CDs, but I do believe that the great model figures of one's youth and student days should endure only so long as their subjective interpretation does not intrude upon the composer. By today's fashions Furtwängler's style was very individualistic. It is unlikely that a press corps that lifts Roger Norrington to the pinnacle of Beethoven expertise would have much use for the ways of a conductor whom we at the State Academy and many others in Europe adored. To try consciously to imitate the ways of another musician is irresponsible and dishonest, and it also does not really work.

In my early seasons with the BSO I once made an awful faux-pas. With me at the piano, the first cellist was rehearsing his solo part in *Don Quixote*. In the slow variation I did not particularly like the uneven rubato; I thought this was overdone and I said so. The cellist replied that his great model was Gregor Piatigorsky and that he always endeavored to do anything and everything as close to Piatigorsky's way as possible. I replied that when a man from St. Louis, whose ancestry is part American Indian, attempts to imitate a Russian Jew, the result will never be the same. A little while later the cellist left the orchestra and went to Philadelphia.

The artist who plays, or conducts, or sings a quality composition has a first responsibility to the composition and to its composer. All other responsibilities mentioned heretofore are secondary. Returning to the quoted passages that opened this essay, the "theoretism" so little-loved by Bakhtin has invaded music as the "early music" experts, whose contributions, unquestionably worthwhile in the beginning, have since bloated into preposterous "theoretism." The world of music has welcomed the incarnations of academics who flourish in an era when it seems uncomfortable to "respond to the irreducible particularities of each case." This means, in effect, that there are no rules governing the playing of all clavier works by Bach. As recently as sixty years ago the most lauded and exciting renditions of Bach's *St. Matthew Passion* were prepared and guided by the great conductors of that decade. Having attended as many of those concerts as possible, I am still deeply moved by certain unforgettable passages. I also know, however, that the perpetrators of those renditions would nowadays be escorted to the city limits by the apostles of the new purism.

Having been instructed by a pianist who considered Bach's clavier music as essential to one's musical health as a dietitian considers bran and fresh fruit, I am eternally grateful for having been able to digest so much of Bach's music at so young an age. I am also aware, however, that we (both teacher and pupil) were woefully ignorant of certain notational conventions that still puzzle musicians when they appear in music written one hundred years after Bach died. Several years ago I sat at

Carnegie Hall for a concert performance of Handel's *Semele*, with Kathleen Battle singing the title role. The concert program featured a learned essay that ended with the remarkable statement that the performance that evening would feature tempos that were faster than usual, according to the "latest findings."

Then came the music. To my surprise and relief, most of the tempos seemed normal. I use the term "normal" advisedly, since there is in most pieces by good composers a motion that elicits an instinctive response from the collective groups of choral singers and ensemble players. It was pleasant to hear fine music being sung and played naturally and convincingly. A few days later Ms. Battle arrived at a private rehearsal for a joint appearance at the New York Philharmonic. I complimented her on *Semele*, also mentioning that the statement in the program book had not apparently been realized in performance. Ms. Battle replied that the experts had indeed started with the faster tempos, but that she had declared that she neither would, nor could be rushed through the music. If this had to be, she had declared, they would have to look for another Semele. They had elected to retreat to "normal" tempos.

If Richard Wagner is correct in saying that the right tempo is more than half of musical interpretation, then the first responsibility above all others is that of self-reliance from the performer. No study with records will do any good. One major problem for conductors in America is the dearth of opera companies. These are the only real training ground for musical leadership, and this is partly because of the importance of the vocal cast.

Singers cannot be forced into one tempo; in every individual singer there are weaknesses that must be respected, and there is no point in following arbitrary concepts that cause the principals on stage to turn blue in the face. My first encounter with this occurred in 1939. The question of tempo on that occasion was partly a ruse by certain vocal stars who wished to replace me with an older conductor (Fritz Reiner). In the end I was rebuked by Lauritz Melchior, who told me, "Your tempos may be truer than Bodanzky's [my former chief, who then had just died, leaving the whole repertoire of Wagner to me] but with those tempos nobody can sing tiring Wagner roles three times a week."

He was right, too. It may be that great voices were always independent and did not hesitate to make their requirements known. The
first tenor who was slated to sing *Tannhäuser*, Tichatschek, declared to
Wagner that one strophe of the "Hymn to Venus" must be cut or he
would not undertake the role. Wagner accepted.

YOUNG CONDUCTORS

A young conductor who is still searching for his certainties cannot start
on the concert podium. Nobody will ever correct his tempos, and he will
suffer instant loss of credit when his lack of assurance is revealed. With
some orchestras it takes no more than the first fifteen minutes of the first
rehearsal for the thumbs to be turned down on a newcomer. At an opera
house, however, the same young man will have served a season or more
as a coach or otherwise aiding and assisting the chief before being called
upon to conduct a children's matinee of Weber's *Der Freischütz* on the
following Sunday. He had also better be sure not to change any tempos,
as the cast members would be used to those of the chief after seven
previous performances.

Carping by singers about tempos is not limited to young musicians on
the podium. It is also addressed (albeit a little more politely) to any older
conductor whose tempos (or one specific tempo) do not allow the singer
to do his or her best. A good, experienced opera conductor does not
have to wait until such protests arrive. Karajan, Walter, and indeed all
conductors with solid opera biographies guess at once when a tempo is
uncomfortable for a particular singer. With aging vocal stars it can
become a little sticky, as they tend to hurry over passages that are no
longer comfortable. It is relatively easy to make an adjustment in such
cases, although sometimes the composition is pushed toward breaking
point.

Normally, however, the vocal department (even choruses) can and
will bring any wrong tempos back to normal. Because of this tendency,
many European conductors start in the pit of a musical theater, where
their responsibilities for a proper flow of the music are shared by the
singers. This also buttresses my opinion that one must not rely on recordings. One who has learned *Aïda* with a recording by a tenor who has a

long breath and takes it slower than others will be very unhappy when he arrives at the first (and only) rehearsal with "his" tenor to be told "Maestro, questo movimento non va" (Maestro, that tempo won't work).

During three festivals I assisted Arturo Toscanini at the piano for every piano rehearsal. I can vouch that the stories surrounding his unyielding severity were not just legendary. When I was in my early twenties I witnessed one tantrum directed at the "Ford" of the *Falstaff* cast, a baritone named Badini who had no mean temper. Yet Toscanini was an experienced opera conductor, and during that limited period of my presence at his rehearsals I found that he treated artists of deeper understanding rather differently from the way in which he treated those of a rather shallower understanding. Having also been a witness to the varied quality of Toscanini's casts, I could not but admire the fact that his first priority (responsibility) was the flow of performance, not the self-assertion of conductors who think only of their stature and how it might one day look in a musical encyclopedia.

When it comes to leading a symphony orchestra, success or failure is determined by qualities quite different from those which determine the fate of the lyric maestro. During the decades preceding the Second World War (and probably going back to the turn of the century), conducting careers were invariably begun in the pit. Anyone who is judging by American experiences only must realize that in Europe the symphony concert was, in nine out of ten cities, a spin-off for musicians of the opera orchestra who were perhaps glad to sit on stage for a change. They could be visible and were not bound to play uneven rhythms merely to suit the vocal fancies of an aging baritone.

To explain the differences between orchestral setups in Europe and in the United States would require a whole chapter by itself, and the careers of Americans who have every right to make conducting their life's work have been gravely jeopardized by this lack of operatic experience. Let it suffice to state that the main difference is that the opera conductor can lean on the musical "lead" (the voice which sings an aria or the six voices who sing the sextet in *Lucia di Lammermoor*) while on the concert platform the conductor simply cannot "lean" on the first oboist for the slow movement of the Violin Concerto by Brahms. There are many fine oboe players about, and all can stand up at a moment's notice to play that solo passage. In the context of that concerto and of that very delicate slow movement, however, it would invite disaster for the ensemble if the conductor decided to "lean" on the oboist to set the tempo and to phrase the long passage.

If, in a performance of *Aïda*, the "Nile" aria were to be performed erratically, (and there are many opportunities for this), the chances are that nobody in the audience would notice or blame the conductor, since all anybody cares about is the high C of the soprano. In Brahms's First Symphony there is no soprano, so nobody has to worry about the high C, but even the average subscriber will notice the conductor's authority, or lack of it. I should add, at this point, that I have been surprised many times by lay listeners with no pretense to connoisseurship, who spontaneously give very perceptive opinions. Unlike some critics and some self-styled experts, such people are not influenced by publicity or prestige, and so voice their opinions like the child of Hans Christian Anderson's *The Emperor's New Clothes*.

A Crisis of Authority

Authority is the one quality that is indispensable for anyone who occupies a position of leadership. Authority in music can take many different forms, but in the professional life of a conductor, authority has always been taken for granted as a necessity.

It seems to me that there is today a crisis of authority. If we are ever to reverse the fragmentation of our musical life, particularly in the realms of composition and music management, we must resolve that crisis.

These days one often sees backstage a little box sitting on a little table with the following little sign attached: "Conductor's Evaluation Votes." How this phenomenon first came about I have never tried to ascertain. It is admirably democratic in intent, but to me it seems unlikely that one hundred orchestra members can give meaningful guidance whether a conductor should be reengaged. One of my recollections in that respect goes back to the time of George Szell's death, in 1970. His tenure in Cleveland had lasted twenty-four years and had been characterized by enormous energy.

He had persuaded the board to make improvements to the hall and increase the number of players (Rodzinski had previously fought in vain for both), and he had elevated the Cleveland orchestra from the status of a very good orchestra to that of a world-class ensemble that one could confidently term "as good as the best." I read about Szell's death in the newspapers while staying in Switzerland. Among the eulogies there was a press statement (allegedly issued by "the orchestra") stating that they, the orchestra members, hoped that the next music director would be less authoritarian.

Now this little statement raises a question that is central to the conductor's role: how does one exert authority without being accused of authoritarianism? It is undeniably true that certain people do express themselves in a manner that may be perceived as contemptuous, even if that is not the intent. From one or two incidents in my experience I can identify with those who protest and object to the authoritarian manner. Very early in my career I was engaged in San Francisco, charged with assisting Fritz Reiner in the preparation of his operas. To make the job more appealing to me the general manager, Gaetano Merola, had agreed that I could conduct Debussy's opera *Pelléas et Mélisande*. Before heading west I visited Reiner at his Connecticut home. Our conversation turned to the subject of recordings, and he played for me his issue of Richard Strauss's suite *Bürger als Edelmann*. Afterwards I praised, in very precise terms, a passage in the overture where Strauss had written a transition passage of unusual complexity.

Reiner's only reaction was to say: "And I thought that only my pupils at Curtis [the Curtis Institute of Music] would notice this." To which I confess I replied (my sense of right and wrong getting the better of me): "That's one of your troubles. You think you are the only one who knows something." It is true, however, that many Central Europeans are unable to conceal their disdain for persons who, on first encounter, are less overtly knowledgeable than they. Reiner and Szell are among those who have not only stored up much trouble for their successors in this respect but also done harm to the essential concept of authority.

In 1989 I read, in the *Neue Zürcher Zeitung*, an essay written by a musicologist on the theme "The Reception of Mahler in the United States." I was so incensed by certain references to the so-called immaturity of the American public of the 1930s that I was moved to write a reply. The writer in question had taken as his only reference point a small magazine issued by the Bruckner Society, which, like many such house organs, propagated opinions that were partisan and inappropriate for scholarly dissertations. Learned Europeans should be more aware that they are not alone. In America it is considered good form to carry one's knowledge lightly.

The conductor Herbert von Karajan was for many years considered a great authority on musical matters. One need only cite as evidence his control of his recordings, his opera productions in Salzburg, and his superb concerts with the Berlin and Vienna philharmonic orchestras. I first met him in 1930, when I attended his courses at the Mozarteum, during the summer weeks of the Salzburg festival. Karajan was just twenty-two at the time, but he already impressed me in two ways: his musical tastes seemed highly developed for one so young, and he also had a great deal of self-confidence. Our personal meetings were very few, but I felt from our very first meeting that here was a young man who had the authority to go far.

Edward Bernays once told me that the aim of publicity was to engineer consent. It was this that Karajan did to perfection, and he was rewarded with a pedestal reserved exclusively for the invulnerable.

In today's musical world authority will always be awarded to the best-publicized holder of the baton. It is odd that Leopold Stokowski, whose personalized interpretations were never offensive to a liberal mind, became known exclusively for his excesses. I believe that during the years 1911–36 (Stokowski's tenure in Philadelphia) the American press preferred to demonstrate their academic competence rather than give credit to a personality who perfected a type of glamour that was both conspicuously absent and mistrusted by experts seeking to appear orthodox, purist, and devoted to the literal translation of a score into sound. There is sufficient evidence that Gustav Mahler acted in a more cavalier fashion with symphonies and operas than Stokowski ever did. Evidently the perception of authority was higher in the case of Mahler.

TOSCANINI

One of the most prominent examples of publicity-driven infallibility is that of Arturo Toscanini. The received wisdom ahead of his New York appearances (my testimony dates from 1937 only) was of a musician so fastidious that he would not dream of changing the tiniest element of any score. How odd, then, that in the library of the New York Philharmonic there is a score of Debussy's *La Mer* with many instrumental retouches by Toscanini, in red ink!

While nearly every conductor has his or her ideas about retouches in the orchestral works of Beethoven and Schumann (retouches that are fully explicable given the limitations of wind and brass instruments and are otherwise almost universally accepted even by the sourest of pedants) nobody has ever thought that Debussy needed any help. Toscanini nonetheless evidently felt that his concept of textual clarity was valid, even though the impressionists themselves would not have agreed with him, and it was his authority that carried the day.

Under the impact of such an overwhelming personality and of such an unremitting propaganda bombardment, hardly anybody dared to mention reservations, however minor. An additional factor was that Toscanini constantly assured anyone present that his was the only correct version while all others (with particular reference to eminent fellow conductors) were fools! Ultimately Toscanini's authority was certainly real and solid in both Verdi and in Beethoven. I well recall his Bayreuth stint of summer 1931, when I was there as a private coach to the tenor Gotthelf Pistor. Toscanini was wooed and adored by the elderly relatives of Cosima Wagner, and whatever he did with *Parsifal* was lauded to the skies. At nineteen years of age I had no right even to hold, let alone utter, critical opinions about one so eminent. I later reevaluated many of my early impressions, but I will limit myself to those concerning the concept of authority.

The interpretation of Beethoven's works for orchestra and of his opera *Fidelio* gained immeasurably from Toscanini's contribution. The entire German-Austrian music establishment had long been (and in some cases still is) under the influence of Richard Wagner's ideas on how to perform Beethoven. Wagner's writings on the subject combined excessive romanticism—especially regarding tempos—with a diatribe against Felix Mendelssohn.

It occurs to me now that modern, so-called authentic interpreters of the classics are much closer to Mendelssohn's ways, if one can judge from a few rather nasty paragraphs in Wagner's *On Conducting* (1897)—as always a work mixed with a subliminal message of anti-Semitism. In Vienna, where I studied and heard such music, Wagner's ways with Beethoven constituted our tradition. When Toscanini visited with the New York Philharmonic to play an unforgettable Seventh Symphony, the reading of the second movement (Allegretto) caused all but the most stubborn traditionalists to look at the scores with completely new eyes.

The first comments emphasized "Mediterranean clarity," but then the hegemony of Richard Wagner's ideas on Beethoven was gradually destroyed. This tribute to Toscanini's influence was mentioned by George Szell in a televised eulogy delivered after Toscanini's death in 1957. Szell, having been a child of traditional musical education, knew just how the classical repertoire was performed here, there, and everywhere. When he credited Toscanini with having emancipated us from Wagner's ways he therefore knew very well what he was talking about. As it turned out, Szell was quickly established as the living image of an authority on the great classic repertoire.

THE "AUTHORITATIVE" VERSION

It may have been in 1983 that I prepared a program, for a New York visit with the Cleveland Orchestra, featuring Mozart's overture to *The Magic Flute* as an opener. After the first rehearsal the concertmaster, a wonderful musician, who had been Szell's appointee and was one-hundred-percent loyal to Szell's memory, told me that for some reason the overture had been programmed by Szell several times but always taken off the final set of selections. Why? Because the opening fanfare never "worked." I asked him how Szell had conducted those opening measures and learned that he conducted "four-in-a-measure with a subdivision for the upbeat to the next measure." I instantly knew where the dog was buried, as it were. Szell, like Walter and other great figures of the generation born around the turn of the century, did not believe the alla breve of the adagio opening. Those conductors tried to take the upbeat sixteenth-note literally as a sixteenth, which will not work because the alla breve is merely a signal that there is double dotting. Since I accepted this as valid there was no problem with making the overture "work."

I am well aware, by the way, that for nonprofessional readers the preceding passage might as well be written in Volapük. I promise it will not happen again (at least not until the next time). The point is that whereas Szell was unquestionably a great authority on Mozart, when it came to interpreting the (apparent) combination of adagio and alla breve his knowledge had apparently not kept pace with some of the findings unearthed with the baroque revival.

Mozart's music provides another fine illustration of the potential vagaries involved in the notion of authority. This example occurred in the 1930s, when I was assistant to Bruno Walter in Florence for his rehearsals and performances of Mozart's *Figaro* at the regular Maggio Musicale Fiorentino. The casting, which had (perhaps) been discussed with Walter months earlier, was carried out according to the Ricordi printing of the opera.

The result was that the Countess was to be sung by a dramatic soprano who, though of great repute, was vocally rather past her best. Even in her heyday her voice could not possibly have sung "Porgi amor," the much-feared opening aria of act 2. The soprano was replaced, causing Walter to be greatly concerned about political backlash (of which there was none). The other casting horror, however, was that of a basso cantante who was very fine for the grand old men in Verdi, but vocally much too heavy for the Count and hardly of the physique for the part, being somewhat more peasant than aristocrat in appearance and demeanor.

Now there is no one edition of *Figaro*'s vocal-piano score that may be accepted one-hundred percent, but Ricordi's edition disregards a few basic facts, and this was the source of the miscasting. In Mozart's operas, as in all eighteenth-century lyric works, the rank of the role determines which voice in the ensembles the singer has to learn. The Countess should have the lead line, the Count should have the line of the baritone, then Bartolo, then Figaro, and so on. Because the Ricordi edition gives the lowest line as "Il Conte," however, somebody in the impresario's office had read "Il Conte basso"—hence our squinting basso cantante count.

Figaro was played by the baritone Mariano Stabile, whose repertoire was determined by his personality and flexibility, by his marvelous acting, and by his wonderful diction. Stabile was beautifully cast as Figaro, never mind that he was not a basso. Knowing that Stabile was the conductor's choice for Figaro, however, the role of the Count should have been sung by a lyric baritone. So whereas in Florence we had a great conductor with a reputation as an unimpeachable authority on Mozart, in Milan there was a casting maestro who knew little about Mozart outside his Ricordi edition. In such cases we have the advantage of musicologists who can be very helpful as long as they do not go too far and do not establish too many new verities. Piano music has had to withstand a variety of so-called authorities trying to earn royalties by transferring their interpretations of Beethoven or Chopin (the two most edited composers) to the footnotes.

Neither a conductor nor a pianist should need to rely upon the interpretations of authorities. Hans von Bülow annotated the piano sonatas of Beethoven for the Stuttgart publisher Cotta, and these were published in five volumes in 1872. I bought a copy once in a second-hand music store because the physical aspect of all Cotta editions (including its editions of Goethe) is most elegant and attractive. On the first page of the Piano Sonata, Op. 111, which is subjected to musical analysis in Thomas Mann's novel *Doktor Faustus*, von Bülow has this to say:

> This last piano sonata of the master is, not without reason, considered by some to be the most accomplished work of the "third" period. In this work one finds a combination of the most profound content and a plasticity so that any aesthetic-poetic comments toward a keener comprehension seem superfluous.

This did not, however, deter von Bülow from adding, right there on page one, about 350 more words, and in the following pages many thousands of words of wisdom such as he had defined as unnecessary. One can nevertheless be quite sure that in his day this elegant and magnificent-looking edition ensured that he was the supreme authority on the subject. Every cure seems to produce new ailments, and so it is with new complete editions of the great classics.

Although the text of those editions printed prior to the war is perfectly fine, the most recent gigantic editions of Bach and Mozart have acquired instant (and quite undeserved) authority. These editions reflect the work of many editors, and if some are excellent, others may be frankly disregarded. So effective is the publicity machine at manufacturing authority that even some very serious and critical musicians took some convincing that certain Mozart works in the new edition are quite unacceptable for performance. The simple prescription for any serious professional performer is that he or she first create personal authority. This authority can be obtained by studying until one achieves trust in oneself.

The best, and yet perhaps the most embattled, example of this is the good old metronome. Beethoven welcomed its invention, believing that it would settle doubts about composers' tempos. Most musicians do not even look at metronomes. Whenever Beethoven is involved one assumes that since he was deaf he had no idea what he was doing. Even that fine and noble musician Carlo Maria Giulini stated, about his 1992 performance of the Ninth in Lucerne, Switzerland, that Beethoven's metronome markings were wrong. Beethoven's metronome marks are not wrong, because he inserted them into the score after, or while, reading.

Reading is not the same as playing or singing. If one reads a score with one's eyes and mind (with one's inner ear, so to speak), there simply is no arguing with the composer. On the other hand, there are also those zealots (including some from the "Schoenberg circle") who maintain that every metronome must be observed as printed. I would dispute their claims. Here again is a lesson for all those aiming to be professional performing musicians: authority is not to be bought, it must be acquired by study and imagination.

AUTHENTICITY

A rather dangerous form of authority has been acquired by those who hunt for authentic renditions of old music. I have no quarrel with even the most opinionated of those groups and individuals, as long as they stay with the baroque alphabet from Albinoni to Zampieri. I become less tolerant, however, when they tackle the music of the Viennese classics (Haydn, Mozart), and even less tolerant when they begin to show how Beethoven, Berlioz, and the-Lord-knows-who-else should be performed.

Their greatest error has been to assume that Johann Sebastian Bach may be reconstructed out of the research library. Nineteenth-century believers in Mendelssohn's great performance of Bach's *St. Matthew Passion* may well have been wrong by today's standards. I am sure that today the great figures whom I heard performing the *St. Matthew Passion*, the B minor Mass, the *Magnificat*, or some of the bigger cantatas would not earn a single complimentary review for the style of their interpretations.

When I happen, however, to hear on the radio an "expert" playing these notes with all the correctness (and all the finesse) of a typist, I feel quite certain that musicians of a former age, notwithstanding the errors of their ways, understood more about Bach's monumental works than these modern performers. Those modern specialists have serious fans and many critics behind them, so they have accordingly gained admittance to the brotherhood of infallible musical authority. It may sound risky to say this, but I believe that very few, if any, rules may be laid down concerning authority. In a musical repertoire three hundred years old, not even the subtitle "in A major" is an unequivocal term. By the time Mozart wrote his famous Piano Concerto No. 23 in A major, K. 488, the A had gone progressively higher. This is one reason why vocal music by composers writing before 1800 is becoming increasingly difficult to sing. The human larynx has not, unfortunately, gone up with the A.

A notable exhortation of many famous conductors used to be: "Play only what's printed." Karl Böhm was most consistent, to the degree that in some Mozart recordings you can even hear the misprints. Conversely, I recall that in the second movement of the Fourth Symphony by Robert Schumann, Furtwängler labored to distinguish clearly between the sixteenth-notes (pizzicato) and the triplet note in the solo cello and oboe. This is as wrong now as it was in 1930, but then there was no great concern over eighteenth-century notation of certain rhythmic figures.

These conventions were carried over into the nineteenth century and used by Beethoven, Schumann, and Schubert, and replaced by our modern notation only in the works of Brahms. The authority of Böhm and Furtwängler was so absolute that even if somebody had put down in writing that these were errors, he or she would have been dismissed as a pedant. These days similar vituperation would probably be reserved for the person who tolerated such errors. My point, however, is that one should be wary of regarding the fruits of musical research as the equivalent of authority.

TEMPO

I maintain, then, that each person must acquire personal authority rather than hang on the coattails of others. Another area in which this is crucial is that of tempo indications. Although all composers use the same words and signals, they often use those signals for different purposes. I have found, for example, that the two meanings of the word *adagio* have not always been recognized.

In several of Mozart's introductory passages (whether as part of an overture or a symphony), in the introductions to Beethoven's symphonies, and indeed in all movements in which the composer precedes the exposition by an introduction, there is a tempo marking which is invariably much slower than the main allegro of the first movement. Sometimes that marking is andante, in Beethoven's Seventh Symphony it is un poco sostenuto, and in his First and Second it is adagio molto. Yet when one checks Beethoven's metronome marks (which one can do with a stopwatch) one finds that the tempo is not nearly as slow as one's ears remember from numerous concerts and recordings heard on the radio. The truth of the matter is this: when the word *adagio* is used over an introduction, it means "slow," but when it is used, for example, over a slow movement in a Beethoven string quartet, in the "Eroica" symphony, or in the "Ghost" Trio, it signifies a piece that dives into the deepest recesses of human emotion. I recall once having turned on the radio and found myself transported by chance into a magnificent rendition of the third movement of the String Quartet in F major, Op. 135. Such playing takes one into spheres where no introduction to an overture or any other work is supposed to take one.

One might even reduce this point to the following simple, rough-and-ready formula:

Adagio for intros = Slow
Adagio for a second or third movement in a symphonic
structure = Deep

Beethoven's slow movements revolutionized the four-movement symphonic structure, elevating his works for piano, quartet, and orchestra to an instrumental pinnacle never reached before. Scholars may with justice call this revolution the greatest contribution to romantic composition, and it is perhaps understandable that conductors, pianists, and even some quartets crave more of these incomparable pieces. It is essential, though, that their "intros" not be dragged.

The term *authority*, which is not used primarily or exclusively in the world of music or the arts, is frequently misused in political debate. In music it has often replaced the word *specialist* to indicate a source of reliable knowledge. One needs to think only of figures such as the pianist Artur Schnabel, who established himself as the ultimate authority on Beethoven, to see where our musical vocabulary lost its way in this respect.

Whereas a specialist is a person who prefers to perform the works of a single composer, an authority is the exact opposite: an encyclopedist, a musician who seeks to be comfortable with Beethoven, Debussy, Britten, or any composer of quality. My lack of confidence in the notion of the specialist originated in a very personal experience. No sooner had I conducted three or four works by Wagner with some approval than I found myself dubbed as a Wagner specialist.

Had I chosen to, I could have coasted along for years on the back of that specialist tag. Fortunately I possessed sufficient pragmatic brain cells to realize that at the age of twenty-seven I could not remotely qualify as a specialist of anything. The experience did, however, illustrate clearly to me just how easily one can become a "specialist." Artur Rubinstein, for example, used to appear in quiz shows labeled as a "Chopin specialist," which in the first place shortchanges his talent and in the second place originated from the simple fact that he is Polish. Whereas there have been other Polish nationals who played Chopin well and there have been other Polish nationals who did not, Artur Rubinstein was a world-wide success because he played an extremely diverse repertoire superbly.

There are several great figures whose renditions of Beethoven were considered authoritative. My experience with this phenomenon has taught me that the cult of special authoritative interpreters is a mixture of solid fact and hype. On one occasion I turned on my radio in the midst of the first movement of the aforementioned Piano Sonata, Op. 111, by Beethoven (one of the classic test pieces for any musician). It really was one of the most masterly renditions of the piece I have ever heard. Whenever I miss opening announcements I derive a modest amount of satisfaction from guessing the identity of the player. On this occasion I was obliged to wait until the end to learn that the pianist was Arturo Michelangeli—not a Beethoven specialist but rather, like Rubinstein, a virtuoso player of a broad repertoire.

My distrust of the specialist stems also from the fact that limiting oneself to a small range of music must become tiresome with time, leading almost inevitably to exaggeration and distortion. This is not an uncommon phenomenon among symphony orchestra conductors, one or two of who are content to travel the world with repertoires that could fit onto a calling card. Their small range is usually rooted in the fact that learning new material takes a long time and constant travel does not allow time to concentrate sufficiently on the task.

I have often found it amusing, though, to read the list of candidates drawn up by the music critics whenever an important orchestra was seeking a music director. Their lists almost invariably included several conductors with the calling-card repertoire, and if those men had ever been foolish enough to accept an appointment as music director, they would have run out of music in six to eight weeks. I can live with many different traits in musicians, but the combination of fine musicianship and very slow learning frankly puzzles me.

It may be that conductors who stay for a long time in opera become accustomed to working only with singers, coaching them. This experience is a helpful process of teaching and learning simultaneously. Smart coaches (conductors) realize, however, that the average singer is a slower learner than a fully schooled conductor. For concert preparation, a conductor has no singers to learn with and, unless fully prepared at the first rehearsal, should expect no authority, no credit, and no mercy.

CASTING

In my relations with RCA, the record company with whom I made most of my recordings, I noticed that their casting of the operas often lacked any artistic authority because they would select singers on the basis that one well-sold album fully justified their casting the same star artist in an entirely different role. I regret that several of my opera albums have failed due to truly idiotic and naive casting. RCA had a contract with the BSO for more titles than they felt able to sell annually, and so decided, in 1965, that they would combine three releases by recording us playing an opera. *Lohengrin* was the choice.

Following their philosophy that a singer who has sold well in one role will automatically sell well in any other future role, they cast Leontyne Price as Elsa and Rita Gorr as Ortrud. Seven months prior to the recording dates, Leontyne Price, wiser than the high command of RCA, canceled her engagement. In the late summer of 1964, while spending a few days in Paris before flying home, I had to attend a performance of *Don Carlos* at the Palais Garnier, with Gorr as Eboli. I was so appalled by what I heard that I sent an urgent message about Gorr and Ortrud, addressed to those who had, as always, made casting decisions without consulting either conductor or producer. I later learned that the recipients of the cable had smiled and declared that Leinsdorf was exaggerating as usual, whereas to me they said simply: "Let's wait until she has sung the opening at the Met." "And what is she singing at the Met?" I asked. "*Delilah*," came the answer. It little availed for me to explain that a part for contralto required different vocal equipment from a part for heroic soprano, and after the opening at the Met I was assured triumphantly that Gorr had been wonderful and earned rave reviews.

A great deal of time had been allowed for the recording the following summer, but we had to repeat the two crucial, short, dramatic outbursts of Ortrud so many times that we compromised other portions of the score. The replacement Elsa, moreover, was no more than a brave pinch hitter. A five-disc album, with both leading women below the level expected by RCA, the BSO, and indeed the conductor, represented, in my judgment, a total loss. Words cannot describe either my pleading with them to change the opera or the smug, self-assured replies of men who could not read one line of a full score.

It is small comfort to anyone who likes to make a good recording that within a decade these authorities of operatic casting had steered the recording division so badly that the mother corporation decided simply to cast out the problem child. Some readers may be asking why such curious and virtually incompetent authorities were entrusted with the responsibility of selecting highly paid singers and contract recording sessions at enormous cost. This practice goes back to the mid-1930s when RCA was led by David Sarnoff, a man whose ambition it was to make RCA the best in every field of communication. If I recall correctly, however, Sarnoff knew a good deal about the technology of communication but next to nothing about communication through music.

In February 1937 Toscanini returned to Italy after leaving his post with the New York Philharmonic the previous year. As I was between engagements and enchanted by a young singer I had met during the previous season, I followed her to her home in Rome. This also gave me the chance to see Toscanini, with whom I always had to discuss details of the forthcoming summer in Salzburg. At our first meeting Toscanini told me: "Can't stay in Rome, must hurry to Milan, Chotzinov is coming over from New York to bring me a proposition from Sarnoff who wants to form an orchestra for me." At that point I had no idea who Chotzinov was, but met him later that year when I arrived in New York. He was a critic for the *New York Post* and a former accompanist of Jascha Heifetz (whose sister Pauline he had married).

Samuel Chotzinov became the minister responsible for convincing people that Toscanini was one of the wonders of the world, never before equaled and never to be equaled again. I do not know exactly how he became appointed as Sarnoff's emissary, but I can imagine that Sarnoff, searching as ever for "the best," may simply have seized the moment of Toscanini's resignation from the New York Philharmonic and decided to go after him. For Sarnoff it was a great triumph and for Chotzinov it was a job at NBC in a key position for which he was not suited. Then, little by little, other figures, whose only merit was that they admired Toscanini, joined the artistic high command of RCA's recording division.

I was also witness to how NBC dissolved the orchestra formed for Toscanini, proving that the entire exercise was not serious and not motivated by any wish to please the American admirers of a great maestro. They simply found Toscanini a burden when they expanded their TV programming. I do not remember the year, but I do remember the day when I called on Toscanini at his home in Riverdale and was treated to a bitter diatribe by the maestro, who complained bitterly that they had taken "his" studio away. His concerts then returned to Carnegie Hall until that terrible day in April 1954 when he suffered a lapse of memory.

On the eve of that day I received a call from Ernest LaPrade, whose exact function at these broadcasts I do not recall. He informed me that Maestro Toscanini had been upset by bad news from Milan and asked me to take over in case he was not able to go on. "Since it was an all-Wagner program and you know the orchestra, we come to you," he said. This was in 1954, sixteen years and many waters down the Hudson River, and yet still the dog tag of the Wagner specialist was so strong that I was being asked to take over from Toscanini without rehearsal, "just in case."

As I have already mentioned, this tag of the "Wagner specialist" was always an embarrassment to me, even at the point when it promised to carve out a career for me. Consider the following story: A Korea veteran returns to his small home town and is greeted with a big party. An old buddy from high school asks him, "Frank, how come you have all these medals? You were never such a courageous guy, you were never any good in athletics, how did it happen?" The veteran replies, "I'll tell you the truth. Here I have a salad of twenty-seven medals or ribbons; the first I was given through an administrative error, and the other twenty-six came gradually just because I had the first one." This is the story of many an authority.

A magistrate marries the couple standing before him with the words, "By the authority vested in me by the State of. . . ." There is nobody, however, to invest authority in actors, singers, directors, conductors, or (perhaps most importantly) critics. If a critic is not an authority, then his or her critique—whether good, bad, or indifferent—becomes irrelevant.

This is part of the current malaise in the musical world, certainly in Europe and America. Of other lands I know nothing, mostly because I do not read the languages.

THE SPECIALIST

In my student days we still debated the merits of an old Viennese critic, Julius Korngold (father of the composer Erich Wolfgang Korngold). We who attended the standing room of opera and concert halls were put off by Korngold's arch-conservative opinions and by his apparent habit of writing whatever might help his son's chances. Many years later I read a book of Korngold's selected reviews and changed my opinion somewhat about both aspects of his writings. The prejudice regarding Erich Korngold still seemed rather unacceptable. As for his conservatism, however, I happened to be reading the book at a time when New York could boast the single most brilliant music critic of all, the composer Virgil Thomson.

Thomson declared quite openly that he took a more favorable view of artists who acknowledged and performed his compositions. This attitude made him, in my view, an honest critic. That he was also an authority may be questioned only by believers in objectivity. I look for and find the authority of a critic in his or her standards, and those standards should be acquired from the only possible source: the composer. This does not mean recordings, even if they have been authorized and led by the composer. Ideally, a critic should be able to read the composer's scores and understand them, then make a further judgment after hearing a live performance. Many critics today compare several recordings heard prior to the event covered. This is not the same and their criticism is bound to lack true authority.

The composer's score is the one and only dispenser of authority. If the critic or the conductor (or pianist, or violinist, or so forth) relies on other "authorities" the only result will be a dodging of responsibility and an admission that one lacks security. When I insist that much musical criticism in dailies and weeklies has become irrelevant, I can cite, in my support, one New York–based magazine critic who lamented that a new opera production at the Met continued to be sold out as if the reviews had all been laudatory, although it had been unanimously savaged by the reviewers. He was very bitter and well he might be, because he understood that he was no longer writing for the readers of his publication but for the birds in Central Park. This has transpired because traditional decisions about success or failure have been transferred to public relations operators who brainwash the public to the point where the critic cannot prevail.

There are one or two critics who write with obvious authority, but to do so one must have no fear of saying unorthodox things and a keen sense of what is significant. Such critics are also not swayed one way or another by insistent audience receptions. In any case the applaudometer is notorious for its fallibility: loud ending = loud applause, soft ending = soft reception. Korngold, no matter how we disliked his utterly conservative views, stuck to his standards. This made him an authority since "authoritative" does not mean "to be right," but "to be sure."

THE "AUTHORIZED" VERSION

In the world of criticism one quickly reaches the point at which there is no longer right or wrong. Take, for example, my experience with the final pages of Beethoven's Ninth. In a previous book, *The Composer's Advocate: A Radical Orthodoxy for Musicians* (1981), I gave a detailed account of a terrible error that had become the unchallenged, traditional manner to close the work in performance.

If my demonstration made any impact, I am not aware of it. Perhaps it has been decided that habit and the lack of any serious challenge between 1830 and 1980 had gradually transformed the traditional way into the "right" way. The great performances of the Ninth by the great authorities of the early part of this century (Nikisch, Weingartner, and so forth) were followed by those of the generation of recorded authorities. It seems clear that an account published in one or two books, no matter how well documented, will never shake the accumulated authority of a galaxy of personalities whose authority, springing from their cult status, has become infallibility.

Having read an absurd essay on certain aspects of conductors' careers, I came across a paragraph that accused Weingartner of having distorted

Beethoven and treated his scores with inexcusable emendations. The accepted professional view has been that Weingartner, in his small book *Ratschläge zur Aufführung von Beethoven's Sinfonien* (Suggestions on the Performance of Beethoven's Symphonies), did a singular and definitive service to the scores of Beethoven by adding notes and completing phrases at the point where the composer reached the limit of the instruments available to him.

Weingartner was known in Viennese critical circles as *the* perfect classicist. In this he was contrasted with Furtwängler and other romantics who naturally took their approach more from Richard Wagner's ideas about Beethoven. Here we have a well-documented case in which several authorities are in considerable disagreement. I do not hesitate to call them authorities because their certainty and inner security projected to the public the feeling that "it had to be that way." Arguing in print that so-and-so erred in some way simply makes no impact. As for what Toscanini achieved with the second movement of the Seventh, perhaps a massive tour with many performances in many music centers might do the same trick today, but there would have to be a great deal of advance drum beating.

In the world of music, authority should be asserted in performance—not in print, not in lectures, nor in any other medium. That this is not the case in practice is one reason why critics have lost out against the publicity industry. One of that industry's most efficient agents is the company that records a specific artist. I could well imagine an interview with some rising star who, upon being asked by a journalist how one so young could already be so expert in the works of Bruckner (or in Schubert songs, or in Chopin ballads, or whatever), might reply loudly, "By the authority vested in me by Telshark, Inc."

The authority accorded to recordings has become great indeed. I recall, for example, how one of my New York Philharmonic programs was built around three pieces about Orpheus. There was a Liszt tone poem, the Stravinsky ballet score, and the overture to Offenbach's *Orpheus in the Underworld*. These selections being too short for a full evening, I added the *Sinfonietta* by Poulenc. This, I thought, would allow for an intermission and a transition between the two serious and frivolous selections. A journalist who used to write little previews for the *New Yorker* magazine called the Philharmonic's artistic administrator, wanting to know what the *Sinfonietta* had to do with Orpheus. Assured that it had "nothing" to do with Orpheus, he proceeded to dismiss it as worthless.

Why? Because the Poulenc piece had not been recorded and was thus automatically inferior. It does not matter so much here that I have frequently performed Poulenc (including the American first performance of his *Dialogues des Carmelites*), but it does matter that an unrecorded score was declared without value by one who had not heard it, and judged according to the notion that record companies are the ultimate arbiters of musical authority.

Ten

Toward a Brave New World of Music

Modern Music

Ever since 1925, the year in which I began to take my music studies seriously, I have been close to many individuals and groups who fought for avant-garde music trends. Despite many years of involvement (both as performer and as participant in numerous discussions and interviews) I am as puzzled now as I was in 1925 by the apparent failure of the musical public to come to terms with much new music. That failure has been as apparent in Europe as it has in America.

When Leonard Bernstein declared that the symphony was dead (it must have been in the late 1960s), his remark was not taken up with great enthusiasm by the media. Perhaps it was assumed that Bernstein was merely trying to justify his leaving the directorship of the New York Philharmonic. I recall wondering whether his words referred to the form of composition or to the organization that presents orchestral concerts, though I rather suspect that it was the former. At this point I hasten to remind the reader that virtually all concert music is symphonic in form. According to the *New Grove Dictionary of Music and Musicians*, for example, any piano sonata could be called a "symphony for piano" just as any orchestral work, such as a symphony, could be listed as a "sonata for orchestra."

The musical term *symphonic* is as firm and descriptive as the terms *nude* or *still-life* in the world of painting. Defined in the simplest terms, the symphony is composed of several movements, which began to vary only with Beethoven (1770–1827). Any number of Haydn's symphonic works, for example, conforms to the following classic pre-Beethoven model:

    I. Sonata (with or without a slow introduction)
    II. Slow movement as a lied (with or without minor variations)
    III. Minuet
    IV. Rondo

Mozart's symphonies follow the same pattern, with some slight exceptions (No. 34, for example, has only three movements). Beethoven wrote five movements for the "Pastoral" symphony and he also reversed the "slow-fast" order in the Ninth, which includes the following:

    I. Sonata
    II. Scherzo
    III. Adagio (Variations)
    IV. Variations

The traditional pattern was followed more or less to the letter by the various symphonists of the nineteenth century. Johannes Brahms (1833–97) does replace the Minuet (or Scherzo) movement with a different third movement that is more or less patterned like his Intermezzi for piano solo, but it was not until Gustav Mahler (1860–1911) that the standard symphonic form began to decline. My use of the word *decline* does not in the least reflect a lack of admiration for Mahler on my part. Mahler brought something entirely new to the composition of music for orchestra—something that anticipated the future just as the works of the Viennese School anticipated the horrors of the Great War. The four-movement or three-movement symphonic forms were clearly insufficient for the expression of the contemporary problems with which Mahler was concerned.

The "novel" symphonies of Brahms and Anton Bruckner (1824–96) elicited a certain interest, but this interest quickly waned at the deaths of those two composers. The emerging music of Mahler was initially regarded with extreme caution, and most of his works (excepting only the First Symphony, which was heard first in Budapest) were first heard in small or far-off provincial towns. By 1918 the Great War and the consequent end of the aristocracy's domination of patronage had hastened the demise of the traditional symphonic form.

One might say that the modern musical universe has three dominant features. First, many composers now write only for professional performers, neglecting the amateur sphere (the magnificent piano compendium by Bartók, Microcosm, is an exception to this). Second, the absence of tonality has taken away one of the central supporting pillars of the musical edifice. Third, the fate of instrumental music with a highly complex formal structure is now dependent upon elite patronage and does not fit into the new order of society. Only a handful of the best-known classical pieces—Beethoven's Fifth Symphony; Brahms's First; Mozart's No. 40 in G minor, K. 550; and the last three by Tchaikovsky—have been welcomed into the world of the modern popular concert. The Boston Pops, for example, would venture only as far as the most famous concertos; but their concern, at least, was such that table service was stopped for the soloists, and the doors were not opened as they were for the orchestral selections.

Also, some writers on modern music appreciation assume that only fragments of larger structures are of interest—length is thus perceived as a forbidding factor. The entire sense of a symphonic form is lost in the notion that recognizing a few tunes, themes, and other melodic or rhythmic ideas can provide an enhanced understanding of the whole. The original intention—to make the works easier and more accessible— was well meant, but it has done little to improve the public's appreciation of music.

The postwar breakdown of the old Central European social structure was the catalyst that liberated the works of Mahler and others from the restrictions that had been imposed upon them. During the years of the

Weimar Republic (1919–33) several conductors and champions of Mahler broke a few batons (if not lances) for these demanding scores. Mahler is not the only composer whose works were viewed with skepticism by a public nostalgic for its past (the Vienna Philharmonic did not play his Sixth Symphony (written between 1903 and 1904) until 1933). It was only through the influence of the Philharmonic's Clemens Krauss, who knew Brahms, that that composer's works were played by that orchestra.

Also in 1933, Krauss gave the local premiere of Debussy's *Ibéria*, a work that provides further evidence of the often decisive influence of politics upon music. The members of the Austro-German music establishment have always been firmly convinced that theirs is the only school of composition worthy of the name. In more recent years, the writings of Theodor Adorno and Carl Dahlhaus have served only to bolster this conviction, but the Austro-Germans' immense pride in themselves has also been accompanied by something rather different—namely, a neglect and a disdain for the entire French school of composition. Since that school includes Claude Debussy, a great "modern" composer and in my view one of the all-time greats of music composition, I would like to share a few incidents from my past that illustrate the classic Austro-German approach to that composer. The incidents are also instructive of my general theme.

I will begin with a story about Arthur Nikisch, who was chief conductor of the Berlin Philharmonic from 1895 until 1920. During that quarter of a century he conducted the Berlin subscription concerts in ten seasonal programs (except during the later war years when there were only six). I have studied those programs thoroughly and can report that in a total of around 230 programs the name Debussy appears just once—in November 1908 with a performance of the *Prélude à l'après-midi d'un faune*.

Seventy-five years or so later the senior management of the Berlin Philharmonic asked me if I would include *Ibéria* in one of my programs. I never thought to ask how familiar the orchestra was with Debussy, having assumed that after thirty years with Karajan they would be familiar with the broadest international repertory. We were given the customary three rehearsals, but during the intermission of the second rehearsal I was visited in my dressing room by a delegation of the players, who told me that they felt unable to learn the piece in the available time. Since there was no chance of being given more preparation time, I was asked to change to something else. I praised them for their conscientiousness and pulled *Ibéria* from the program.

In 1933 I graduated from Vienna's State Academy of Music. During my two years of study with that institution's professor of orchestral conducting (a prominent, excellent, and active conductor) Debussy was never even discussed. Furthermore, the student orchestra never had a Debussy score on the music racks. Forty-five years after graduation I undertook a lengthy guest engagement in Vienna and was invited by the then Rektor of the Academy to give a talk to the graduating composing-conducting class. When I asked them what they wanted to talk about they replied, "Tell us something about Debussy, whom we never study, alas!"

While in Vienna I often used to sneak into orchestra rehearsals. Sometimes I would hear the music director of the Vienna Symphony and of the Radio orchestra—an excellent man with the works of Bruckner, Mahler, and other romantic repertoire—preparing a French composition. On one occasion, unhappy with the players' approach, he told them (in good solid Viennese dialect), "Chentelmen, chentelmen, French mousik, bubbly, bubbly, like schampain."

In 1930 the director of the Vienna Opera, Franz Schalk, conducted a French composition in Salzburg. I sat at the rehearsal and saw how he used a small pocket knife to cut open the score's pages. He remarked to the players with a smile, "Gentlemen, tomorrow I'll know it better."

During one of my many visits to Vienna I once went up to the library of the Musikfreunde, which has an almost complete set of programs for concerts that have taken place in their grand hall. The programs describe not only the pieces performed but also biographical material and music examples illustrating the composer's main ideas. The program for the premiere of *Ibéria* also featured a Brahms symphony. Whereas the Brahms piece was given the full treatment (doubtless for the umpteenth time) there was not one word of commentary on the Debussy premiere. Under the composer's name it was mentioned merely that he died during the bombardment of Paris. That was it. That this "bubbly" music was extremely complex and worthy—in the circumstances—of more commentary than the thrice-familiar Brahms piece did not seem to concern the program's editor. Perhaps the editor would excuse himself by saying that Debussy's publisher could not be reached for permission to reproduce the music.

In 1976 I was asked to help after another conductor canceled a pair of subscription concerts of the Vienna Philharmonic. I quickly devised a program, but when a friend saw that I had selected Debussy's three *Nocturnes* he strongly advised against performing that composer with a Viennese orchestra, no matter how superb they were at playing other music. I retained the piece and to my enormous satisfaction the performances turned out as splendidly as I could have wished—a fact that proves merely that the neglect and disdain for French music emanates not from the orchestra but from "above."

My last tale concerns something I read in the *New York Review of Books*—an extensive review of Carl Dahlhaus's *Nineteenth-Century Music* (1989). The review, written by Philip Gossett, dean of music at Chicago University, notes Dahlhaus's declaration that beyond the main line running from Bach to Schoenberg most other music belongs on the trash-heap of history. Gossett then adds that by some odd coincidence that trash-heap would be mostly—if not entirely—filled with non-German composers (Moussorgsky, Bartók, Debussy, and of course Stravinsky).

Some of those little incidents are perhaps rather less serious and scholarly than they ought to be. I guess I have never stopped wondering whether the Germanic stranglehold on music might have been weakened, or even broken, if only the Weimar Republic had survived a little longer. As it turned out, the sole beneficiaries of that short-lived republic were those great creative talents (Dahlhaus's trash-heap crew, incidentally) who composed neither symphonies nor concertos.

Before Debussy's heyday, French contributions to the soloist or orchestral repertoire were mostly on a relatively small scale. Among such works one might include Fauré's *Ballade*, Franck's *Variations symphoniques*, Chausson's *Poème*, and Ravel's *Tzigane*. Even before the so-called *fin-de-siècle* era, French composers had perhaps already signaled that bravura music need not be thirty-five, forty, or more minutes long. Saint-Saëns is an obvious exception here, but then his music is as un-French as César

Franck's *Symphony*. Public taste in France seems to favor vocal music—a fact that may account for the relatively few French symphonic compositions.

As for the Italians, a splendid summary of their preferences can be found in a letter written by Giuseppe Verdi to his former schoolmate, the lawyer Giuseppe Piroli, on 2 February 1883. The composer writes that the world has only two real schools of composition (the Italian and the German), that all others derive from these two schools, and that Italian music is distinct from German music in that its home is mainly in the theater, not in the concert hall.

It is also interesting in this context that for a very long time only those Mahler scores with a vocal element were performed with any degree of regularity (these include his Symphonies No. 2, 4, and 8, and *Das Lied von der Erde*). The Symphonies No. 5, 6, 7, and 9 had to wait much longer before being generally accepted, and their acceptance was often gained only through retrospectives (which, by the way, have become an effective means of bringing to the attention of the wider public the less accessible works of otherwise popular composers).

The Soviet Union's *kultura* commissars insisted that composers deliver long, patriotic diatribes disguised as symphonies specifically to challenge the established bourgeois musical order. The years of the Weimar Republic brought new waves of composition, but due to the limited talents of the Honeggers, Milhauds, and others, the concert repertoire created in the 1920s never approached the miraculous relevance and immediacy of, for example, my three favorite works, Stravinsky's *L'Histoire du soldat*, Alban Berg's *Wozzeck*, and Kurt Weill's *The Threepenny Opera*.

When I listen to the symphonies and concertos of, for example, William Walton and Ralph Vaughan-Williams, I am more than ever convinced that in the postwar era the very vitality and communicative power of the symphony have been exhausted. With a few notable exceptions, the current generation of composers seems to look only backward, as if longing for the return of a pre-Hitler music world. One senses a general nostalgia, almost a Proustian *Recherche du temps perdu*.

Perhaps the main reason for the inertia of the music repertoire has been (and continues to be) the detached manner in which critical treatment of music activity is carried out. By "detached" I mean "ivory tower" —a manner that contrasts starkly with that in which literature and the pictorial arts are criticized. There is no doubt that music, as composition, is more difficult to "describe." Even the emptiest work of Mondrian can be described in words by anyone capable of putting a visual impression into words.

Music, however, is clearly different. Since the late seventeenth century the world of music has produced compositions that have remained vibrant, alive, and therefore immortal. Orbiting gamely around this immortal core are many secondary works, which are frequently summoned to fill up music events that could not otherwise function as regularly or frequently as they currently do. Commentators, radio announcers, and newspaper critics alike are frightened to speak in anything but the most reverent tones about even the most negligible products of the great masters.

The Mozart bicentennial celebrations of 1991 were a prime example of this. I was horrified to see how even learned musicologists fell into line—not one dared hint that not every Mozart divertimento had the ideas and the sparkle of *Eine kleine Nachtmusik*, or that the five best-known Mozart operas were superior to the other sixteen. This apparent compulsion to elevate the gifted composer into some kind of infallible superman has the effect of distorting both the critique of new music and the debate about music's social function. Until music (its composition, performance, and critique) is treated as part of society's overall arrangements, composers will always be confused about their place in society.

The three composers who in my view set the pace of twentieth-century music (Bartók, Debussy, and Stravinsky) wrote very few scores that were not intended for immediate use. Both Bartók and Debussy were pianists (Bartók's wife inspired some of the two-piano music, including the masterpiece, the Sonata for Two Pianos and Percussion) and consequently produced a great deal of eminently accessible works for that instrument. Stravinsky, for his part, guaranteed performance of his works by hitching his wagon to ballet. For purely orchestral works (without soloists, singers, or dancers), the harvest from the three composers is relatively poor. Bartók needed a commission from Serge Koussevitzky combined with dire financial and health crises before he could write his

Concerto for Orchestra (a work considered by most Bartók-watchers as inferior to his concertos and to *The Miraculous Mandarin*). Claude Debussy's purely orchestral compositions are four in number (the *Images*, *La Mer*, the three *Nocturnes*, and the *Prélude à l'après-midi d'un faune*). Stravinsky waited for many years before giving us his two orchestral masterpieces. All three masters knew that orchestral compositions in the symphonic mold were not in demand, and all three consequently incurred the wrath of Theodor Adorno.

At our particular point in the history of music there are probably as many styles and manners of composition as there are types of mushroom. Most are equally perishable. I confess I often feel slightly uneasy watching a subscription audience sit in a kind of semi-comatose rapture during a Dvorák symphony only to return after the intermission to give the most earnest and concentrated attention to a piece by Anton Webern, Elliott Carter, or any similarly "demanding" composer. It has become fashionable to hurl unkind epithets at such audiences, but there are signs that musicians, too, have begun to treat the latter works with caution. A labor dispute, involving the freelance personnel of several New York orchestras, was solved by a settlement guaranteeing the musicians a slightly higher rate of pay for every hour of rehearsal or concert performance that was due to the "more demanding" music fare. Is it not a little strange that the pay rate of a musician should vary with the (assumed) complexity of the task at hand? In fact, most contemporary pieces for orchestra, judged according to the criterion of relative complexity, are unquestionably easier than the best-known scores of Mozart or Beethoven. I am aware that most people who are not professional orchestra conductors will probably not accept that point, but I believe it is an eminently provable one.

I recall one occasion when the manager of a fine orchestra's summer season engaged a music director who was deeply committed to modern music. In a cycle of twelve orchestral concerts spread over three weeks, that music director presented various operatic works by minimalist composers, followed by act 3 of *Tristan und Isolde*, but featuring singers trained to sing only the minimalist works. The public of the resort would have none of it, and the orchestra spent much of its time playing to five hundred people in a pavilion holding ten times that number. When asked why he selected such a program, the manager replied that one "must make a statement" (meaning that one is obliged to present modern and contemporary compositions). This attitude, however, ignores any concern for potential or actual public demand. After all, does anyone feel the obligation referred to above? The manager knows the answer to that question but is reluctant to give it openly since it might be too embarrassing. The public certainly does not accept any obligation to purchase admissions for certain works and often skips "modern" programs on their subscriptions. Performers do not generally refuse to perform the works, either out of conviction or out of sheer necessity (they do not wish to miss out on other coveted engagements). If this is rarely admitted by the critics, it is for fear lest the writer be accused of philistinism. Too many hasty judgments have been made by critics in the past. Posterity has never forgiven the culprits, and music critics have consequently grown frightened of making any extreme statements about new music. Sitting awkwardly amid lobbyists and pressure groups, they are only too aware of the precarious nature of their position. The program annotators have their task made easier by extensive notes supplied by the composers themselves, but those notes rarely constitute the kind of valuable critical introduction to which lay public and expert listeners alike are entitled.

The current situation reflects a perversion of cultural values, and the critic, by fighting mindlessly for works that are not wanted, makes himself neither pathfinder nor missionary. I recall seeing a play in which a single incident was acted out several times to reflect the perspective of each participant. Perhaps one might use the same approach to establish accurate musical terms, values, and philosophies and to rediscover the true purpose of composing and performing "serious" music.

Broadening the Repertory

Since conductors earn their living from the orchestral repertoire, they can hardly be expected to support a music policy that will make large orchestral programs an exception rather than the rule. I believe that such a policy is nonetheless justified.

My argument dates back to 1913 and the sensational premiere of *The Rite of Spring*. I have always maintained that this event signaled, not the beginning of a new era, but the grand closing of the large orchestral world. It was the end of the "monster" band, as conceived by Berlioz and given life in Wagner's *Ring*, Strauss's *Elektra*, the efforts of Mahler and Schoenberg to outdo Beethoven's Ninth by adding vocal parts, by Messiaen, and so on. Many conductors still sustain entire careers by repeatedly serving up this sumptuous musical feast, but though audiences may find such fare deliciously satisfying on occasion, it evidently does not constitute a healthy and steady diet. A system that builds a seven-month season on a symphony orchestra with piano and violin soloists, plus an occasional oratorio, will no longer work, regardless of economic conditions. In its place I propose mixed media "academies."

As an example, allow me to show how one might present the eternally popular all-Beethoven program. Instead of the trite combination of Overture, Concerto, and Symphony, I propose the following program:

1   A few excerpts from *The Creations of Prometheus*, Op. 43.
2   A reading of Goethe's poem.
3   Beethoven wrote two sets of variations on two pieces from Mozart's *The Magic Flute*, for cello and piano. For each of these pieces the original Mozart should be sung with orchestra. A cellist and a pianist should then play the Beethoven pieces. (It is to be hoped that the regular cellist and pianist on the orchestra's roster are capable of playing these pieces. Such solo appearances are a strong boost to orchestral morale.)

Interval

4   The narrator returns to read about Goethe's *Egmont*.
5   The orchestra plays the complete Beethoven score of *Egmont*.

The narrator should introduce each piece of music in such a way that the public can connect Beethoven's music with the setting of the drama's specific scene. There are not too many possibilities for such topical programs and they should be carefully spread out over the season.

Another major departure from the permanently exhibited full orchestra might be an assiduous regular scheduling of baroque music of the kind that has captivated younger generations who like their classical music "neat." I refer to the works of Vivaldi and his contemporaries, which does not demand the broader cultural awareness necessary for the understanding and enjoyment of music written in the period between 1760 and 1910 (to which the vast majority of orchestral scores belong). With this baroque plan goes another very urgent solution; it has been made clear by every orchestra that the relentless sequence of rehearsing, performing, and learning new pieces is exhausting and probably counter-productive. As a result the actual presence and participation of players do not correspond to the terms of their contracts. Whereas top-flight European orchestras consist of two virtually complete casts, the American orchestras do not.

Under the severe strain imposed by the annual contract, American orchestras have established alternating casts, which are not equal to one another musically. In doing so they have relieved the music director of yet another musical decision, since the sections themselves do the cast-ing. In this context I well recall the occasion when Herbert von Karajan, after thirty years at the helm of the Berlin Philharmonic, asked the city to spell out his contractual rights. Despite the millions that he had put into the pockets of the players and the numerous other tangible benefits of his success and conquest, he was still not able to engage a new clarinet player, because he had been defeated by the orchestra's veto.

If orchestras were to include more baroque programs, they could split the big band and thus provide necessary time off. The result would be a program featuring fifty percent conventional, twenty-five percent "Academy"-type, and twenty-five percent baroque-type fare. In certain cities the seasonal program might even be divided into thirds.

It must be obvious that the individual who designed and executed such scheduling could never be an active conductor—there can be few people, after all, who would willingly prepare their demise. Baroque music does not need a conductor and assuredly not one whose great strength is the period 1760–1910. The Academy-type program would need the conductor, but in a rather different way than in the past. Sir Winston Churchill once declared that he had not become the King's first minister to preside over the liquidation of the Empire, but the Empire was done for just the same, and Churchill showed merely that he had not understood how the world had changed. Good conductors, so the orchestra players say, are in ever shorter supply. This does not mean, however, that those music directors who were promoted as indispensable stars by the publicists really are indispensable. I can guarantee that a good recording engineer can make a first-class record with an ensemble, a leader, and a soloist who are not beneficiaries of the Madison Avenue Music School. Only the symphony boards in the United States have been deceiving themselves on that point.

Central Europeans have always insisted upon seeing a concert as a rite akin to the Christian Mass (hence the reason some orchestra leaders see themselves as High Priests). Of course, there were many sacred and quasi-sacred compositions that provided plenty of reasons for turning what had been an eighteenth-century pastime into a nineteenth-century edifying experience. In the past, this process may well have had convincing reasons or offered superficial advantages, but in America it has had the disastrous consequence of misleading people as to the real nature of symphony, chamber music, and instrumental presentations in general.

The oft-heard slogan "we must educate the audience" is plain nonsense. An educated public is a necessity just as an educated electorate is a necessity. Voters cannot be educated during the weeks or months preceding actual election, just as audiences cannot be educated by little essays in the playbill handed out by the ushers. The symphony orchestra, the string quartet, and the piano virtuoso are all, by definition, entertainers in the same sense as an actor is an entertainer. A good actor is able and happy to alternate between Prospero and Falstaff, as a Basso Cantante should be able and happy to alternate between the Grand Inquisitor of Verdi's *Don Carlos* and Don Basilio of Rossini's *The Barber of Seville*.

There is no natural border separating serious music from pop music. There are extremes that nobody is likely to confuse, but nearer the center the only dividing lines are those of prejudice, snobbery, and a regrettable inferiority complex according to which the word *imported* automatically means superior. When one thinks of influences from Europe, one generally thinks of a specific country (in music, either Germany or Italy). It is

obviously quite impossible to apply examples from one country to a
continent as vast as America or to attempt to bring to fifty multilingual
states something that is written in a single language. Unless government
can be convinced that funding of minority values is more important than
the objections of regional disinterested hostility, I see no point in trying
federal subsidies at all.

There is another key point to note regarding the so-called
Americanization of music. Despite numerous outstanding conservatories,
no first-class orchestra can field a first-class string-instrument choir without immigrant musicians from East Asia or, more recently, Russia and the
former Soviet Union. Players in the wind and percussion sections know
that their only possible career is within the orchestra, but violin and
cello students will always dream about solo careers and chamber music.
One would need a sociologist, a psychologist, an education expert, and
probably an anthropologist to fully fathom why violin and cello players
do not appear to consider the orchestra a desirable career. In both Europe
and America the turnover in these instruments is constant.

It is my firm belief that many of these deep-rooted problems can be
alleviated—perhaps even solved—by extending the repertory range of
orchestras beyond their present narrow confines.

Crying Out for Leaders

The impresario Sol Hurok was a fascinating figure. A throwback to the old
movies, he always wore a fedora (or top hat), cape, cane, and boutonnière,
and always drank champagne—as if the presentation of musical artists
was one long party. I believe he was a great impresario, but is an impresario also necessarily a leader in the music world of his country or city?
The answer must depend on how one defines musical life within a given
demographic unit. If a series of six to ten events constitutes musical life,
then the impresario is a leader. If, on the other hand, musical life is somewhat broader than this, then we must look elsewhere for leadership.

In the communities where music institutions function, an impresario
with his events can be a nuisance. By music institutions I refer to opera
companies, symphony orchestras, choral societies, or chamber music

groups attached to the local university or conservatory. The impresario's events can and do upstage the offerings of the local musicians (it is not just the snobs who opt for the international *olla podrida* in preference to the home-grown product). The clear and easily identifiable leadership of yesterday has now been terribly fragmented.

During my long career in the American music establishment I have observed two real leaders: Arthur See in Rochester and Rudolf Bing at the Met in New York. They differed from each other in virtually every respect, and yet both proved to be solely responsible for all decisions affecting the well-being of their respective institutions. Arthur See demonstrated that the specific problems and difficulties of a community are not necessarily the same as those of the neighboring towns (in Rochester's case, Buffalo to the west and Syracuse to the east). Nobody could say that See would have been as effective elsewhere as he was in Rochester. What he did display, however, was a masterful way of manipulating adversary forces, and this happened also to be the great skill of Bing, who handled his board of directors like some operatic Machiavelli. It was Arthur See, not I, who captured several beneficial recording contracts for the Rochester orchestra.

Perhaps it is no accident that the current manager of the Met, Joseph Volpe, was chosen for his proven effectiveness in union matters. This skill has been particularly valuable for the making of operatic recordings (a bonanza that had eluded previous management). The splendid preparatory work of James Levine could not have produced those recording sessions without Joe Volpe's skill. There must be other real leaders in this field, but I prefer to limit my narratives to experiences for which I can vouch. There is at least one more piquant similarity between what I saw in Rochester and what I saw at the Met.

After Arthur See's death the board of the Rochester Philharmonic set out to engage a successor. Since I was never consulted I must conclude (admittedly from very scant evidence) that they went about their task without really understanding the nature of Rochester as a place. They hired a salesman who had been with the gigantic road organization known as Community Concerts. They thus confused the basic function of a local manipulator—which a manager must be—with a person who might sell a modestly budgeted music ensemble to the glamour spots.

Between his appointment in March 1953 and November of the same year, when I arrived back in Rochester for the new season, the man was already gone, discharged by a board comprising men with much egg on their faces.

After Bing ended his twenty-year tenure at the Met there must have been similar infighting among the board members. They ended up with people whose sole distinction was that they were as readily acceptable on the society pages as the older scions. In fact, Bing had been able to mask his non-society background because of the knighthood earned for services to Britain's Edinburgh and Glyndebourne festivals. By the way, if anybody wonders why society never has any qualms about the proliferation of European Jews in positions of music direction, the answer is simple: whereas a manager must be present at board meetings, this is rarely the case with music directors.

I first came to the United States in November 1937 and quickly learned that there were numerous legitimate leaders of American musical life. It was a difficult era as the Depression had left budgets in great disarray. Yet, there was Koussevitzky in Boston, Eugene Ormandy (who had followed Leopold Stokowski) in Philadelphia, Artur Rodzinski in Cleveland, and Gaetano Merola in charge of the San Francisco opera season. Then there was the Met, where I served for some six seasons under a troika comprising an ex-singer (as impeccable frontperson), a somewhat dubious box-office manager, and an *éminence grise* of a caliber rarely encountered in any corporate configuration. The latter's name was Edward Ziegler, and he was generally feared, hated, and resented because he dealt with adversity by saying no to nearly everything that ventured into his office. Yet he was a man of singular honesty, totally incorruptible, appreciative of quality in any form—a unique personality.

The conductors I mentioned above were also leaders in the sense that they managed their organizations, often against all the instincts of their boards. This I know from conversations with Henry Cabot, chairman of the board during my Boston years, treasurer during Koussevitzky's years.

The successor to Koussevitzky, Charles Munch, was the very antithesis of the leader: a musician who found the work too much and who spent thirteen years doing too many concerts and too few rehearsals. During his tenure the playing deteriorated, nobody was pensioned regardless of age and frailty, and *vieux copains* from his Paris days were permitted to remain in key musical chairs even though they were no longer able to turn pages. Munch was among the last conductors to reside in the city where his major opportunities and income were located. Among his greatest moments was the occasion when the trustees used their Washington connections to have a law passed allowing Munch's French cook to work for him in America (as an antidote to Boston baked beans). This tale was told to me with great feeling by the orchestra manager, who had been assistant manager under Munch.

Today the most distinguished posts in American symphonic organizations are treated by music directors as "second jobs," with their European engagements taking clear and unequivocal precedence. This state of affairs is perfectly logical, and it is perfectly understandable that conductors should wish to divide their time thus. The horror of it all, however, is that the boards of directors do not draw the one obvious conclusion: an absentee cannot be a music director. Guiding a symphony orchestra musically through the year is a civic task that requires the physical presence of those who do the guiding and make the decisions. As for the music coaching (rehearsing an orchestra is the same as coaching), there is no doubt that the constant disruptions caused by guest conductors do more harm than good to the music ensemble. Like members of any team, musicians must learn to adapt their individuality to the psychology of the overall group.

This process of adjustment has, in the first instance, nothing to do with the conductor. A new first woodwind player who finds that the other fifteen woodwind players have been together for a few seasons needs all his or her musical wits if he or she is to adjust successfully to intonation, attack, dynamic levels, and so on. This adjustment must be made regardless of who stands on the podium.

Making music with more than one person means a constant shift from leading to accompanying, from individual assertion to the suppression of individuality to better accompany those who have the lead. In orchestras where the music director's authority is on another continent, musicians fight over these questions. When the director stays away too long, they give up and become indifferent. Their playing deteriorates in consequence.

Many new chief conductors find it urgently necessary to reseat the players. Sometimes when I finish a guest engagement and the next guest conductor has a rehearsal the following morning, I like to sit in on the proceedings. I recall one such occasion in Boston in 1992, when I was quite amazed to find that the next man had totally reseated the players. It so happens that Symphony Hall in Boston is a marvel of acoustics for the public, but not for the players on stage—it is hard for the musicians on the right side to hear those on the left, and vice versa. The guest conductor who reorganized the entire seating scheme had done it (as the players confided to me) to humor his somewhat unprofessional inability to adjust to ground rules that were not his own. I did ask one of the orchestra's music administrators why this had been permitted, only to receive the reply that the music director tolerated it from that particular conductor.

Leadership of any civic enterprise is unthinkable with an absentee head. A symphony orchestra is a civic enterprise in the same sense as an athletic team is a civic enterprise. The great conductors of the past rightly resided where their orchestra lived and took barely any time off during a concert season. It is obviously impossible to make judgments and decisions about assisting artists and personnel problems during the absence of a music director. The constant disruptions to the physical conducting of the ensemble keep musicians in a state of uncertainty about strictly technical and stylistic approaches to music. Ultimately it all justifies the general verdict of the American music critics who find that their orchestras have a "neutral" sound that is distinct from the "individual" sounds of visiting bands.

American orchestras play a much larger repertoire than their European colleagues. There is a fairly rigid schedule of preparation that never allows enough time to learn new music. String sections in the better orchestras are constantly losing good string players to higher-paying ensembles, and a small but significant number of younger players are reading the classic repertoire for the first time. On my first road trip with the Rochester Philharmonic the large string section was augmented by excellent graduate students from the Eastman School of Music. That season I had programmed a complete cycle of the Beethoven symphonies, which had required many extra hours for rehearsal. At an after-concert party I happened to ask why the graduates of such a famous music school did not know the symphonies of Beethoven. To which the first oboist, Bob Sprenkle, replied with a deadpan face: "But they know the symphonies of Howard Hanson."

The aforementioned music directors of the 1940s had to master a much larger repertoire because they stood much more often before the same subscribers. In those years subscribers bought series of twenty-four, eighteen, or sixteen programs, whatever the local band's season. Music directors like Frederick Stock performed a repertoire that was sufficiently broad to maintain variety through decades of tenure without boring the public. Today's chief conductors do not master a large enough repertoire to get through more than a dozen programs a season before starting over from the beginning.

Modern subscription series are usually for six programs, and the generation that used to take twenty-four or sixteen is no longer with us. After the older guard of music directors had passed on or retired, the new boys began to accept posts only on condition that they could retain a European tenured post and restrict their presence at home to an acceptable minimum. That minimum generally varied between twenty-five and fifty percent of the home season. There was one music director who grazed the meadows of music with the same few pieces for years.

Another would demonstrate tremendous éclat at every debut, but could rarely follow up to any great effect since he knew only two symphonies. If the second did not suit the host there was little to do but cancel. The very idea of leadership has been discredited by the actions of a few practitioners, but music and musical planning must involve clear and unequivocal leadership or it will not be tolerated by the public. The problem for the presenters and the entrepreneurs is to find a way of providing that leadership while also allowing room for the recognition that every member of a team craves.

If I were the attorney for the orchestras that had their music directors for only twenty-five percent of their seasons I would accuse conductors of flagrant dishonesty in accepting a responsibility they can have no intention of fulfilling because they simply do not have enough time. I would have to argue that the players were justified in complaining about overwork and a lack of proper guidance. If, on the other hand, I were

defending these conductors, I might protest that nobody wanted continuously involved music directors any more and that many music decisions
had been taken over by external forces, especially the record companies.
I would argue that musicians want an authority to guide them only when
it is convenient, and further that this is unrealistic.

If I were the judge in this case, I would conclude thus: Even if a
conductor were to be continuously present throughout the season and
utterly devoted to one organization, in the manner of Frederick Stock,
the time is long gone when a conductor could be the music director of
any music association. My reasons for saying this are strictly artistic, having nothing to do with finances, the unions, or diplomacy. The largest
and best-organized venues may still laugh at my findings for several years,
but the second and lower echelons are going to fail fast if they do not
reform and realize that the figure of the music director as international
personality is as dead as spats.

Index of Names